Becoming a Glo
Executive Office

A How to Guide for Next C ...ration Security Leaders

Becoming a Global Chief Security Executive Officer

A How to Guide for Next Generation Security Leaders

Roland P. Cloutier

AMSTERDAM • BOSTON • HEIDELBERG • LONDON
NEW YORK • OXFORD • PARIS • SAN DIEGO
SAN FRANCISCO • SINGAPORE • SYDNEY • TOKYO

Butterworth-Heinemann is an imprint of Elsevier

Butterworth-Heinemann is an imprint of Elsevier
The Boulevard, Langford Lane, Kidlington, Oxford, OX5 1GB, UK
225 Wyman Street, Waltham, MA 02451, USA

ISBN: 978-0-12-802782-0

Library of Congress Cataloging-in-Publication Data
A catalogue record for this book is available from the Library of Congress

British Library Cataloguing-in-Publication Data
A catalogue record for this book is available from the British Library

For information on all Butterworth-Heinemann publications visit our website at http://store.elsevier.com/

Contents

About the Author

Roland Cloutier is one of the world's most foremost experts on corporate and enterprise security, cyber defense program development, and business operations protection. Roland specializes in the development, implementation, and management of global converged security programs and has held positions as the chief security officer for major multina tional corporations such as EMC Corporation and ADP, LLC. He has been responsible for the protection of trillions of dollars in global money movement and critical infrastructure technologies that protect hundreds of thousands of companies' and governments' interests in more than 120 countries.

Roland's diverse career spans more than 25 years in the military, law enforcement, and the commercial sector. Roland started his career in the US Air Force as a combat security specialist and then worked with the Department of Defense as an aerospace protection and antiterrorism specialist. Roland continued to work in federal law enforcement with the US Department of Veterans Affairs, specializing in fraud and health care crime, with special assignments to joint task force operations in counter-narcotics, and he was assigned to special security functions at the 1996 Olympics in Atlanta, Georgia.

Roland has been featured in leading industry and news media, including the *Wall Street Journal* and the *Financial Times*, and he has contributed articles for *SC Magazine*, *Human Capital Insights* magazine, CIO Review, and *CSO* magazine.

Roland is active in multiple security industry associations, serves on several advisory boards, and is the recipient of numerous security awards:

- #1 Security Executive of the Year by ExecRank
- Tech Exec Networks' Information Security Executive of the Year
- Most Influential People in Security by *Security Magazine*
- *CSO* magazine's Compass Award Winner
- Evanta CISO Breakaway Leader

Roland's education includes studies in criminal justice at Holyoke Community College and computer sciences at Boston University. He has guest lectured at Boston University, Worcester Polytechnic Institute, Northeastern University, Babson College, and the MIT Sloan School of Business. He has been sought after as a speaker for the RSA Conference, Interpol, ASIS, ISACA, the Global CISO Summit, FINRA, GFIRST, *CSO* magazine, CSO Standard, CSO Top40, Secure World, *SC Magazine* Congress, ILEA, IDC, the John Hopkins-APL Kossiakoff Conference, and I4 conferences.

Roland, a New Hampshire native, lives in Tampa, Florida, with his wife Laura and two daughters.

Chapter 1

Business Operations Protection: The Future of the Security Executive

In the opening chapter of this book you will be introduced to the concept of executive security management using the methodology of business operations protection. This focus is to guide you to an understanding that leading security risk and privacy programs within businesses or government agencies is as much an integral part of operating the overall business as any other front or back office function, such as finance. In this chapter you will learn about business value chain assurance and the role the security executive plays in it. You will also discover core principles and security business operation effectiveness, including attributes for a world-class program, such as risk management, operational excellence, security transparency, security intelligence, and the integration of normal business imperatives, including service management and what the future of leadership in our profession must embody.

As the title of this book clearly indicates, this is a how-to guide for those men and women who have decided to dedicate themselves as leaders in the diversified disciplines of security, risk, and privacy. However, it may be slightly misleading. If I were to focus on only those three simple words—security, risk, privacy—I believe I would be doing you a great injustice. For many years our industry has been teaching basic theories such as "align to the business" and "business impact." Our industry's continuing education models have been based on decades of strict security management fundamentals that are necessary and critical to the development of any practitioner. The problem is that executive practitioners need a model that integrates discipline excellence with business context to ensure that our focus is truly on the entirety of the company or agency that we serve using a holistic approach of security and business management. When you successfully create a security management model that is designed specifically for a business through the entirety of its life cycle, and you successfully create security as a component of cross-functional business operations, then you have graduated from being just a "security executive" to an industry leader in Business Operations Protection.

THE TERM AND THE FUTURE OF YOUR PROFESSION

The term *business operations protection* implies a significant change in how we think, develop, and deliver security programs. But as you continue along this path of next-generation learning and advanced security management concepts, there is a simplicity in the primary function of the mission you support. Your job is simply to ensure the prevention of negative impact events that would otherwise affect the security of your business's people, process, or technologies, or ultimately threaten the continuity of operations of the business you serve.

The Complexity of Protecting a Business

However simplistically articulated the bottom-line requirements of a security executive's job may be, reality is steeped in the complexity of understanding what it actually takes to protect an entire business. If protecting a business were as simple as deploying technologies such as firewalls, intrusion detection systems, and secured development life cycle processes, or implementing intellectual property protection programs and workforce safety programs, this would be a short book. But protecting an entire business truly means understanding the end-to-end concept of your company's business lifecycle and any operational value chain associated with it.

The following simplistic depiction of a technology manufacturing company's business value chain is an illustrative look at the extent of core business operations that really make up a company.

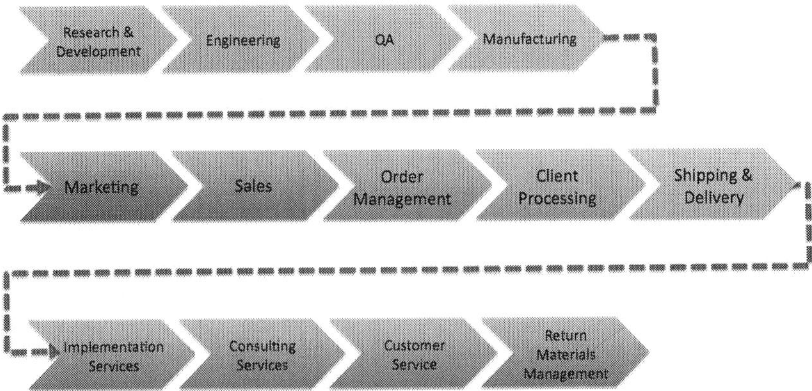

As you can see, from the time a product is engineered, designed, and developed, it has already gone through three different and distinct business processes. Once a product is ready to go to market and is marketed and sold, it is already gone through five independent business processes, often with different management, profit and loss statements, and executive responsibilities. As the product is delivered and implemented, and services are applied, the business expands its scope of security requirements beyond the walls of the organization and into that of its customers, wherever they may be. When a client calls a call center for service or returns a product, different requirements to protect each of those independent operations—such as call center security, authorized material return loss prevention, and client data security—all come into play. By the time you end the total business life cycle to the point of revenue recognition, you have traversed 12 different business functions and elicited the necessity of security services, from product security engineering, through intellectual property protection, through workforce security, to advanced security functions such as fraud prevention, client data privacy protection, and even financial crimes monitoring.

The science of applying security risk and privacy service delivery to the holistic business process is called "business operations protection."

Understanding the complexities of business operations protection through the lens of business process analysis is the foundational requirement necessary to begin on your path to creating a next-generation security program. Other complex security and business components cannot be neglected because they also are core to creating a context-based enterprise security program.

The first of these is the realization that security is not a *static condition*. Evolving threats, both virtual and physical, against any business are constant and unpredictable. As quickly as defensive and detective controls are developed and deployed, those seeking to harm your business are working just as hard to circumvent those controls to meet their end-goal criteria. Add in the unprecedented level of technology change and you can see the exponential mathematical equation of potential risk issues facing your business today.

As important as developing a security program specific to your business is, individual industries have complex specific issues that need to be taken into consideration as well. Industry-specific knowledge applied to technologies, threats, threat actors, regulatory concerns, privacy, and so on need to be applied to your program. Remember that issues that affect other businesses or agencies in your sector or industry will also affect you. Your knowledge of external conditions that could affect your business is just as important as knowing your own business. You *are* the expert for your company, and therefore you need to take time to establish your expertise through education, information sharing, research, and applied knowledge. Using peers and resources from the industries you operate in, serve as force multipliers and as an asset-leveraging tool. This is smart business sense and exponentially adds capacity and capabilities to your business defense program.

As you begin to take on the challenge developing a business-specific security program, the topic of privacy must be foremost in your planning preparations. Although not always security specific, the crossroads of security and privacy often meet at an operational level, and failure to address both specialties can severely affect your business's ability to compete, deliver, or service your clients.

In any business, a security executive must understand that the services you provide are simply a component for consideration, not a hard and fast requirement for the business. With the exception of a few industries, such as financial services, health care, and other critical infrastructures, most businesses in private industry, both large and small, are not constrained by law for the entire security program. The implementation of security programs and controls should be based on fact-supported risk management evaluations in the context of the entire business, not just an immediate threat or vulnerability. For instance, you may want to implement a new fraud control that reduces or stops the ability of criminal actors to defraud a certain portion of your business. If the downstream residual risk or risk of financial loss is not material enough to warrant the spending required on the fraud control function, the business may accept the loss as a part of their expected loss ratio and choose not to implement the control you selected. In Chapter 7 we cover operational risk management and the integration of enterprise risk into business operations protection programs.

Service Ownership

The next core consideration for transforming your security program into a business operations protection function is the concept of service ownership. Within corporations, the functional description of end-to-end service ownership is certainly not new. Major functions such as manufacturing and information technology (IT) long ago adapted to frameworks, like ITIL, founded on the principle of delivering service products to internal and external constituents as a mechanism for operational efficiency, assurance, and quality.

Those same theories can easily be applied to security. In fact, the following is an easy way to think of service ownership for the delivery of business operations protection: Consider yourself the CEO of a security consulting and services company within a company that has a captive client. The quality of your product, the consistency of your service delivery, and the management of your business operations are imperative to the success of ***your business***. Later in this book we review business management functions not always thought of in the context of security, such as unit cost measurement, efficiency growth reinvestment, and total shareholder return. These are concepts that the business you support managed themselves, and you must manage your own internal business the same way.

EFFECTIVE RISK MANAGEMENT

Another "religious debate" in the areas of security risk and privacy centers around the question, "Who should do risk management?"Certainly, the science of risk management, the broad implementation of enterprise risk management programs, and specific disciplines in the area of risk, including legal, finance, tax, IT, and operational risk, often require trained, dedicated risk experts to manage holistically implemented programs. As a next-generation security leader acting as a chief security officer (CSO), managing any business operations protection function in any size company, you need to know that the term *chief security officer* should be congruent with the term *risk execution leader*.

CSO = Risk Execution

In the course of any day or week you will be required to make many decisions that affect the security operations of your business. It may be how to interpret policy, a decision on the changing of standards or what level of response is appropriate for any given incident, or an evaluation of the organization's defensive posture against a new industry threat. Whatever that decision is, it's your responsibility to ensure that the decision or opinion you provide is based on fact and done in the measured context of the company's interests. This is risk-based decision making and is a skill that every chief security officer must learn, embrace, and advance in their operations to ensure action-orientated prioritization of the many issues at hand.

Measurement of Accountability

The second important function of using risk management fundamentals as a basis for decision support structure is the need to create a culture of accountability within your company or agency. The security executive of the future will need to migrate his or her business from managing lists of risks and to-do's to creating an active mechanism that fairly measures, processes, and articulates a broad variety of risk issues while engaging and enabling other business leaders to be accountable for those decisions. This measurement and assignment of accountability related to various business risks is an underlying requirement of most compliance and regulatory doctrines required of businesses today. In addition, through the board of directors, accountability—and evidence thereof—are expected and necessary to ensure the interests of the shareholders and those various agencies that provide lawful oversight.

Complex Mechanisms and Complex Algorithms

The final component when articulating the criticality of operations risk management in the context of the future security executive is to establish a clear understanding that risk management is, in many ways, a science. Yes, risk is a business tool used to understand futures, effects, liabilities, and many other quantifiable outcomes of actual or proposed conditions; but the capability to do that, use the measurements and algorithms necessary to make informed and correct assumptions, and achieve the analytical capabilities and experience needed to interpret that data is much like a science.

Therefore, risk programs, services, and actions should be considered a critical component of any business operations protection framework, and those performing risk operational services need to be trained, educated, and credentialed professionals. As a chief security officer, risk officer, or privacy officer, you will provide critical data to business leadership, allowing them to make strategic, financial, and critical decisions for the business. Doing that hinges on your ability, or that of your teams, to apply these sciences in the form of enterprise risk articulation, using industry-based frameworks to measure, analyze, and articulate risk.

Business operations protection is all about creating and enabling your business's ability to operate as needed, when needed, and where needed, unencumbered and without significant risk. When you enable and integrate operational risk as a part of how you deliver services and get it right, you tangibly reduce risk, prevent bad things from happening, and deliver on the commitment of protecting your business.

THE IMPERATIVE OF OPERATIONAL EXCELLENCE

As you expand the operational footprint of the security risk and privacy programs you deliver to your business, in accordance with the concept of business operations protection, the imperative to ensure you efficiently manage your operation becomes critically more important. As a business leader—not just a security leader—you are expected to operate in a manner that continues to drive financial and business value into your company. Examples of this include leveraged resource efficiency evaluations, increased automation, and committed financial efficiencies as either givebacks or mechanisms to support expansion requirements of your program. The phrase "doing more with less" has all too often been bantered around like a negative attribute of a business society that overly demands unrealistic expectations, with the sole focus of reducing cost for margin expansion. As a business leader, your responsibilities include continuously driving operational excellence through process improvements, innovation, automation, and efficiency design attributes that better the services delivered through delivery improvements, quality improvements, standards improvements, time improvements, and cost containment. That is both smart business and the mark of an intelligent executive focused on the success of the business.

Equity and Efficiency

The long-term financial impact to an efficiently run operation with respect to security functions cannot be understated. Later in the book we discuss unit metric costs in other financial measurements of your programs, but the two outcomes you should focus on when driving operational efficiency are residual value and total business value.

Businesses can be measured in many ways. As in any investment portfolio, the longer the value of your investment remains, the more financially productive your entire portfolio is. As a security executive, selecting the right investments that support multiple functions—that can be used, reused, and remain productive components of your protection portfolio—provides increased residual value to your entire program. For instance, investing in a security operations center that then can be cross-utilized to support other functional areas, such as physical security monitoring, crisis management operations, and incident coordination, increases the residual value of an existing investment through operational and program efficiency, which in the long run helps reduce the total cost of operations for the business.

Effective program management and efficient operations also contribute to the overall business value of the investment your company or agency has made in your program. When you think about extended business value, put yourself in the shoes of your internal client. How does a business executive interpret your value to them through the use of your services? Is your security program seen as the bearer of bad news or as a service partner they can depend on to help enhance and expand their business portfolio? An example of this is extending the consultative use of your existing resources to support your business's customer interactions when it comes to issues of security, risk, or privacy. For instance, your business may get questions during the portions of their business life cycle process while dealing with clients before sales, during delivery, or after sales. Often these client interactions are done without the support of a security professional, slowing down the close process with regard to contracts or even delaying delivery or implementation times, which affect revenue recognition. By creating a process, communication methods (such as group email or an 800 number), and training your practitioners how to support your sales or delivery organization, you can allot a portion of time to create a new customer security service management team that engages directly with the client on a peer-to-peer basis, reducing missteps and misrepresentation from non–security practitioners, reducing the sales cycle, and increasing client satisfaction. Not only have you effectively used your resources to increase business value, you have created additional mechanisms of trust that support your company's move to the market and make your executive business partners look at your program in a very different light.

Being a Business Leader versus a Security Person

Another attribute of the security executive of the future is a focus on being a business leader beyond a security manager. Driving significant and broad change across any organization requires core leadership skills.

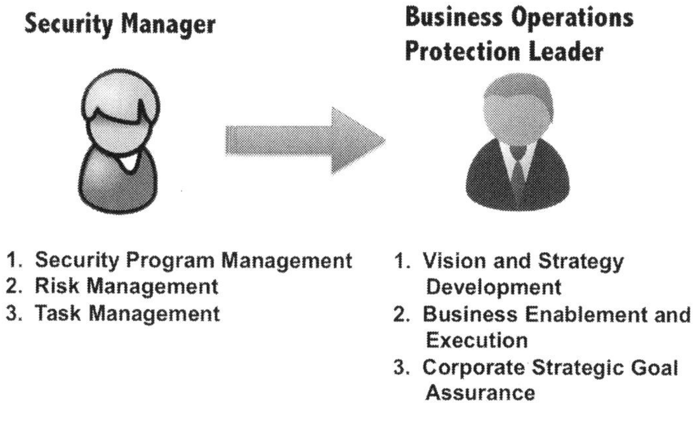

Security Manager

1. Security Program Management
2. Risk Management
3. Task Management

Business Operations Protection Leader

1. Vision and Strategy Development
2. Business Enablement and Execution
3. Corporate Strategic Goal Assurance

Attributes like these are required to change the DNA and culture of an organization to embed the concepts and designs of security functionality within its business value chain. As you transition from security manager into business leader, you can actually start to distinguish yourself with a career in leadership. This career has three main delivery requirements: vision and strategy, enablement and execution, and a specific goal.

As a professional leader, the expectation is not just simply to lead your people to a focused outcome. The function of a leader is to be able to provide the required vision and "over-the-horizon" thinking that betters the organization as a whole. True leadership means true thought leadership, and as you expand your area of responsibility from security executive to business operations protection executive, you need to enhance and expand your leadership capabilities in that light. Further, as you create vision, the technical aspects of this area require your ability to deliver the strategy to effect that vision.

Your next delivery requirement as a business leader is enablement and execution. This is often confused as simply "just getting the job done." As you expand your span of controls, operational footprint, and cross-discipline oversight, the reality of you as an individual simply rolling up your sleeves getting it done (whatever it may be) becomes less and less tangible. At this level of leadership, enablement must focus on your capability to create opportunities and mechanisms that enable your team to execute the functions required of them. From relationship development, through political minefields, to resource assurance, your job is to create the operating environment platform for your people to deliver from. That is enablement and execution from a cross-discipline executive leader.

Later in this book we spend a lot of time on people development. But we can't leave the discussion of advanced leadership development for the next-generation security leader without touching on this topic. I said at the onset that sustainability was a key mission imperative for any security, risk, or privacy executive. Sustainability takes on many forms, and perhaps the most crucial factor is the people who deliver business operation protection services to your business. Millions of books have been written and published on leadership, and I would guess that for the majority of them one of the most critical aspects of a successful leader is always the individual's ability to build other leaders. People development in our disciplines is critical because of the nascency of our industry and the significant gap in the pipeline of qualified practitioners across the multiple disciplines we support. Even more critical at this juncture, however, is ensuring that we have in place the appropriate future leadership that can understand and execute a converged security model methodology.

Technical excellence in any discipline you lead is always a core requirement and should be something you consistently strive for as the senior expert within your discipline inside your company. Business leadership skills equal total business success in the context of business operations protection.

TRANSPARENCY

Early in my career, the discipline of ensuring strict adherence to operational security was instilled deep into my character. Certainly, as a young Airman protecting my little sliver of the nation's critical air defense posture, the requirement for secrecy around our methods and tactics were required and necessary. What is interesting is that, like many others I have worked with over the years who came from like backgrounds, as I continued my career, the shroud of what security does and how it does it made its way from military operations into commercial business. Now, in some instances, and certainly at a deep technical level, the confidentiality of tactics, techniques, and procedures in the defense of any security risk or privacy program need to remain private to ensure the integrity of operations in the protection of the defense of architecture. There is, however, a difference between protecting critical confidential tradecraft and sensitive detailed architecture and enabling a transparent dialogue between you and the business you serve.

Transparency of Operations

Your goal as a business operation protection leader and the "CEO" of your security services business is, first, to appropriately affect your mission and, second, to have happy clients. Happy clients require a good product, an investment, partnership, and mutual feelings of value and respect. Key to this formula is your ability to show them the value of their investment, understanding of what they are "buying," and fair measurements of the quality of the product you are delivering. A single word that describes all of this is *transparency*.

Let's face it: Delivering security services into a business is not top secret. Businesses know they need workforce protection programs. They understand the need to defend their technical platforms in operation through advanced cyber defenses. Your shareholders expect you to have antivirus, firewalls, and crisis management capabilities. By disclosing your programs to the right people at the right time and being transparent about the investments and efficacy of the programs you manage, you don't risk causing a massive security failure; rather, you enable a trusted partnership in preparing an avenue paved with success.

Transparency of your programs and operations prove several things to your executive management teams and internal business partners. First, you are making a statement that their opinion matters and you are open to input from those who are essentially the buyers of your services. This shows a level of maturity in partnership that supports strong and sustained relationships within a business environment. Another major positive outcome from a policy of transparency and sharing is that others often make decisions and assume that because you are so transparent and open to dialogue, you must know what you're doing and are a true professional in your area of expertise. Although that may not always be the case, the fact remains that human nature is what it is, and assumption of expertise and knowledge goes a long way in reducing pushback, opposition, and political battles based on a concern that you are not capable of making the right decisions.

Understanding the Importance of a Value Chain

The obvious to-do in the area transparency is, as previously discussed, is to enable bidirectional communication as an opportunity for those you serve to understand your capabilities, services, and program efficacy. But getting there means developing a program based on the context of your business's value chain, and that takes a whole new type of transparency. The type of transparency I'm speaking of is your view into the detailed schematic of your business's core operations and delivery mechanisms, commonly referred to as your business value chain. This view is your mechanism to understanding what your business is and how it is delivered. Without this, you cannot truly create a business operations protection plan that encompasses all requirements specific to your company. Sure, you can institute basic protective technologies or operations, but to make truly appropriate investments, define risk-based priorities, and establish definitive and measurable improvements in the protective posture of your company, the value chain risk model is key to your success.

In this context, the more and broader the transparency is, the more effective you will be at utilizing your resources to accomplish your mission. To apply advanced concepts (described later in this book), such as critical asset protection programs, active fraud defense platforms, and binding corporate rules for authorized global data movement, the use of value chain definition and assessments is a prerequisite. This value chain methodology enables a transparent view into where operations, data, people, and issues are, which then enables you to deploy resources correctly.

To enable business operation protection, you must understand the value chain concept. The value chain is your mechanism for understanding what your business is and how they deliver it. Advanced concepts such as critical asset protection and fraud defense require an understanding of the value chain, which provides a transparent view to where operations, data, people, and issues are enabling you to deploy your resources correctly.

Root Cause Management

The previous two points about transparency covered the who and the what. This next area is all about the why. Often in businesses we create measurements that are totally performance-based rather than efficacy-based. For instance, an IT helpdesk may look at the total number of calls and the speed at which the call are closed, and never look at important information like what caused the workload in the first place. Whether you're in a large multinational company that spends tens of millions of dollars on security programs, or you are a two-person shop that begs, borrows, and pleads its funding from every other budget in the company, your responsibility as a next-generation security leader is to ensure the effective and efficient use of resources, and the betterment of the environment through reduce recidivism rates. The only way to accomplish this is through a transparent view of root cause analysis.

An appropriate root cause management program provides two key mechanisms for effective security management. As mentioned above, reducing future events by root cause remediation lowers the overall total cost of ownership of security through the reduction of continuing remediation costs and response costs for incident and other related financial and resource impacts that otherwise could quite reasonably continue if the root cause issue is not addressed. This simple program is often overlooked, and many practitioners find themselves in a continuous cycle of discover, repair, and response over and over again for what eventually is identified as the same issue.

Root cause transparency has a silver lining. Once a root cause has been determined, the security executive has the opportunity to look broadly across their enterprise, operations, and business value chain for current gaps and previous issues, and to quickly resolve and defend against the defined gap. From a reporting and regulatory perspective, there is no better outcome from a gap discovery than when you can go back and make definitive statements, such as, "we broadly looked across our organization using the data from our in-depth root cause analysis process to ensure we had no other similar issues within our environment."

Used properly, root cause transparency programs actually increase the level of security by quickly identifying and reducing like risks across your enterprise. In the following pages we connect the dots on how to enable transparent root cause analysis through the use of extended data collection and security intelligence platforms focused on creating transparency, truth in services, and a better decision-making capability for you as a business operations protection executive.

Truth in Services

The final area of providing transparent operations your business is the critical component of truth in services. Truth in services is the ability to provide insight and measures a protection program's abilities, efficacy, and effectiveness. Executives in any part of a business often provide high-level data that show the programs or projects they have implemented yet lack the transparent truths around how holistic, how global, and how effective those programs are. As a security executive responsible for multiple disciplines, your ability to attest and to hold yourself accountable to the organization's ability to defend itself and respond to critical issues is paramount for several reasons.

Let's first look at what truth in services really means. Often, people align this to a capabilities maturity model. But that tells only part of the story. Appropriately designed truth in services matrices take into consideration a holistic view of people, process, technologies, capabilities, global reach, and efficacy of the program attributes to attain the committed level of delivery. Of course, the biggest question you must answer is what is the effectiveness of your programs and services. The figure below is an example of a purposely built truth in services measurement model for a technical security organization. Notice that it has multiple columns with simple measurement criteria. This allows downstream management practitioners to participate in the discussion in a simplistic fashion that ensures that truth is not just a measurement of what the executive sees but is what is happening at the ground level.

Sample Maturity Measurment Chart

Program	Service Catalouge Item	FTEE Assigned	Division 1	Division 2	Division 3	Service CMM	Program CMM
Policy & Standards	Policy Development & Management	0.5	3.0	3.0	3.0	3.0	3.0
	Standards Development & Management	0.5	1.8	2.6	1.9	2.1	
	Education & Awareness	1.0	4.0	4.0	4.0	4.0	
Cyber Defense Operations	Host Based Defense	2.0	3.0	3.0	2.0	2.7	2.9
	Network Protection	1.0	4.0	4.0	2.8	3.6	
	Hosting Protection	1.5	3.8	2.6	4.3	3.6	
	Security Intelligence Operations	1.0	1.5	2.0	0.0	1.2	
	APT Defense	2.0	3.0	3.0	3.0	3.0	
	Vulnerability Assessment & Management	1.0	2.0	2.8	3.0	2.6	
	Operational Sustainability Services	1.5	4.0	4.0	4.0	4.0	
Monitoring & Response	L1 -3 Monitoring	4.0	3.0	3.0	3.0	3.0	1.7
	Advacned Threat Hunting	1.0	1.0	3.0	1.0	1.7	
	Cyber Incident Response	0.5	3.0	3.0	3.0	3.0	
	Forensic Services	0.5	0.5	0.5	0.5	0.5	
	Incident Response Training	0.0	0.5	0.5	0.5	0.5	
Product Security	SDLC Consulting Services	1.5	3.0	3.0	3.0	3.0	3.1
	Developer Training	0.5	3.0	3.0	3.0	3.0	
	Code & Pen Testing	2.0	4.0	2.0	4.0	3.3	
Customer Security	Pre-Sales Security Support	0.5	3.0	2.3	2.7	2.7	4.1
	Customer Questionnaire Management	1.5	4.0	4.0	4.0	4.0	
	Customer Security Marketing Services	0.5	1.5	2.0	1.0	1.5	

Perhaps the most critical reason for you to be transparent about your service capability and delivery models is the implications to the business. Your business makes strategic and operational decisions based on many factors, one of which is the protection or capability of the business. Often you may not even be aware of decisions that are being made for extraneous reasons that are not directly connected to security yet are based on, at least in part, the executive leadership's view of the company's ability to protect its operations or deliver secure product or services across the globe. For instance, articulation of a specific cyber defense that was implemented to ensure the denial of intrusion may be used as part of a calculation of the level of insurance required for errors and omissions or cyber incident coverage. Another example is that, based on your articulation to provide public safety and facility security controls, your business may use that information in the decision of where to build a new office building or whether to consider international operations in a high-risk environment.

As the "CEO" of your captive security company within your company, it is your duty to ensure that your customers understand the level of service they can expect, the type of products they can expect, and where you can deliver them. As you develop your plan and program, remember to take into account contractual relationships you may have with external third parties. For instance, you may have forensics capabilities within the domestic United States; however, you have a plan in place to use a consulting organization in the European Union if necessary. Although not a direct delivery option, documentation in a contractual relationship means that you do have service capability in that region.

For many of you with boards of directors or those in public companies, the questions, "How secure are we?" and "How do we know?" will be repeated to you quarter after quarter as you deliver your "state of security address" when requested. The implementation of the truth in services monitoring program amounts to a constant monitoring oversight program that can be used as part of these critical discussions. The data collected and described will serve you well as you create business cases to support the expansion of the business, make resource decisions based on business priorities (whether or not additional funding is provided), and respond quickly to questions around your business's ability to protect its operations.

THE POWER OF DATA

The most powerful tool of a chief security officer is the use of data and information as a core part of business operations protection programs. From intelligence operations, through decision support, to process automation and even controls assurance, the use of cross-business data elements enables critical areas of your service delivery and business effectiveness. Data is the most leverageable and readily available resource at your disposal. Often ignored, untapped, and reputed as a "paperwork exercise," security executives risk the inability to obtain true business transparency, completion of critical operations, and valuable details that are easily available through the expert use of data analytics.

The following section covers the top four areas of using data for a converged security program, including intelligence, decision support, metrics, and key performance indicators. By understanding and implementing data-gathering, data manipulation, and data analytic services, the use of advanced security information becomes a force multiplier in day-to-day operations and program management, increasing business effectiveness, security defense, and overall program transparency and effectiveness management.

Intelligence

The term *intelligence*, when used in association with commercial business operations programs, often brings to mind a massive global company and the protection of a business within the defense industrial base. But the term itself simply signifies the use or collection of information and data for a specified outcome. To do your primary job, which is to prevent bad things from happening to the organization you work for, you must understand the totality of what is happening within the world you operate in. If we as security executives look only at data points coming from those tools we deploy within our business, then we are seeing only a microcosm of our business in the industry in which we operate.

When you think about the use of data and intelligence operations, consider it in the capacity of resource management. Through the combination of understanding external trends, external threats, and internal situational awareness, you gain the ability to deploy, migrate, and move resources to prevent, detect, and deter issues or incidents happening outside your control. From a cyber perspective, think of it in these terms: if you enable an intelligence service that looks at other like businesses for ongoing attacks against services or technology in use at your business, you can better predict future attacks against your business and proactively implement controls to reduce the possibility that what occurred to another company happens at your company. In the use of intelligence for corporate security services, consider the use of a simple operation, such as business travel security and safety. If the simple use of intelligence monitoring was enabled for travel issues in the areas where employees travel, you can reduce the possibility of sending an employee into harm's way by monitoring available data such as political stability, weather events, and general travel disruptions. In almost every portion of your operations freely available information, fee-for-service information, and basic technology capabilities can be used to enhance the ability to predictably understand threats to your business and reduce or remove the potential impact of those threats.

When we focus on the internal use of data intelligence and analytics, we create a spotlight effect. This is the ability to shine a light on the needle in the haystack, that is, creating the ability to differentiate and identify abnormal business operations or situations that are potential threats to the business. The best way to understand this concept is to go back to the previous section that described business process risk management. If as a security organization we can understand key components of our business operations process and what norms are expected in that process, then we have the ability to understand what is not normal. By instrumenting the program with analytical capabilities that look for abnormal operations, you often can quickly sift through millions of pieces of information, transactions, and other data points to focus on those that are not like the others, often indicating a problem within your business. Further, by infusing external intelligence information with algorithms built specifically to understand your environment, once again you have created a force multiplier with known external threat information, enabling you to make quick and informed decisions.

Decision Support

The use of information and technology to make informed business decisions dates back to the 1950s and 1960s, when the Carnegie Technical Institute first created a theory then applied that theory to technology, spawning a new discipline of business science. In the 1980s and 1990s technology and data acquisition continued to advance, and business intelligence functions within IT organizations became a normal service delivery area within large businesses. Today, an entire industry has been created to support the ability to identify, collect, process, analyze, and make data a valuable informational asset and strategic component of how businesses make decisions.

As a chief security officer, you are in the business of making decisions. You are required to understand complex risk issues and unclear threat considerations, and make effective business decisions to ensure the continuity of operations and safe business practices of your company. It is nearly impossible for any single individual to truly understand all of the diverse aspects of those key considerations, drive on-the-fly risk modeling, and make informed decisions without the use of available data and technology.

First, let's start with the basic concept that more data equals more perspective. Simply put, having a system that combines a large aggregation of relevant data in the right algorithm to an interrogation of that data provides intricate insights that would otherwise not be available. More relevant insight around any specific matter creates a broader perspective and, in turn, a better decision.

When we speak of more data equaling better decisions in terms of converged security operations, consider the application of decision making for a complex security incident across your organization. For instance, imagine your security operations center informed you that they were seeing a malicious virus in parts of your business across multiple geographies. Although your security alerting system identified the progressive virus through your malware alert system, how are you going to make the decision of where to deploy your resources to enable prevention, containment, and cleanup operations? If you have a data repository available to you that enables cross-query of security information, IT information, bidirectional Internet access, unstructured and structured data access management information, computer system logs, network flow data, and technology in software information, it may be possible for you to do the following:

1. Know exactly where each download occurred
2. Quickly decipher exactly what type of computers (hardware/software) are susceptible
3. Know exactly the population and potential threat surface of the incident
4. Gain immediate insight into hosts that have been affected and correlate configuration likenesses
5. Understand from those affected machines the behavior of the malware, including command and control, lateral movement, cross-system communications, and other key indicators
6. Deploy network blocks, including firewalls, proxies, and other key technologies, to disrupt the spread and contain the issue
7. Create a probable target definition based on alignment of infection with user correlation
8. Create an incident cost management report based on affected operations, systems, response personnel, and business impact

This is just a small sample of how cross-business data can be used operationally to make better security risk and privacy executive decisions, even during crisis.

The use of this type of decision-making process also extends the use of those data with new partners. When well-established data aggregation and interrogation platforms are available, the reuse of that data for other applications outside of your core area of operations often are big business wins. Key partners in these areas often include the IT organization to help understand how to better align their controls architecture in the management of the services they deliver. Your audit organization can use a large data repository with critical information around security, controls, and configuration data to increase the efficiency of their operations in the overall validity of the data they require to make key decisions. Your legal teams will be interested in the supporting documentation, validation, and evidentiary capabilities that a security intelligence data warehouse provides in the context of litigation support and legal risk management.

The use of data and security intelligence as a decision support platform provides great opportunities far beyond incident response and basic security program management. As a chief security executive, discussions with the business around risk and security matters often are tenuous and at times combative. The basic cause of this type of interaction can sometimes be linked back to a lack of understanding or available data in business terms. When you use quantitative and qualitative information obtained through a security decision support platform or security intelligence data warehouse, you enable a transparent and data-driven discussion with your business partner. By showing them the information and aligning it to the way they are used to looking at business information, you create an opportunity to speak on their terms to solve your problems.

As a security operations executive, the use of a decision-support architecture enables you to make accurate and informed decisions in the deployment of resources, the continuing investment of operations and technology, and the prioritization of security risk and privacy imperatives. Through the active use of data from across your business you can answer questions often asked by executive staff and board of directors: "Why?," "How do you know?," and, even better, "What is the probability?"

PEOPLE, PROCESS, TECHNOLOGY

The future of business operations protection involves an ecosystem of technologies, processes, and skilled individuals driven to successfully enable businesses, organizations, and agencies to deliver their services and products broadly and securely. These varied and diversified components in each area of people, process, and technology will become the lifeblood of the operational success of next-generation security leaders. Through the development of the right balance of these three, and their applied execution as well, security risk and privacy executives of the future must successfully create their own operational ecosystems that reduces complexity, leverages resources, and advances performance in all three areas.

The Importance of All of It

Over the next few chapters this book describes at length how information security, corporate security, and other similar concepts can be refocused into this concept of business operations protection. The diversity of our companies in protective work efforts forces us to extract ourselves from a common, single discipline practitioner model into a converged entity that understands the end to end business process that is the business we serve. As our practice transforms, critical transformational necessity is how we create a bridge between the successive knowledge gap in the capacity of practitioners of today.

As a start, senior security executives must consider the application of the fundamental knowledge management theories associated with people, process, and technology. At the most basic level, knowledge theory can be defined as the practice of organizational learning and innovation. As mentioned earlier in this chapter, functional business knowledge in multiple categories such as finance, business modeling, service and delivery, and business strategy become critical elements in the architecture of preventative security models focused on protecting an end-to-end business process rather than a technology stack or directed people operation. Knowledge theories enable our understanding and management of integrated transactions across diverse areas of business functions, expanding our knowledge capacity and capability in areas such as information economics and process innovation. In our quest to create dynamic capabilities we must use advanced learning concepts that support structured knowledge enhancement for these diverse organizations and strategies.

The use of people, processes, and technology is equally important, and all three are required to be successful in delivering this comprehensive set of next-generation security risk and privacy services. All three clearly relate to each other in your overall operation, including your ability to measure it and consistently improve, which allows for a cohesive interoperable business protection platform. Your success in the management of these functions will be measured in your ability to create an appropriate balance between the three. This balance is important to reduce friction within your operation, create the capacity for problem-solving within your operations, and allow you more time as an executive to focus on your areas a responsibility.

Practitioner Pipeline Management

Of the three areas, people leadership and practitioner management is by far the most important and the most relevant. Throughout the course of this book we will cover many aspects of managing and sustaining human capital investment. Although any leadership or business reference material would certainly agree that people are typically your most important asset, the reality within the security risk and privacy arena is that it is indeed people who deliver the services you manage every day. In fact, in the future implementation of business operations protection programs, the diverse sets of skills—from thought leadership to technical service delivery to analytical thinking—will all serve as the foundational structure of your service delivery capability. Your job as a leader is not only to have the right people to deliver the right services at the right level when needed; it's also to have the capacity and the forethought to build the right people within your organization to deliver continuity of operations, organizational intellectual property enhancement, and over-the-horizon position development for next-generation services you develop as a part of your ongoing quality improvement and advanced services capability.

From individual contributors to leaders, it takes extreme effort on your part to create a people pipeline that meets the operational, cultural, technical, and business needs of your operations. You need to learn to use the support of your businesses, the industry, and your peers to find, retain, and develop them for managing your people sustainability needs. This book will teach you critical elements of and a simplified approached to human capital management.

As you can see just from this chapter, the security executive of the future is an incredibly exciting and complex function. From core practitioner practices, through advanced business theory, to human capital management and advanced business intelligence programs, the demands of a business process protection leader requires diverse skills, critical capabilities, and a unique approach. This book walks you through each element of the core principals and pillars that make that possible.

Chapter 2

Converged Security: The What and the Why

Apply to any MBA course and one of the first things you learn is the concept of business, financial, and strategic leverage as a fundamental need in the success of any business. Leverage and leveragability at times can seem like abstract terms, but in the most pure sense, from a business perspective, leverage really equates to this: creating multiples with shared assets to further the business advantage of profits.

Now ask yourself: "As a next-generation security executive, how do I apply the principle of leverage to supporting my companies pursuit of furthering their business advantage and profits?"

This question, and its answer, is at the core of this chapter, which explains the why and what of a converged security program. Perhaps one of the most controversial strategic models in our profession today, the converged security program and the security executive are not easy to implement or find, yet they both are critically important to the functional success of next-generation security, risk, and privacy programs. This chapter we take a deep look at what converged security programs bring to the corporate table and how they deliver transformation and operational success and drive exceptional management practices. We sort through the history and variations of converged portfolio implementations and cover the business case attributes from a finance, metrics, and business effectiveness point of view. In addition, we cover foundational design requirements such as governance and oversight, navigating choppy political waters, and even basic negotiating principles for those executives looking to create a converged security platform.

OPERATIONAL AND ACTION TRANSPARENCY

In July 2004 the 9/11 Commission released its report including findings relative to intelligence and operational failures that, in part, enabled the horrific terrorist attacks perpetrated by Al Qaeda operatives in the United States on September 11, 2001. The following year the Government Accountability Office of the United States released its report on the failures of interagency coordination as a result of the 9/11 Commission's findings. In both cases the common theme around degraded capabilities to detect, deter, and respond on the part of the

United States were the result of lack of cross-coordination and unified efforts, communications, expertise, and—worse—a culture of secrecy and entitlement within the organizations charged with defending the US homeland.

In the years following great emphasis was placed on creating cross-agency cooperation, communications and intelligence-sharing platforms, and, most of all, enforcing and establishing a culture of operational and action transparency. This is the foundational element of converged security programs.

From business management to the operational level there can be no greater leverageble asset then transparency. The problem is, because traditional security, risk, and privacy programs inside corporations have their beginnings in two very different legacies, with two very different executive makeups, the very same issues determined by the 9/11 Commission with regard to US federal entities are alive and well within corporate America today, albeit at a different scale.

What are these two different factions at a high level and why do they tend to look so different in corporate America?

> First, let's look at the traditional "corporate security" entity. Many refer to this part of our profession as "physical security" or "corporate investigations." Whatever the given title, the function is the formation of traditional and historic general security, public safety, facilitates security, intellectual property protection, travel security, executive protection, and similar programs that defend and protect the physical operations infrastructure and assets of any given company. Although there is a deep pool of global industry experts who are career corporate security executives, the history of many leaders in this function aligned to that of former senior executives from military, law enforcement, and intelligence agencies.
>
> The second area, often referred to as "information technology (IT) security," has a very different history of functional and executive leadership. For instance, this side of the house is steeped in deep technical knowledge of business platforms and architecture and historically has been focused on information security, IT risk management, network security, data protection, disaster recovery, business continuity, and cyber threat management. A nascent career field in comparison, this budding practice started in the late 1990s as a career field by predominately technological engineers from several disciplines of the IT community. Although specific executive leadership career tracks have altered whereby IT security leadership is obtained, the abundant number of incumbents are still sourced from technology leadership, business leadership, and even financial leadership.

Most organizations today still have parallel organizations focused on "security", and in many cases their operations our entirely different. Although at some level they may in some ways share intelligence, people, and infrastructure, many do not share common missions, operating platforms, budgets, communications platforms, standards, or goals. Further, complications of some assumed requirement of autonomy and secrecy on both parts reduce information exchange, shared intelligence, and operating principles basic to the necessity of creating a converged leveraged asset for a corporation.

The responsibility of the next-generation security executive is to create an organizational architecture that ensures the sustainability of a global security program that leverages assets and resources from a multitude of disciplines into a shared operational model, creating a holistic business operations protection program. That is the definition of a converged security leader.

The Single Most Important Attribute

This leverageable effect of transparency is perhaps the most important and obtainable attribute of a converged security program. The ability to communicate, share information, and jointly solve problems is an undeniable by-product of the simple act of sharing insight. Even without a directed command-and-control structure under a single security executive, the effect of this type of unified effort of joint experts and "interagency" coordination can greatly expand the effectiveness and speed at which corporate business protection teams are able to prevent issues with negative impacts from occurring within the business.

No security issue on either side is independent or exclusive of either operation. When was the last time that a corporate security investigation did not require technical evidence supporting an end-user action, email, cell phone, or personal computer? When was the last time that a data protection program did not involve the physical protection of facilities or data centers, or physical access to media and documents?

The world we live in today is a converged world, and all aspects of security operations rely on both the physical and cyber disciplines. To add complexity, the way in which we manage information, data, and people are subject to regulatory and privacy considerations that mandate the inclusion of privacy experts as a component of the ability to deliver resolution to complex business issues. The following are important attributes when considering the joint leadership team under converged security program.

> *One Table*: In my tenure as a chief security officer responsible for converged security programs, every week the heads of every operational and business-supporting security, risk, and privacy function sit (either physically or virtually) at a table and discuss incidents, issues, operations, and critical concerns in front of every other security leader. This exercise creates a unilateral transparency across disciplines, enables real-time leadership discussion and decision making, and results in joint resolution management, defined ownership, and faster action planning. The one table concept supports unified leadership and cross-discipline learning opportunities, enforces the principles of shared accountability, and prepares leaders to operate in a matrixed environment. It also establishes a sense of aligned missions and creates a top–down message to practitioners within your organization, as well.

Interconnected Issue Problem Solving: As a business leader your job is to create solutions and solve problems. In this line of work "problems" is your middle name. The broad span of problems needing to be resolved that will come to your attention is at times mind-boggling, and the impact those issues may have on your business at times will be very broad and critical. Often these issues cross multiple disciplines within the security, privacy, and risk segment. In a nonconverged organization each component of the problem-solving effort often is managed in separate discipline teams. In a converged organization each part of the problem is identified as a joint mission objective and, through the use of interconnected resources, becomes a leverageable asset that speeds the time to problem resolution through the joint knowledge of the disciplines. As a practitioner you will see the value in reducing the threat and risk impact to the business or agency you serve, but as a businessperson you will grow to recognize that speedy resolution equates to speed to business value and it is through your growth as a business value proposition that you truly become a valued part of the executive leadership ranks.
Active Decision-making: If you look at the science of decision-making in general you'll soon find that decision-making is simply the process of identification and choice using knowledge, values, preferences, and other similar attributes of the person making the decision. Active decision-making is considered that same cognitive process that uses decision-making infused with specific selection criteria, beliefs, or planned courses of action in parallel with alternative options. It is believed that this type of decision-making in general speeds time to a better decision and adds to future decision-making through additive intelligence as a direct result of the cognitive computations made during the process. I bring up this point specifically because group decision-making in an active decision-making context for a converged security entity; the additive capability of the education, experience, and combined knowledge of the cross-discipline security leadership group makes for a powerful, well-thought-out, and broad response assurance to a wide variety of security issues. This type of speed, action ability, and certainty in decision-making can make a significant difference and a successful outcome of the negative impact event that you are responsible for managing. From life-saving responses in the context of your public safety responsibilities to financial devastation avoidance in an active cyber incident, the use of active decision-making by a cross-functional team as a processing capability parallel to your decision-making process reduces thinking overlap in unconnected decision-making bodies, provides active iteration to your decision-making process, and adds intelligence growth characteristics to your team at the same time.
Link Analysis: Perhaps you've heard terms like "good police work" or "old-fashioned police work" on television or in something you have read. The terms often reference the use of tried-and-true investigative and operationally sound criminology processes to support policing in criminal investigations. These elements are broad and expansive, including

such components as cataloging, canvassing, interviewing, researching, reviewing, collaborating, informants, intelligence, and so on. Although technology has changed the results of these elements, processes and operations provide either a directed or implied link analysis capability from theory, to evidence, to crime, to conviction. Today, technological applications provide data analysis and evidentiary link analysis through complex algorithms in scientific mathematics that tease out the darkest secrets in any given problem. But human link analysis cannot be forgotten as a readily available resource for decision support, complex decision-making, and solutions engineering. In the context of a converged security leadership group and organization, the exponential leveraging of this multidisciplinary link analysis capability creates a formidable interconnection of an incredible depth of job knowledge and historical considerations across multiple disciplines and multiple industries that allow you as a leader to chase problems rather then be chased by an inability to understand a diversified converged problem set.

Creating Business Simplicity from Issue Complexity

There is no denying that every area within security, risk, and privacy compose complex issues that most businesspeople find difficult to interpret. The fact that our disciplines are not an exact science or technology field, and outcomes and measurements often are measured in algorithms that talk about probability, risk prioritization, and likelihood, added to what is often interpreted as a convoluted approach, increases businesses confusion over how to relate security and privacy problems to business resolutions. Imagine that you are an executive in a company that has three different security executives—one for cyber, one for privacy, and one for corporate security—providing independent updates across a multitude of significant issues that affect your organization. You've just multiplied the complexity to a factor of three and have in turn divided the minimally available attention span of the requisite executive by three. All the while the executive is internally wondering whether he has heard a portion of this before from somebody else, is trying to consider to whom he or she should listen most, and worse, has tallied up the number of independent issues. This executive begins to get sense that the security aspects of the business have become too complex and wonders whether they have the right security leadership in place.

This is where the converged security program provides some of the initial business benefits that organizations recognize when they create a singularly led, joint discipline security program. This deconflicting, demystifying, normalizing, and cross-prioritizing ability across these multiple complex disciplines allow businesses to focus on the priorities at hand and ensure a level of focus needed for critical issues. But the simplification aspect goes far beyond decision-making, an executive focus. It also provides an optimal experience for practitioners, clients, and external partners alike.

Let's start with security, risk, and privacy practitioners. Although the converged security program supports many areas and reduces the complexity for employees, let's focus on conflict reduction, shared intelligence, and mission priorities. It is often in these three areas where siloed operations tend to drive confusion, frustration, and duplicative work streams that waste valuable resources and increase the load on any given functional area.

First, the ability to engage expertise and drive shared functional accountability within a project or a problem set becomes limited when the functional resource elements report through entirely different structures. This is not to say that a well-run company with shared visions and objectives cannot overcome a matrix management environment, but the reality of like discipline executives managing independent groups of people competing for budgets, accolades, and success often leads to a less optimal experience and pressures that roll downhill to the individual contributor. When you remove fiscal, political, and competitive employment boundaries of the leadership, the necessary focus of mission objectives and success tend to become the priority and the focus of the organization.

In the end, transparency drives simplicity, understanding, and speed to resolution.

THE BUSINESS OF THE FUTURE

The goal of a converged security executive is to create a sustainable, multidisciplinary security service entity focused on protecting and enabling the business of the future. Therefore, of course we must ask, What is the business of the future? Does it really matter if convergence is considered as a part of the organizational makeup? There are three undeniable characteristics of any business that enforce the concept of a necessary converged security program: advanced technology, global by default, and increased regulatory considerations. The three of these together continuously cross boundaries within multiple security sectors and create substantial workload and elevated priorities for businesses in almost every size and industry category.

Technical

Although I have a technical background I'm not jaded enough to believe that every business in the world must have technology. But when you start to review, research, and simply ask how technology is used from a five-person mom-and-pop store to a multinational public corporation, it is amazing how uniquely dependent each organization is on technology. When my eldest daughter entered college, focusing on agriculture, I thought it would be great for me to learn a little bit more and to see if in any way our worlds would cross. I started with what I considered would be the most common area in agricultural safety and intellectual property protection assurance. What became interesting to me as I continued to read, educate myself, and research was that the agricultural industry had an incredible history of, use of, and future in technology. From daily operational crop management through global distribution platforms, and even into decision support systems for agricultural sustainability, technology is and will be one of the most important levers in the future of sustainable food sources. In almost every industry and size of business that statement still rings true, and by default that has deep implications for the global economy.

Businesses of tomorrow will depend on technology that delivers critical resources and assets that enable their business, move their money, draw their clientele, and deliver their services simply because of the adoption technology in human existence. The security and privacy implications will go far beyond the major multinationals that focus on these areas today and will affect organizations large and small.

Technology in Business

As we consider the impact of advanced technology within the business of the future, for the purposes of this book, we must consider the implications or areas where technology becomes the concern for any given security service. The easiest way to conceptualize this is to take a given business, map out their actual business process, indicate where technology is used, and underneath that create a matrix that lists any given security, risk, or privacy service on the *y*-axis. Then, under every process area, make a checkmark where a security service may be used in the support of technology operation platforms within the business. You will quickly realize that, from people management, through business operations, into the sales arena, product development, go to market, service operations, transaction management, billing, funds management, and so on, technology is riddled through every aspect of the business.

Technology support is not limited to just cyber defense, information assurance, and like services when it comes to security. For instance, when we think about ensuring the continuity of business operations in the full spectrum of business resiliency, necessary services need to be provided to ensure business continuity planning, disaster recovery management, and the ability to manage a crisis. If you are supporting a company that deals with financial money movement, you must consider the applicable services mentioned previously, but look at additional services such as fraud management and financial crime investigative services. If your company deals with sensitive, protected individual data, then data privacy functions must be engaged to ensure the correct handling and security of the information applicable to regulatory mandates. The lesson to be learned is that the business processes that involve technology are not solely the responsibility of information security or cyber services, and it takes every part of a holistic security delivery model to provide a secure and resilient business process that relies on technology.

Technology and the Human Process

The advancement of technology is a direct relation to the interactions that humans have envisioned, innovated, and demand as part of their work life, private life, and society as a whole. As a security practitioner it is important to recognize that evolving technology is the process of human and societal evolution. There was a time when protecting a business entity was focused solely within the confines of the business itself. Whether it was the brick-and-mortar company's defense and protection of its facilities and campuses or the computer infrastructure that was dedicated solely to the purposes associated with that business, our jobs were limited to the confines of that business. The evolution of the continuing development of technology and integration into the human process, however, blurs the lines between individual's personal actions and those associated with work. From work-from-home scenarios, to integrated technological devices that support both personal use and business use, to technology that better manages the tracking and management of the human condition, such as "wearables," the extensive use of technology in the day-to-day life both people will greatly affect and influence the services necessary to secure and defend the businesses of tomorrow.

As a security executive of the future, you must consider these implications as the cornerstone of your program development. Where do your responsibilities begin and end? What are the implications of diverse work locations as the "campus" of the future? What are the regulatory considerations and data protection issues associated with private corporate data comingled with private individual data? Part of your job is to establish the guidelines, thresholds, and service scope requirements for your company. Issues such as jurisdiction, data ownership, privacy limits, electronic discovery capabilities, safe work environment limitations, and many others will be greatly affected by how the integration of technology and the human process continues to evolve.

Technology in Crime

As I think back to when I started in my career in law enforcement, the concept of technology in relation to crime predominately was in law enforcement's use of technology rather than technology as a component of criminal actions or the investigation thereof. Oh, has the world changed. It is truly difficult to think of any criminal or policy violation action that you may be required to investigate that is not in some way—and in the context of this chapter—affected by technology. Compile that with the use of technology as a decision support infrastructure for public safety and security management, and technology suddenly becomes a large part of how crime is operated and managed.

Let's start with something as simple as petty theft on a campus. When investigating petty theft, the use of technology has become critical to the ability to quickly narrow a suspect pool, provide intelligence, verify facts, and gather critical evidence. For instance, if a facility was experiencing a rash of these type of thefts, we would probably use technology to validate who was in the facility during the given periods of criminal activity through the badge access system. We would also probably use network video-recording capability as part of the facility monitoring to attempt to identify criminal acts or suspicious behavior. Once people or surveillance targets have been identified, the use of advanced video surveillance will most probably be used, and even technology-laden "honey pots" could be used as a mechanism of criminal identification. Later in the investigation, the use of electronic discovery such as email reviews or social media reviews may be required to create the case. All of these real possibilities and we are still just talking about petty theft. From egregious criminal actions, such as assaults against people, to high-tech crime, such as the theft of intellectual property or cyber attacks—the use of technology across all criminal actions will only increase.

In the context of this chapter, the complexities that technologies introduce across each area of technology investigations, privacy investigations, criminal and civil investigations, policy violations, and general crime and public safety management demand a method, structure, and service architecture that meets these needs. This structure must have integrated operations capabilities, access to intelligence across a broad span of programs, and resource management that is not interfered with by political, jurisdictional, or budgetary boundaries. This structure can be obtained only through the use of a converged security platform.

Technology and Multidisciplinary Security, Risk, and Privacy Operations

As we consider the value of converged security programs, we must also consider the use of technology in cross-discipline security, risk, and privacy operations. Although later in this chapter we cover in-depth converged security technologies and reducing operational costs by leveraging platforms, the advancements in cross-discipline technology use is a key consideration in the discussion of advancing business technologies. In many respects it is our profession's ability to institute business protection services that enable our companies to expand operations into new markets, product sets, and physical operations around the globe. Our ability to solve problems, leverage resources, and extend an effective operating range is enabled through the use of advanced technology sets. Consolidating operating platforms, integrating information management and intelligence management solutions, and automating processes across disciplines that ensure effective controls are designed and implemented in a timely and cost-effective way enables our profession to move nimbly yet with great effectiveness for our business or agency. Compare an organization that has segmented operating, control, and monitoring technology platforms for each of their security areas. If the business has to consider the cost of extending operations to a specific region or market by replicating platforms for each given security discipline, and the time to deploy each independent system, as a prerequisite to their expansion, or they have the opportunity to use a converged security technology architecture that supports all given disciplines, which do you think they would choose?

Global By Default

The next element of key concepts for businesses of the future in relation to security services architecture development is global by default. No matter what size your business is (with some exceptions), in many respects your security responsibilities become global by default, even if your operations are in a single town or in a single country. The implications of an interconnected financial ecosystem, interconnected web of technology, and global supply chains that support even the smallest of operations, you must think like the chief security executive of a multinational corporation when developing your security program and plan. It is, perhaps, not that you will be providing services in multiple countries, but more that your company or agency can be affected by many forces far beyond your control and far outside the nation state in which you operate.

In the previous section we talked about technology as a part of any business in one form or another. If we accept that technology is a part of any given business, then in effect we are global by default. Consider the most basic of operating infrastructures required to run a business—such as Internet, email, telephones, electricity, public services, financial services, and so on; these are dependent on the availability of those services to you, whether managed internally or externally. Those services can be greatly affected by global issues such as Internet cyber attacks, global supply chain incidents, cable cuts of major international telecommunications services, and global cyber crime or nation-state espionage aimed at the markets you serve or the markets of the providers that deliver your services every day. Your business depends on your ability to defend against these international threats and business-impacting issues. That may not mean you actually provide the defensive service capabilities or active services, but rather that you consider the greater external view of your threat surface and your operating requirements and service options as you create your business operations protection plan.

Regulation

Next we focus on the implications of continuing expansion of regulations for commercial entities. Although every business must, for the most part, adhere to basic regulations in support of employment issues, human safety issues, and other business requirements, major regulations with regard to specific physical security, cyber security, or privacy operations have mainly focused on sector-specific businesses in areas such as the defense industrial base, finance (such as banking, money movement, and insurance), publicly traded companies, and critical infrastructure entities as determined by independent regulatory authorities in any given jurisdiction across the globe. Advanced political and public pressures in response to the impact of cyber, privacy, and financial incidents around the world, however, have created an onslaught of new regulations that have unfocused business sector–specific requirements and created broad and sweeping requirements for any entity of any size in specific areas, such as protecting identity information and private health data.

These newer consumer protection regulations are what is believed to be the beginning of a new governmental capability to regulate private entities to ensure the protection of the public interest. Consider US regulations that define what health data is, how it must be protected, and what public or private entities must do if that information is somehow breached. The common businessperson may pay no attention to the changing requirements until an incident occurs that demands their attention, but as the senior-most security executive, your job is to keep abreast of these industry changes and how they affect your company's go to market and risk positioning. In addition, the translation between regulatory compulsory requirements and real-world control, monitoring, and reporting requirements (or components thereof) may fall to you. These broad requirements often cross areas of responsibility in data privacy, data security, compliance, reporting, investigations, and forensics. Companies that can reduce organizational complexity through convergence often have a higher propensity of successfully meeting requirements since management ensuring the enforcement, monitoring, and reporting of controls occurs under the authority of a single executive.

Interconnected Business Ecosystems

The last area to consider as we think about the future of what businesses will become is a simple concept that demonstrates that nearly all companies, big and small, are not insulated from the impact of technologies, regulatory issues, and global implications simply because they are "doing it right." The reality remains that through the simple ways that businesses operate and will continue to operate, we must consider the fact that the world is an interconnected business ecosystem where security concerns that affect another company have ripple affects far beyond their walls and could affect your business. A kinetic terrorism attack against a power grid could stop your business dead in its tracks. A cyber attack against the telecommunications company that delivers your telephone and Internet services could also stop your business. Or perhaps a data theft from a key partner that manages components of your go to market could introduce disastrous and costly legal and regulatory actions. Establishing broad business operations frameworks that take into consideration the totality of your businesses architecture, go to market, and operating footprint requires the ability to nimbly operate across historically independent operating groups.

THE COST OF GOODS SOLD

Making the case for a converged security program often hinges not on the security reasons to make the switch, but rather the smart business reasoning behind the decision. In commercial entities (although the same school of thought follows in governmental agencies) cost containment isn't an "every now and then" thing; it's a basic element in the survival of free enterprise. Each industry has its own measures of financial success, but every business depends on the margins between the cost of making the product or providing the service and the profit from the sale of the product or service, commonly referred to as margins. Each business has different levels of sensitivity to these margins, but they are the basic measure by which a company becomes profitable.

As a security executive, decisions you make must consider how your expenses and investments affect those margins and the cost of goods sold (COGS). It is your responsibility to understand the financial measurements of your company to better articulate the impact of your spending in the same manner the rest if the business is also measured by. Do you know whether your costs are considered general and administrative nonsales expenses or are added as a component of COGS? Have you broken down the different areas of your budget to differentiate what supports business operations, product go to market, facilities management, presales support, and so on? Knowing these things is important because how your business recognizes, amortizes, and reports those costs requires your ability to provide them in a format that makes sense to financial professionals.

Having a good understanding of your program's financial picture and how it affects the overall company financials is import for planning, leveraging your resources, and supporting the business while making smart, risk-based security decisions. It shows increased business acumen on your behalf and demonstrates that you consider yourself part of the business and hold yourself and your operation responsible for the financial success of the business. In the next section we relate how converged operations makes this process easier, more transparent, and more efficient.

Efficiencies to Drive Investment

Now that you understand margins a little better, it's time to explore the implications and opportunities associated with security, risk, and privacy functions. The cost basis of any security organization has been and will always be a complex issue within businesses. Even in companies that have a higher risk of impact if a negative impact event were to occur, there is always a fine balance between security spend versus total realized business risk. Often, security investments are not as immediately tangible as other investments, and the discussion about how much is enough or too much will always be a concern. Yet this does not need to be the only discussion, nor should it be. During budget season, better discussion topics are things like "we've become 14% more efficient in our security spend through XYZ programs and we are seeking to reinvest in these three gap areas." Responsible business management equals responsible financial management, and that is the sign of a successful security executive. Detractors to this process or ability at a total company level, however, are often the complexity and confusion that multiple security functions create, thus detracting from better investment and financial management conversations.

From a basic financial discipline point of view, multiple security organizations in a company drive more costs. From duplicative full-time equivalent employee costs, such as executives, administrators, operations support, project management, and so on, to basic operations management functions, such as reporting, demand additional time, effort, and costs inside and outside the organization. These costs are often difficult to quantify, but when they are done, they represent a significant opportunity for reduced duplicative functions and costs. In addition, until a unilateral cost evaluation is complete, it is not possible for a business to define its total cost of business operations protection spend and even less possible to align that spend in the different areas of financial reporting.

Additionally, with multiple security silos also come independent operating platforms including prevention, detection, monitoring, reporting, incident management, incident response, risk management, labor management, and similar technology stacks. These different parallel and often like operations drive costs because of segmented purchasing decisions, independent operating teams, and even duplicative maintenance and depreciation costs. Through simple platform consolidation and maximum leveragability of resources and technology across like required functions, the total cost of security ownership for your company can be reduced dramatically through simple and effective smart business management.

Finally, from a financial perspective, the negative impact of a bifurcated security, risk, and privacy program is not always measured in the straight costs of the profit and loss statement; many times it can be measured through the inefficiencies in time to resolution of a complex, multidiscipline issue that extends the duration of exposure and increases the likeness of exploitation simply because of a lack of decision-making and the independent implementation of fixes required by all parties. Those waters get more muddled when security executives in each independent area disagree because of ideological, political, or self-preservation concerns. These extended exposures have tangible and intangible costs that need to be considered as your organization heads toward a converged approach.

LEADERSHIP

The core concept of this book is training you to be a security leader for the future. The critical concept here is leadership, and as we explore the necessity of convergence as a fundamental component of the future security program, we must address clear differentiated leadership principals that highlight the effectiveness of the converged security leader. For the most part, we can sum up the advantages of convergence using a comparison to water. The larger the body of water, the larger the selection of diverse and component talent to select from, and terms such as diversity, leadership, and capabilities should not be taken lightly.

Capabilities and Diversification

"Diversity," a term often overused or overlooked, it is most often referenced when considering the management of people by a race, religion, ethnicity, or similar measure. But the science of diversity in leadership and management goes far beyond the color of skin or the measurement of who works for you. Diversity, when truly embraced, allows you as a leader to create a competent tiered organization with diverse knowledge, skills, thought processes, and capabilities. Diversity of leadership ensures that nepotism, bias, and extremism are muted and removed from your decision-making and management process and expands the combined knowledge base of education, practical experience, and individual strengths that help you make better decisions more quickly and with a greater cross-discipline landscape.

In traditional insular security programs leadership selection often comes from within the linage of the specific discipline programs where like backgrounds, experience, and education are the baseline to which future leaders are groomed and from which they are recruited. If you are an IT security leader, perhaps your career path meant a BS in Computer Science, a postgraduate degree in Management of Information Sciences, and previous IT and security positions. If you are on the Corporate Security path, perhaps you have a history in government service with a degree in Criminal Justice or Homeland Security. Although this may seen as an overtly biased depiction, in my experience, I have often seen similar narrowly focused predefined leadership criteria in singular functional teams.

The clear cross-discipline integration of work issues, work efforts, and hard business problems of the future business entity does not allow us the luxury of partisan approaches to secular decision-making. By creating a cross-disciplined leadership team in converged leadership architecture, you create a diverse pool of knowledge and expertise with broad experiences that can deliver faster solutions, more complete decisions, and a broader business-centric approach to business protection.

Talent and Succession

Better and faster decision-making won't be your only concern as a future security, risk, or privacy senior executive. As a leader, your responsibilities to organizational sustainability demand that, in addition to the services you deliver every day, you must ensure the success of the future operation with our without you at the head. This means that talent and succession planning are at the top of your agenda every day, but in one of the most growing professions in the job market, pipeline development of leadership is easier said than done. It is not unheard of for a senior security position to be open for up to a year because a lack of a talent pool, and when working through internal succession development and planning, the smaller the organization, the smaller your leadership team and the less ability you have to draw future leaders from it.

Consider the following as minimum capabilities of a future successful security executive. These skills are necessary to effectively navigate your position as a senior business executive who has broad responsibilities and is positioned to drive change across companies, not just manage a security function:

1. Deep business acumen
2. A clear grasp of technology and technology futures
3. Over-the-horizon thinking
4. Knowledgeable in functional regulatory and legal issues
5. Deep financially based decision support
6. The ability to connect, translate, and capture
7. Force multiplication engineering

These seven staples of the "security change agent" in tomorrow's businesses create an instant uphill struggle in terms of finding like attributes in potential talent, acquiring that talent, educating and advancing them, and retaining them for potential succession positions. To make the problem more difficult, the smaller your organization and the smaller your leadership team, the less ability you have to draw from that internal pool, driving higher search and talent acquisition costs and reducing your training investment and institutional knowledge bank.

There are only two ways to accomplish this: (1) hire resources with the requisite talent and experience or (2) train promising talent with the necessary skills. It's never an either/or situation, and your leadership positions must be well mapped out to determine which positions require which skills in support of your operations. Once you have mapped out required positions to skills and at which level they must be competent, you can determine where those skills exist in your organization, where they need to be developed, and how long you can take to build required skills into your leadership team.

Converged security teams assist in diversification and talent development in several ways. The most obvious is that the expansion of your responsibilities means an expanded leadership team, from which you will have a larger pool of resources that you can acquire and "build to suit" the future needs of your business. By simply moving from 2 or 3 areas of responsibility to 6–10, you are provided with a wider pool of leadership candidates and a broader selection of talent, including technical, operational, business, and converged.

The successful attraction, acquisition, and retention of talented human capital in the security industry is not limited to just money. Often, factors far outside compensation attract the type of long-term, dedicated practitioners you are looking for and keep them on the team for many years. In my years as a chief security officer I have found that the five following areas are most top of mind for practitioners when selecting new jobs:

1. A forward-thinking and advanced security program
2. Opportunity to expand knowledge and practitionership
3. Leadership progression
4. A mission-focused organization
5. Ability to participate in decision-making

These are consistent both among individual contributors and across leadership paths and should serve as a reminder that as the executive responsible for sustaining an operational security program, you need to consider what type of foundational organizational characteristics your program will be recognized for. Each of these program attributes takes effort, resources, and action to develop and maintain. By prioritizing which attributes are most important to those candidates in your industry, then establishing a baseline gap assessment, you can quickly develop a plan that creates those program characteristics. As you progress through this book we discuss in detail how to develop these attributes.

As important to the discussion of why talented people join an organization, how they know what their opportunities are is also key. I am referring to the clear establishment of job families and career paths that, in themselves, demonstrate opportunity and knowledge development expansion possibilities. This becomes exponentially more powerful in a converged organization. For instance, if you are in a siloed security organization, such as information security, typically you are limited to positions specific to engineering, operations, analysis, architecture, and management job families. In a converged organization you may have management and leadership positions in many other disciplines such as risk management, facilitates protection and public safety, criminal and civil investigations, fraud management, crisis management, business resilience, client security, privacy, travel and executive protection, and other functions specific to your company's needs.

Beyond the addition of cross-discipline leadership functions, a converged security program offers promising management leadership candidates with a well-rounded education in all aspects of a professional security career. A broad-based job family enables you to create unique career ladders that help develop these leaders of the future by generating career path guidelines that establish expectations in cross-functional knowledge achievement. As leaders under your command rise through the ranks, they should be expected to go outside their comfort zone and take leadership positions in areas adjacent or even foreign to their given discipline. From manager, to senior manager, to director, and on to the executive core, a converged security program enables you to ensure that your future leaders experience professional training and on-the-job education in multiple disciplines of security, risk, and privacy leadership.

Leading a converged security program can be exciting and rewarding in many ways. Certainly one of the most rewarding is creating new leaders that will take our profession further in the years to come. Job families alone do not create leaders. Your hard work in architecting your leadership schema, creating opportunities, and making good choices in human capital management will create the security executives of the future.

OVERSIGHT AND GOVERNANCE

The function of security, risk, and privacy programs in corporations and agencies is essentially a risk management program, as mentioned previously. Depending on the type of industry, the type of business, and the size of the organization, the security concerns in focus areas, as well as the risk measurements, will be different. The reality is, however, that, in general, business executives do not segment the word "security" as much as security practitioners do. When a business has siloed security programs, this often results in duplication of oversight and governance processes that thereby result in duplicate outcomes. Think of this in the context of a financial organization: Does your company have an independent chief financial officer (CFO) focused on procurement to pay and another CFO focused on revenue recognition and compliance with general accounting practices? Of course not. Can you imagine the confusion, the replicated work, the additional effort if those two finance functions reported independently into the same oversight organizations but at different times and with different approaches and priorities?

How is security any different from their standpoint? For the most part it isn't, and in the future it shouldn't be. The concepts of cross-discipline security risk and privacy operational issues should be apparent and easily articulated, reviewed, and processed by governance and oversight groups. When companies and agencies establish multiple leaders and segmented security operations programs, they often lead to bifurcated decisions, segmented and fractured strategies, and a poor ability to cross-relate risks and priorities and ensure compliance.

Focus from Executive Committees and Boards

Later in the book we learn what appropriate governance and oversight architectures might look like for security risk and privacy programs, but two groups that will always garner interest and need to engage the security executives of any given entity are the executive committee (the chief executive officer's leadership team) and the board of directors (or the similar structure for nonpublic companies). Each of these groups have specific needs and reasons to engaged in an overall understanding of risk issues associated with security risk and privacy functions. One thing will always be true, however: getting the attention of these groups is difficult. When splitting security responsibilities between multiple executives, oversight and governance functions face the problematic of issue of who should they listen to as the foremost security leader in the organization, how should they bifurcate their focus, and who gets a lower priority because in their mind it is simply not efficient to listen to two leaders on what they considered to be the "same topic."

This type of unnecessary decision burden often reflects back on to the company as having security executives that may not have the right level of seniority to be in the position if they are not capable of representing a holistic view of all security, risk, and privacy issues. As security functions mature and become more mainstream business processes, the converged security executive must be better prepared to be that single point of leadership, that senior security executive expert, and the one business leader to deliver the message, drive the conversation, and create clear consistency across all security disciplines for governance and oversight authorities.

CONVERGED TECHNOLOGY AND ARCHITECTURE

Earlier we acknowledged that technology's involvement in all aspects of security functions has become an integrated part of how we operate. Although at times this may seem to drive complexity, if developed and used appropriately, a converged technology and architecture function becomes one of the most significant levers in resource, process, and intelligence management and the linchpin in maintaining consistency in converged program assurance. The concept is very fairly basic: Create a single framework and architecture from which all security, risk, and privacy functions operate. Beginning with the selection of technology, to the development of any given processes, to the use of human, cyber, and business intelligence, you build for the majority, not the minority. By ensuring that development of operational resources are maximized to support all security functions, you reduce overhead and maximize your buying power by forcing the creation of an operating platform that gets maximum cross-discipline use rather than investing in platforms that get singular group use. The following are examples of a few of these areas.

Leveraged Infrastructure Equals Smart Business

One of the most costly areas that you will be responsible for managing is the operational infrastructure and technology that helps you deliver the services you deliver to your business. Any business-replicated infrastructure that is used by only a portion of the organization is a wasted asset, so the focus of a leveraged infrastructure is to reduce wasted or unused portions of your operating platform. Segmented security leadership often leads to independent program and platform selection for each area. The reality is that the core requirements and necessities for why the platforms are being deployed are shared in some form or fashion with each function. By carefully understanding each one of their requirements, creating the solution accordingly, and selecting technology and platform purchases adhering to those criteria, you make a smart investment through a shared service platform that allows not only for better utilization but also for wider transparency across multiple operating areas. Consider the following list of technology and operating platforms and how each disparate security function would be able to use the resource as part of their everyday service delivery.

10 Key Platforms to Consider

1. Detection platforms (Data Leakage Protection (DLP), Deep Packet Inspection (DPI), Intrusion Detection Systems (IDS), etc.)
2. Monitoring, alerting, and response technology

3. Security intelligence and analytics platforms
4. Governance risk and compliance platforms
5. Case reporting and evidence management
6. Facilitates access and visitor registration management
7. Business continuity, crisis management, and disaster recovery platforms
8. Key performance indicator and reporting platforms
9. Program, project, and utilization management platforms

The easiest way to implement this type of converged platform architecture is to create first a singular architect function rather than multiple architects across each discipline. The leader of this function should be senior and experienced enough to grasp the concept of multidisciplinary use of technology platforms across diverse job functions. Second, establish or use extensively an existing technology oversight group that provides guidelines that demand the demonstration of how a technology will be fully used across all security, risk, and privacy disciplines.

Tactics, Techniques, and Procedures

"TTPs" is often referenced by military or government entities as an acronym for tactics, techniques, and procedures. Sometimes it's used to describe the fingerprints of a known adversary or to reference standard operating procedures by which you will lead. In reference to a converged security program, TTPs are the formalized instruction sets by which your operators, analysts, responders, investigators, and in general all practitioners operate for any given scenario within your service delivery function. These are the "how tos" of our business and serve as guidelines, instruction sets, and checklists during normal and emergency operations.

Something that often goes unsaid or unnoticed is that TTPs take a lot of effort, meaning that the development, documentation, training, and organizational readiness require resources, time, and financial support. When you multiply this across independent security functions, the costs add up, and if they are not coherently aligned, during the course of an urgent situation lateral security organizations may find that their procedures do not match up, wasting valuable time, effort, and potentially degrading an organization's response capabilities.

Converged security organizations provide businesses with an opportunity to create a standard set of operating practices that incorporate multiple security functions in a singular process. These converged TTPs create like decision-making standards, create smooth operating linkages between disparate security services, and provide transparency and knowledge sharing for integrated response and operating dependencies. Further, by establishing shared TTPs, organizations gain the benefit of the old Marine saying, "sweat more in training, bleed less in battle." It is through joint training and joint practice that converged security teams create the best leverage of all: shared and expanded knowledge.

Creating Intelligence

The third most leveragable convergence platform opportunity is in the area of security intelligence and analysis. Undeniably, one of the most important leaps in security operations in recent history is the utilization of business intelligence platforms for the use of intelligence creation specific to security functions. In the last chapter we described the holistic approach of the business value chain as a consideration of how we must think of defending an entire business. The use of intelligence operations for understanding external forces, managing internal resources, and deriving intelligence for multiple data sets must also fall into that holistic approach. Even more important, however, how we share and utilize that intelligence across multiple security disciplines creates a resource multiplication effect that maximizes our efforts in collection, analysis, and decision-making capabilities.

The cross-utilization of incidents, actors, trends, indicators, and other similar security intelligence attributes needs to be used, enriched, and evaluated through the lens of a converged entity. The costs associated with collection and analytics for each independent security discipline demand a better approach to an overall intelligence program. Data collection, data storage, data processing infrastructure, analytic computing platforms, and other components need to be shared cross-functionally to reduce the overall cost impact to all security organizations. Further, when data is reviewed and interpreted with a broader perspective and enriched with more data points, the intelligence output is greater and more meaningful than any singular area of focus.

To achieve this, organizations should collapse the fundamental data collection and processing architecture into a single leveraged instance. Standards should be incorporated that determine data collection mechanisms, intelligence sharing standards, external data ingestion mechanisms, and data cleansing processes. Finally, a single security intelligence operations function should be used across disciplines to help create the analytical requirements of any given function, reducing duplication, exploiting existing resources when available, and maximizing intelligence outputs for all converge security entities.

The savings and cross-utilization cannot stop within security practices only. By expanding and extending your operating platform to other organizations within the business itself, including segmented business groups, you are engaging in good business practices, reducing complexity, and developing margins by encouraging the use of resources that are already in place. Is there any reason why corporate audit functions should implement a separate governance, risk management, and compliance platform? Should corporate legal have to go out and independently procure their own evidence management system? Should your procurement organization purchase a segmented risk management measurement application for third parties? Look across your platform; engage executives outside your function who could tangibly benefit from your investments, and force good discussions for the financial betterment of your company.

TIME TO RESOLUTION

Another clear advantage of a convergence security program is the acceleration of the metric time to resolution, commonly referred to as TTR. In service organizations the TTR is often referred to as a foundational key performance indicator that drives client satisfaction and quality metrics, and is also used in the measurement of business financials. The measurement is simple: elapsed time between the discovery of an issue in the resolution of that issue. In security programs the metric TTR takes on entirely different level of criticality of measurement because the actual measurement of TTR not only measures the capability maturity of preventive, defensive, and monitoring controls, it is also a key measurement in risk findings. In the areas of threat modeling, threat management, and vulnerability management, that period of time—or the open window between issue discovery and remediation—increases the opportunity for exploitation, increases the possibility of other threats surfacing, and potentially increases the overall impact based on exposure times.

As a security executive, you are accountable for not only the holy grail of prevention but also for reducing the TTR, reducing the overall risk posture of your organization, and mitigating the potential downstream impact of any given threat. In organizations with multiple independent security functions, the accountability of any given issue may often be bifurcated across multiple executives, and your ability to effectively make decisions to start the remediation process could be hampered by political lines, organizational lines, budgetary lines, and other real or perceived functional decision-making issues. The following further explains why converged programs accelerate risk reduction and program acceleration.

Accountability and Decision Ability

When I speak to new leaders, I often spend a lot of time on the importance of accountability. Accountability to self, to those you lead, to family, to organizations you serve, and to your beliefs. Accountability is a key element in human performance; it serves as a behavioral lever in several aspects of human perception. For instance, accountability may drive me because of a moral standard that I believe is important, whereas in others accountability may drive action as a result of their competitive nature, and yet in others accountability and the results thereof maybe driven simply as a compensation response to their hunter-gatherer complex. The key to any of these considerations is that accountability typically drives action, action drives inertia, and inertia drives the ball forward. Forward momentum, no matter how slight, is momentum, which is what you should strive for as a decision-maker and leader.

Your sense of accountability should drive you to take action that requires your ability to make decisions. Decisions come in all shapes and sizes. Sometimes they are well informed, studied, and agreed on. Others need to happen fast and are based on experience, with minimal information at hand. No matter what the decision you must make, the fact remains that you must be enabled to make decisions, and act on them, within reasonable time frames and with minimal approvals. If you are the leader in an organization making a decision, then seeking multiple approvals does not make you accountable for an issue, it makes you a contributor to a joint issue.

In a nonconverged security company the concept of "responsible–accountable–consulted–informed" (RACI) responsibilities are independently aligned for each security, risk, and privacy discipline. When operational issues across multiple boundaries in organizations get caught up with "who makes that decision" and "why did they make that decision" and "that's not their decision to make," it reduces a leader's ability to effectively move the ball forward and begin problem-solving in an incident management process. In today's world security issues are broad, do cross multiple disciplines, and require urgent action. By consolidating reporting structures in decision-making leadership roles, organizations are better suited to making better decisions faster.

Action and Oversight

The same thought process can be applied to ensuring the actionability of those decisions and the authority for oversight. The decision process is only one factor in driving issue resolution and management. In the action phase resource utilization, direction, and task management are also critical in getting the job done. Just because a decision is made does not mean that a disjointed and comingled working group will get to end of job in a timely manner if their leadership groups are not aligned. Converged security organizations resolve these types of issues by using codeveloped, cross-discipline standard operating procedures by diverged practitioner areas and operating as a single unit rather than multiple units introduced only at the time as needed. This type of multidisciplinary, single-unit approach has worked exceptionally well in elite military units for many years. When special operations groups are formed for specific missions, members of those groups may come from different military services and military occupations such as antiterrorist specialists, forward operators, K-9 units, medical experts, demolition experts, intelligence experts, and many other skill sets. But they establish organizational frameworks, joint procedures, joint training, single command structures, and operational accountability well, which enables action-oriented decision-making and delivers incredible success.

As you develop your framework, ask yourself: "How am I going to ensure decision-making success?"

THE TWO-HEADED POLITICAL MONSTER

Politics matter. Some people like it; many of us don't. Some people are good at it, and others struggle their entire career. But the fact remains, in any business or agency, public or private, politics plays a role, no matter how big or small, in the everyday workings inside organizations. In cross-functional operations and corporate positions, the political battleground increases. If you operate in only a single business unit, your politics are typically compressed to that area. If you have global responsibility in a multinational company and manage critical security functions that cross multiple divisions and business units, the political issues tend to be much larger.

In bifurcated security programs that level of "politicalness" is exasperated by competing budgets, political positioning, and a multitude of other issues. When multiple security leaders compete at the highest level of a company for attention, dollars, and decisions, that political positioning can waste precious resources, time, and goodwill that could be focused on the problem rather than the independent security entity itself. Remember that influence, trust, goodwill, bargaining, and favors are all elements of political capital, which is often referred to as the invisible currency of politics. Consider those elements as precious resources there are needed to pay for the missions you are assigned and take on. The reality is that there are only so many resources to go around, and independent political positioning by segmented security groups is a waste of those resources. Converged security organizations with single-stack leadership can more effectively use the political capital necessary to focus on overall prioritized mission objectives rather than issues of self-interest or independent organizational positioning.

This book is not a lesson in the science of the human psyche. It is important to note, however, for the sake of understanding competitive political positions in reference to multiple security leadership functions, how the natural science of the human psyche, specifically the ego, can affect effective leadership. The ego is simply a part of one's personality that coordinates functions such as defense, perception, intellect and cognition, and executive function. It's responsibility is to mediate individual impulsive and instinctive drives and actions with knowledge and intellect for self-sustainability. Think of it as a safety mechanism rather than a selfish mechanism. In fact, well-developed and balanced egos are part of a well-balanced person. The important part in all this is that egos drive action, but typically action focused on the success of a single person. Because of this, leaders with similar functions waste valuable cognitive effort for self-sustainability decision processes to ensure their executive success rather then the success of the entity they are responsible for. This is a human trait, and even converged security leaders apply self-sustaining thought processes as part of ego processing. This doesn't make anyone egotistical or mean that security leaders have "big egos"; rather, this is it simply a subconscious self-preservation exercise. The problem occurs when security leaders are competing for exposure, praise, wealth, resources, and so on and make decisions corrupted with egotistical consideration based on a competitive nature. This can often lead to poor business decisions and detract from effective management.

The final area of interest when considering converged security programs over traditional bifurcated security models in the context of politics is the effort required to manage multiple negotiations across multiple issues. Whether it's the development of policy, implementation of standards, negotiation of RACI responsibilities, or just the agenda at the next security council meeting, negotiations between security groups are a tremendous waste of resources. Single security leadership structures cross-discipline responsibilities that use programmatic and measured prioritization based on business need, and broad-based key performance indicators reduce unnecessary expended energy required for consensus development. Wiser organizations use their resources, political capital, and negotiation skills to solve issues themselves rather than discuss who is going to solve the issues.

METRICS TO THE RESCUE

The final important area to discuss in relation to the need for converged security programs is in the area of metrics and measurements that provide a clear understanding of the risks, resolve, and efficacy of a company's or agency's security, risk, or privacy capabilities. As a security leader, one of your most powerful tools is your ability to use data in negotiations and business cases, and simply articulating and explaining security concerns. A great mentor of mine once said, "Numbers don't lie, and numbers don't have emotions." When you as a security executive master the business principles of going to the table with hard data, established metrics, evidentiary material, and an impassioned approach, you will become an effective negotiator and arbitrator, which will enable you to drive action.

Problems can arise in companies that have segmented security groups because different approaches, mechanisms, and frameworks for how data is gathered, measured, presented, and tracked are often used. For instance, an IT security organization may take a parochial approach, using a specific framework such as Control Objectives for Information and Related Technology or an International Organization for Standardization framework when defining security performance indicators and metrics, whereas a corporate physical security function may use a practitioner-based model specific to an operating area such as physical security, environmental security, or supply chain security. Other specialty disciplines such as fraud and privacy add to the confusion, with their own independent frameworks and models. Although often the multipronged approach is used for the right reasons, the amount of data, the complexity, and the diversity of decisions that need to be made become very complex to the nonpractitioner and subsequently inhibit the security prioritization process and deter focus from the business that is needed to resolve issues in these critical areas.

Converged security programs enable organizations to create cross-discipline measurement frameworks that demystify complex multidisciplinary issues and provide a single representation a non–security expert can understand, as well as a broad set of program and service measurements and indicators that help drive business decisions and provide transparency into security operations. A converged security program can focus on three principal areas:

1. Standards of measurement
2. Efficacy assurance
3. Truth in services

Standards of measurement create a baseline mathematical or measurement function that interprets specific attributes about a service, control, or outcome that can be applied across multiple frameworks and measured in a like manner. For instance, an applied algorithm may include a numerical representation (say, 1–5) for elements such as capability maturity, deployment level, global serviceability reach, automation ability, or other similar measurements that are important. The total sum is a component of the measurement algorithm and creates the baseline metric. Because of the simplicity of the measurement elements, this type of common framework based on a collection of cross-discipline frameworks delivers broad applicability for all areas of a converged security program, enabling you as a security executive to have a simplified conversation with your business partners.

Efficacy assurance is a mechanism aimed at the measurement of multiple parts of controls architectures to ensure that what you have works. Although this may be a simplistic way to look at it, it is truly harder said than done. Most people consider controls as technical controls, but when having a discussion with the business about the investments made in all areas of security risk and privacy, controls may include things such as policy controls, people controls, technology controls, process controls, management controls, and any other number of programs aimed at managing risk. The points that you will be trying to get across are this: Is a control we implemented working the way we expected it to? Does it still reduce risk as intended? In an unconverged company, each security, risk, and privacy executive may provide their own independent answers for those two questions. In the converged security organization, however, through the implementation of standardized efficacy assurance measurements, the senior security executive is better able to make investment decisions against prioritized cross-discipline risk issues that are also measured under something like an enterprise risk management framework.

Finally, the ability to have a discussion around the effective use of resources and an organization's ability to deliver security services requires a standard framework for service measurement. This framework is used for resource management needs, attests to internal and external capability concerns, and generally is a part of a mature organization's decision support architecture. A framework that measures service maturity, service capability, service delivery, and service effectiveness can be used in multiple security, risk, and privacy disciplines, enabling transparency into investment dollars, and can serve as a baseline for prioritization alignment to corporate and agency security needs.

Chapter 3

The Job of the Senior Security Executive

In the previous chapters we touched on the importance of converged security programs and future business operations protection programs. In this chapter we begin to focus on you, the senior security executive. By creating the starting point for developing your personal strategic roadmap, along the way we the hit upon important points that are an important part of creating and developing career momentum. Understanding how your chosen career affects businesses both within your industry and outside your industry, will help you create a more well-rounded approach to security leadership. By diving deep into the role of a senior security executive, we can touch on critical areas such as business needs, driving business transformation, and ensuring strategic executive alignment as you move from operational management to business leader. Establishing baseline expectations and concepts through advanced functional requirements, including executive alignment, specific role functions, and business attributes, and even providing advanced business protection priority development and mission development, this chapter serves as a foundational baseline for the job of the senior security executive.

REALITY: THE STATE OF SECURITY RISK AND PRIVACY TODAY

This section focuses on the history of the chief information security officer (CISO)/chief security officer (CSO) positions, career field, the state of the global technical infrastructure, the availability of solutions for key security considerations, and the evolving diversity and advancement of threat.

Reliance of the Global Economy on Computer Infrastructure

The criticality of the services that a senior security executive delivers to industry every day cannot be overstated. At a global macro level, the defense of technology infrastructures can be measured in the impact on world economics and nation-state gross domestic product. When you pull back from your day-to-day job, from your independent company, and even from the industry you serve, you have to think about how technology moves the world we live in. From small, mom-and-pop stores in your local community to major national retailers, technology delivers goods and manages cash flow. From the electricity that comes to your house to the water supplied to your city or town, technology is required to create utilities, deliver those utilities, and make them safe. Major transportation infrastructure such as highway management, ocean-based shipping, trains, and public transportation all use computer technology and networking infrastructure to operate. The world in which we live, the economies that drive it, and the safety of society on the whole rely on the technology platforms and security defense services you deliver every day.

This is the state of the world today, and as technology continues to evolve and be integrated into our social and human fabric, the criticality of the defense of that fabric becomes significantly more important. In the not-too-distant future the Internet and the integration of consumable electronics will be responsible for important things like home health care, residential food delivery, vehicle safety, and one million other innovative applications of technology into the way we live our lives every day. This means that cyber attack and the threat surface will grow exponentially with those innovations, demanding innovations in the way we defend the world's reliance on global technology platforms.

Human Capital

The next critical component to discuss is people. As a converged security executive, the majority of your focus is on understanding the actions of people, ensuring their safety, and aligning to the needs of the people within your company or agency. In the abstract, the business element of people is often referred to as "human capital." The term "human capital" is simply the aggregated compilation of knowledge and skills that people have to further the goals of any given entity. As the senior security executive of your company, you are charged with ensuring the protection of that human capital, which, as you will soon learn, is ensured through the delivery of many different services, all focused on people.

Until the world creates true artificial intelligence, it is people who will develop, run, and manage businesses. Your job is to ensure that they can do it in a safe and protected environment—whether that's an office, traveling in an airport, or in the field halfway around the world. It is not your responsibility to dictate where your business is or where your company's people need to operate, but rather to be sure that they can operate safely wherever the business requires them to do so.

Further, in the context of people you must remember that, as in any society, organizations have rules and social frameworks to which people are accountable. In the concept of cities and towns, it is the responsibility of the justice system and law enforcement to ensure the sanctity of those frameworks. In the concept of private business enterprises, it is typically the responsibility of general counsel to be the justice system and for you as the senior security executive to manage the "law enforcement" component, providing safety functions, investigation operations, and legal and litigation support for issues from business policy to crime.

The effect of human capital management on your job should not be understated and is a critical component in any business. This is a key job responsibility. Long gone are the days where security leadership does not need significant people skills. By studying how human capital affects your business, you will be better positioned and equipped to create the necessary services to ensure the sustainability of your business or agency.

Intellectual Property

Now that we've addressed the critical delivery mechanism of knowledge and skills—people—we need to focus on the knowledge compilation that is developed as a critical asset to any business. The legal term for the formulation of this asset is "intellectual property". There are many international and domestic jurisdictional considerations for what intellectual property is; however, most agree that the legal frameworks by which intellectual property is governed by can be covered in four basic areas:

1. Copyrights
2. Patents
3. Trademarks
4. Trade secrets

The term itself references property that is actually the creation of the mind. Although a form of intangible property, the protection of these valuable assets is deep-seated in international law and spans every conceivable business entity. From the development of music, to the creation of scientific formulas, to business process development, intellectual property is a protected asset that must be considered as a foundational element of any converged security program. In larger businesses an attorney specializing in intellectual property, or what is commonly referred to as IP law, typically manages the governance process, definitions, and management of all corporate intellectual property. From a security, risk, and privacy perspective, you must be prepared to deal with the enforcement aspects for the infringement or misappropriation of your organization's intellectual property, whether in policy, criminal, or civil form.

As we discussed in previous chapters, business operations protection must take into account all aspects of your business. Significant financial implications are a real possibility when intellectual property is not appropriately identified, protected, and managed. By being a part all of the overall intellectual property defense process, you are better positioned to reduce potential impact through prevention, identification, and detection of intellectual property crimes and supporting external entities, such as outside counsel and law enforcement, and quickly responding and reducing your company's risk exposure.

The Impact of Crime, Terrorism, and Violence on a Business

Understanding how external forces and actions, such as crime, terrorism, and global violence, affect your business is another fundamental consideration of your job. Let's face it: You do not operate in a vacuum. The external conditions of the environments in which your business operates affect your company's ability to deliver goods and services and the cost of doing business in those locations. Further, if you are doing your job right, a consultative approach to informing your business of these types of considerations during the decision-making process provides a critical cost savings and cost avoidance by ensuring the decision-makers are well-armed and informed of issues and situations that could potentially affect their interests.

When developing your program and the support of business intelligence for the purpose of impactful crime, terrorism, and violence, it is easiest to complete your business process value chain analysis first. You will be able to overlay an understanding of how your business works with factual data in the geographies you are responsible for, thereby creating a true actuated risk definition, allowing your business to better grasp the issue. Real risk measurements create a financial screening capability that aligns with how your business or agency often makes critical decisions. Some of the areas you will need to consider and be prepared to support are:

- business operations locations;
- intellectual property protection capabilities;
- employee travel;
- supply chain defense;
- third-party management; and
- technology deployment.

Part of your senior leadership objectives should be to have preposition business support services that help to measure the risks to the business and its operations in the context of these external issues. The sole decision must not be made based on probability and vulnerability to your business alone, but rather on the holistic capabilities that you are able deliver to your business as preventive and protective services in each one of those areas. For instance, are there third-party companies that can support the defense of your operations in any given geography? What are the costs of those and how is that figured into your risk calculation? Is there an acceptable level of risk associated with each one of these components? Is there a defined risk appetite to which you are evaluating?

Your evaluation should be made in conjunction with your businesses approach and the business's strategic needs, and the mechanisms used to evaluate and create your calculated risk measurement should be transparent.

These types of external forces and elements are important to understand as the chief security officer for your company because they dictate the types and levels of services that you must support. This does not mean that you must have specific programs for each of these areas, such as your own antiterrorist team or your own criminal task force, but how you deliver services to reduce the impact of these issues does matter in many areas including the following:

- Public safety and facility security
- Travel security and executive protection
- Business resiliency and crisis management

- Intellectual property protection
- Security intelligence operations

By better understanding the downstream residual effects of these types of external forces on your operations in all aspects of your business delivery processes, you will be appropriately informed to make risk calculations. These risk calculations serve as decision points in security program investments and needs by the business. Using critical information and intelligence services provided by governments and like government entities within the jurisdictions you operate in is critical in understanding those impacts. In the United States, the Department of Justice makes available information by the division of Unified Crime Reporting, which gathers, records, and aggregates crime information from all 50 states and US territories. Internationally, the United Nations and Interpol also provide worldwide data specific to a variety of crimes to help you better understand your business's operating environments and to help you plan for the level of potential impact your business may face.

The Who and the Why

Beyond supporting operations that you provide to the business in defense of criminal enterprises and criminal attempts against your business, understanding who would want to harm your business and why must be more than a conceptual discussion. Criminals and terrorists target different industries, different business types, and individuals for very different reasons. Understanding how your company fits into the crosshairs of criminal operations is paramount in your ability to create preventive operations and to prepare for the eventuality of having to respond to criminal actions.

Although large multinational corporations typically have competitive and security intelligence groups, you need not have a perfect formalized group of full-time criminal analysts in your organization to understand threats to your business. The following list represents excellent avenues from which to derive information about the different criminal threat vectors for your business:

Open Source Intelligence: This mechanism of data-gathering is probably the fastest and easiest, and is a great way to start. Using the Internet, information-sharing groups, and the media to provide a basic look at current happenings, affected organizations, threat actors, and regional considerations can help you narrow your scope of research. As the old saying goes: If it's free, it's for me, and I'll take three. Of course, that needs to be balanced with the level of confidence you give to the information based on where you obtained it.

Industry Intelligence Groups: "Birds of a feather" (the term given to people with similar interests who share information) intelligence sharing is probably one of the most productive uses of your time. Depending on what industry you're in, some of these groups are very formalized, such as in the defense industrial base, financial services, and critical infrastructure. In other sectors they are less formalized with less infrastructure, but nonetheless they still have terrific mechanisms for gathering and ensuring case information, such as methods and objectives, evidentiary data, actors, mechanisms of defense, and even information about which law enforcement agencies support those specific types of issues.

Government Reporting: Another option is to use publicly available and sometimes nonpublic government reports from a variety of different agencies across the globe. Organizations such as the US Department of Justice Bureau of Statistics, Interpol, Europol, the US Secret Service, as well as a variety of other agencies, track criminal and terrorist activities targeting a variety of industries and report a broad span of data about previous incidents and potential future targets. These reports, both classified and unclassified, can largely be trusted, are typically not politicalized, and can be used as a data point in your overall decision-making processes.

Informal Law Enforcement Relationships: Some of the best data I've ever received came through my relationship with peers who fight the same fights I do every day on the government side. Their level of commitment to defending society is always impressive and they typically truly understand the effect commercial entities have when assisting in stopping, preventing, and investigating criminal activity. For each industry, each business sector, and each global market are law enforcement agencies that specialize in crimes specific to your business. In the United States alone there are more than 17,000 local, county, state, and federal law enforcement agencies. Obviously, some are larger than others and all have a varying degree of investigative capabilities. In some instances federal law enforcement may focus better on a specific area; however, in other areas, state or county agencies may have a dedicated task force available to supporting industries specific to your business. Either way, create a list of potential criminal issues that you are aware of or are concerned about and research what agencies investigate similar issues. Set time aside to meet with each of those agencies and begin a relationship. These types of informal touch points and relationships often lead to mutual information sharing, providing quality information from a trusted source.

Formal Government Intelligence Sharing Programs: The opposite of informal government relationships are formal government programs that are set up for public-private intelligence sharing and collection. Some of these require government clearances whereas others simply require mutual nondisclosure agreements and information-sharing agreements. If you are unfamiliar with an agency's effectiveness in these areas, get with other members of or peers in your industry and ask them what they think of any specific program. Those groups that require a clearance and target a small and specific industry or group of companies typically have good and active data that you can use.

Commercial Intelligence Services: The final area of opportunity are commercial intelligence services that provide, for a fee, targeted reports, ongoing human intelligence gathering, automated open source gathering, and entity-specific threat analysis. The major players in this service areas are all very good, are typically staffed by former government intelligence analysts, and utilize automation, technology, and good tradecraft together with data for you or on your behalf. Although in the groups I manage I typically have full-time intelligence analysts assigned, I still use external, contracted commercial intelligence services in gap areas, areas of specialty, or in times where speed to intelligence delivery around a specific topic is important, such as intelligence or criminal activity focused on business travelers in a specific region of the world, or a merger or acquisition in a specific industry. When I need extraneous information not available from an existing method of collection, commercial intelligence services provide surge capability with a high level of confidence of good-quality data.

The Changing Privacy Climate and Its Effect on Sustainable Business Operations

Whether you are a CPO, CISO, CSO, or chief trust officer, the fact remains that data privacy is a very important element of your executive capabilities. At the time of the development of this book, there were more than 37 new privacy laws being written around the globe. Whether it is a nation-state's perspective to implement these regulatory mandates for the purposes of consumer protection, data protection, or digital economic expansion, privacy laws have gone far beyond a set of parameters and guidelines by which to operate and now can truly affect the financial stability of an organization.

Although it may seem provocative that a single regulatory issue can threaten a business, the facts support it. In several jurisdictions punitive and criminal damages associated with some these laws can account for up to 5% of an organization's gross revenues. In addition, the impact to the COGS cannot be underestimated. The requirements to implement prescriptive controls, required infrastructure, mandated operations that support specific notification clauses, and even business operation restrictions can change overnight the cost basis model of any given business.

At a minimum, your protective and response priorities specific to data privacy are required for your own businesses information. Your human resources data, employee health care information, timekeeping data, employee training information, and so on are all subject to privacy legislation. Further complications occur when you are operating as a multinational organization and are trying to manage your global employment information on a single platform. Legal requirements such as safe harbor certifications, binding corporate rules, and filings with data protection authorities in each jurisdiction become an operational and management challenge of their own.

The stakes only increase as you start to consider the client data you are accountable to protect. You need to understand whether you are a data owner, a data steward, a data processor, or a combination of these in each jurisdiction you operate in. You need to be fully versed in understanding contractual language that affects financial and contract liabilities subject to privacy and data protection provisions.

Understanding privacy beyond basic business practicalities is required because your policies, standards, and operational frameworks need to take into account this new era of operational privacy requirements. From privacy by design through operational privacy programs and into integrated data privacy and data protection convergence operations, the next-generation security executive will spend much more time talking about privacy imperatives than network security.

The responsibilities of the next-generation converged security executive specific to privacy imperatives must address at a minimum the following categories:

Privacy Definitions: A working taxonomy to establish meanings, needs, requirements, and expectations across a broad set of jurisdictions and regulatory language.

Privacy Operation Frameworks: A defined approach outlining responsibilities, accountability, and ownership for everything from policy to privacy incident response. This can be self-developed, based on industry standards, or a combination of both.

Privacy Controls: Much like cyber defense and information protection controls, privacy controls and their assurance must be defined, implemented, monitored, and measured. Because privacy controls in the future will focus on data assurance, security executives will likely need to cross-map privacy control sets with others in their wheelhouse. Privacy by design and privacy engineering concepts will be the active result of these control requirements and will introduce new service-offering requirements.

Privacy Operations: In every company "privacy operations" means something slightly different. Simply put, privacy operations is the ongoing efforts of a sustainable privacy program and services delivered by a company. These may be a simplistic as "privacy consulting" services given by the firm's CPO. It can be as complex as the holistic management of a set of an entirely new privacy technology control infrastructure.

Privacy Monitoring: Like privacy operations, privacy monitoring may fall into a couple different varieties. The first is what is typically referred to as continuous monitoring, or controls assurance. This is your organization's ability to monitor internal and external compliance of the privacy control infrastructure needed to support the industries, markets, and geographies you operate in. The second area is literal monitoring. As technology continues developed in support of broad-reaching privacy requirements, businesses are looking toward technology to manage their privacy concerns. These tools and technologies will require some type of monitoring and in most cases can and will be combined with existing cyber threat operations. In both cases converged security executives should be prepared to understand their monitoring requirements, develop and deliver metrics and key performance indicators associated with their monitoring controls, and drive transparency and assurance through effective reporting.

Privacy Incident Response: The final area of privacy that next-generation executives need to develop is the concept of privacy incident response. Cyber response is significantly different than the requirements of privacy response. From notification requirements, to client and customer interaction, to regulatory filings, and even incident problem root cause analysis and investigation, privacy issues and incidents have unique handling requirements. That is not to say that a foundational incident response framework is not a great place to start; rather, I am saying that when a privacy incident is identified, a segmented action plan, work plan, and incident response plan should be available to the incident response team. Some large organizations may be fortunate enough to have independent teams that support either function. In most cases, however, a single incident response group will be responsible for handling both, and special response instructions and handling instructions ensure a legally compliant and appropriate response to privacy matters.

The focus of privacy-related acumen for the next-generation security leader is not singularly focused on data privacy matters. In a converged security environment, groups outside of cyber, including employment law, employee travel security, facilities safety and public safety, and many other areas, have their own unique requirements because of the increasingly regulated areas around protecting consumer, citizen, and employee information. It is your job to know how privacy affects each of the areas you are responsible for.

The Business Ecosystem and the Critical Impact of Trust

There's an argument to be made that perhaps next-generation security leaders should not even be called security leaders but rather trust leaders. In several major corporations, such as salesforce.com and Cisco, executive leadership focus on trusted relationships with both clients and partners as a fundamental element of the business ecosystems they manage. Trust does not always come easy for security practitioners. Often considered to be or referred to as naysayers, Chicken littles, theatrical, paranoid, and a host of other negative disparities, we have a historical (and sometimes well-deserved) bias perspective to overcome. As security executives have successfully made the transformation from a very black-and-white world to an understanding of a colorful world managed by many shades of gray calculated through risk programs, we must now demonstrate our ability to strengthen the ecosystem by being the champions of trust.

There are three primary trust areas ripe for development by the next generation security leader. The first is driving trust within your business.

The next area is trust within your partner ecosystem. You may have only one or two critical supply chain or business-related partners or vendors, or you may have tens of thousands. You help to influence the needs of your business specific to security, risk, and privacy within those entities you do not control through a trusted relationship. Although you may not be able to manage their business, you certainly can manage your own services aimed at supporting that ecosystem. Areas of opportunity include providing transparency into decisions, policies, and operations that affect how they deal with your business. Potentially extending existing services that you have in the support of your overall business, such as user awareness and other like functions, to your partner community shows them that you are not just checking a box but rather are making sure that they are considered a trusted part of the ecosystem for which you are accountable.

The final area that should be a foremost priority in establishing trust programs is, of course, with your clients. With the exception of those businesses or agencies that have a captured clientele or don't need to create revenue, establishing trust with those who consume your goods or services is typically considered a really good thing. As security executives, I argue that it is a really, *really* good thing. Trusted relationships with clients go far beyond reoccurring revenue implications from returning clients. At an operational level, when things go bad, trust often saves the day. When you operate a transparent program that engages your clients, delivers trust through consistency and defined and managed outcomes, and enables bidirectional communication, that communication is even more effective when there is stress on the relationship. I've been in situations in my career where a security incident that has affected several customers had significantly different outcomes based on the levels of trust between our companies. In one case a mid-sized company with which we had not yet established a direct relationship at a practitioner level felt the need to have multiple internal and outside attorneys, most of their executive staff, third-party security firms, and their security director deal with the incident. That call did not go well because of the lack of understanding of the issues and an assumed level of distrust because the incident was our fault. Because they did not know how we operated they assumed the worst possibly behavior from us, which couldn't have been further from the truth. During the same time frame and the same incident, I had that same call with a Fortune 50 company that we had a fantastic relationship with. That company audited us two to four times a year, as we did them. Our practitioners shared technology, infrastructure, and operational programs in a joint effort to strengthen both of our security capabilities. We had formal information sharing in place, and every year they attended a third-party security summit we hosted for our clients and vendors. A call was scheduled for 90 min and we completed it in under 30. We explained the issue, the root cause, the remediation steps underway, how it was being handled within our enterprise risk management system, and the attestations they would receive from us. There were a few nominal technical questions and several operational explanations but that was essentially it. Their level of trust in our ability to defend our environment, provide transparency into our operations and risks at a reasonable level, and execute our commitments made it a nonissue.

Trust operations is not just about getting people to believe you and to sell more. It is about creating financial and operational success through shared knowledge, transparency, and mutual respect. Trust programs reduce costs through the reduction of time and resource effort, enable faster sales and delivery cycles by reducing implementation and COGS, they provide a return on investment by advancing and ensuring client retention.

Technology as a Lever, Not a Solution

Clearly, technology will continue to be a requirement for developing the acumen of security leaders, whether you are within a converged security position or not. As a senior security executive in general, not only must you be the defender of the technology infrastructures supporting your business, your use of technology as part of how you manage your business will be just as important. Today, more than ever, the skill set required of an operational executive is not measured by simply creating solutions for problems sets with technology, but by advancing your operational management capability to use technology as a lever.

Before we get into a discussion of the skill set required for resource, operational, and management leveraging, let's not discount the need for technology solutions to be a lever as well.

Your success when trying to advance security, risk, and privacy levels, standards, or program efficacy during business discussions relies directly on your ability to articulate and demonstrate flexible options that come across more as a selection rather than a forced requirement. Since the car and brake analogy is incredibly overused and abused in our industry, why stop now? Consider when you go shopping for a car. Imagine you're buying a car for your job. One of your requirements is that you need to get between multiple locations. The faster you do that, the faster you make money. When you tell the salesperson your needs, would you prefer that they tell you there is only one vehicle for work purposes and it has very special breaks to ensure that the vehicle can operate at very high speeds? Or would you prefer options? Assume there are two or three options. In addition to the first car there's another car that goes only a third as fast and the breaks are not really good, but that's okay because the car doesn't actually go that fast. There's also a middle-of-the-road car that goes two-thirds as fast as the first one but the cost is still much less because it has fewer creature comforts. Presented with these choices, you can make a better financial decision based on the reality of how fast you can go on public roads, your anticipated breaking requirements, and other things that maybe you have already thought of that the car salesman has not.

This is what we are talking about when it comes to choices of technology lever in the programs that you deliver. By aligning requirements with a set of services or technology delivery capabilities aligned to different risk postures, you create choice and flexibility that enables consumer confidence in the services you deliver.

The other important area in using technologies as a lever is in your operational management capabilities. Although the core part of any operational leader's job is to develop solutions to critical issues, of which technology will always be a part, responsible executive management also includes the use of technology to appropriately manage their business. These two things are not necessarily exclusive, and often when selecting a technology you have benefits in both providing a solution for a security issue as well as leveragable management opportunities. For instance, consider facility security management. Imagine you are trying to solve a multisite issue of badge management because of a lack of card access control, reporting visibility, and identity integration. The solution to remediate this issue may include a centralized badge system whereby individual sites become a slave to the enterprise platform and integrate into your company or agency identity directory. That is a fairly standard approach, and by doing so you get better transparency, more controls, and better reporting. In addition to all that, from the management leverage side, that technology can also be used to optimize security. Today you have five sites and you consolidate them under a single enterprise system. You previously had several people doing badge management at each of those locations. Consolidating to an enterprise platform could potentially allow you to issue and manage badges from one site with specific service-level agreements for delivery and reduce resource expenditure at the other sites. In addition, you probably are required to perform audits for things like regulatory compliance, industry certifications, and corporate controls attestations. If you have five independent sites, that means five independent reports have to be created, normalized, then joined together to create a single report. This single enterprise system will most likely have the capability to run immediately a single report with normalized data for all sites without the need to manually develop reports, again reducing unnecessary resource utilization.

That was a very simplistic view of technology use for resource leveraging. Your job is to map your own business, define where duplicate or manual processes are in use, and evaluate how technology can reduce waste, add efficiencies, automate manual processes, and reduce the total cost of ownership for the services you provide. Technology can be one of your biggest financial levers through work and resource cost manipulation and management. By automating work, adding efficiencies, improving speed, and removing duplicate work, you may be able to increase the optimum output of your organization while maintaining financial cost controls. That is the bottom line of what is expected of you as a business executive in your company.

Market Opportunity and the Supporting Role of Security

Another clear advancement in the use of security, risk, and privacy services by leadership executives and businesses across industries is their use in the decision-making portions and operational imperatives of seizing market opportunities because of the strength of their security position. In fact, the opposite can also be said in this era of continuing onslaughts of security issues that face businesses today, both in the form of cyber as well as physical operations. Those companies that do not believe they have appropriate capabilities to protect their business often make decisions not to seize market opportunities because of concerns that they cannot manage these type of significant hurdles.

Therefore, the question is: "How do you ensure that the services you are delivering increases market opportunities for your business?" The answer is this: Understand the strategy, vision, and business roadmap of your company or agency; research perceived or real roadblocks within your area of operation specific to security, risk, or privacy; and create a plan to remove those obstacles or provide options for reducing risk.

This may be easier said than done, but the process is relatively simple. Consider the following seven-step process as a project outline for strategy and growth enablement programs:

1. *Strategy Review*: Spend time with your corporate strategy group or the senior leaders responsible for its future and expansion. Document markets and geographies, and specifically ask whether they have any concerns around security that potentially you may not even think of.
2. *Evaluate Potential Risks*: Through the use of industry information, intelligence, and other like data, create a list of potential risks for this new or expanded business strategy. This list should be broad enough to address cyber, physical, and privacy issues.
3. *Facilitate Documented Risk Assessment*: Once you have a good list established and qualified, run it through your normalized risk assessment process. Because this is a future opportunity, you may choose to create a "risk assessment lite" to speed up the process. Either way, the outcome needs to be formalized, calculating an actuated risk measurement that can be articulated, defended, and used in risk reduction formulas.
4. *Align Risk Reduction Opportunities with Existing Controls and Services*: Use this step to match qualified risks with existing services or programs you provide your business that can either automatically be implemented to cover the risk or can be extended at a cost. This process serves two desired outcomes. The first is to show your business the flexibility of the investment in your program to support the future needs of the business. The second is to evaluate whether you have that flexibility in place.
5. *Create a Tiered Risk Reduction Options Approach*: Now that you have created a list of gaps, create a measured risk reduction option menu for the business to enable leadership to make informed decisions on their strategy expansion. Remember, risk does not always mean remediation, nor does it mean that the risk must be totally removed. By providing options and showing executive leadership how their risk is lowered and by how much with each option, you become a flexible resource to them.
6. *Document a Simplified Business Futures Security Enablement Plan*: Being able to talk to your business or agency's future strategy and roadmap in the context of your business is very important. A view of how to enable the business should be a tool you keep ready at all times. This should be a simplified document that you can speak to rather than a 10 to 50 page

Powerpoint presentation that you must drag the business through. Consider using the framework of the business's strategy document or a pictorial representation of it, as well as a clear and concise balanced options scorecard based on your assessment and plan, along with your suggestions on risk remediations, timing, and potential costs.

7. *Meet with Business Leaders*: Finally, the business will not know this work by osmosis, and you should not wait until they ask you to discuss it after they have made certain decisions. Be proactive in meeting with executive management to discuss the current business strategy and the work you have done to ensure they are successful, and stress the importance that there are measured approaches to reduce any potential security, risk, or privacy issue that they may be concerned about. Letting them know ahead of time that "you've got this" and showing them your approach will give them confidence in driving the business forward.

The art to this approach is doing it as a normal part of your everyday operations and getting answers ahead of your internal clients concerns. Imagine how you would look if you went into a meeting about future strategies prepared to discuss potential security issues, existing risk reduction plans, the potential financial impacts or necessities pre-calculated as the executive management team is making its decision. That type of forward-looking capability helps your business make faster decisions and execute them more quickly, thus supporting opportunity costs and time-to-market considerations. That is the level of business acumen necessary to be considered a next-generation security leader.

THE CSO AND THEIR ROLE

There is no doubt that the CSO role has significantly developed and expanded in the past decade. From technology, to convergence, to legal considerations, the security executive requires broad, career-focused technical acumen across a large set of service areas while still serving as a business executive supporting the organization's goals and strategies and managing his or her business of security.

No matter how the position of the CSO develops, there are some basic fundamental concepts and requirements of which each senior security executive should be aware. This section of the chapter touches on some of these critical concepts to create a baseline expectation to be used when thinking about how you lead, how you manage, and how you drive your own organization. These expectations are not just assumed practitioner requirements; they are the expectations of your business in how you carry out and assume these responsibilities, which determine the success you have within your position.

To Protect

In a search of any generic explanation about "security" or a similar service, the word "protect" most often is associated—and for good reason. I often respond to messages of thanks with a simple phrase: to protect and serve. Although a bit tongue-in-cheek, there's a lot of reality to that statement. As a chief security executive, your primary duty is to protect. Certainly, one can argue that your job has many more functions—as it most certainly does—and will continue to grow in the future. But that word "protect," that duty of care, the fundamental necessity to protect from harm, is by definition the primary goal of your position. Prevention of negative impact events against people, businesses, economies, technologies, and markets is why our jobs were created.

When establishing some ground rules about how we protect, security practitioners can take their cue from ancient Greek science that is still in use today by doctors who take the Hippocratic Oath. The Latin phrase primum non nocere has been a consistent part of that oath for centuries, and loosely translated it means "do no harm." There is a lot of wisdom in that statement, and for years it has been studied as a part of governmental rule, societal management, and the advancement of human studies. For our purposes, this principle of do no harm should serve as that voice in your head on a daily basis that guides you in delivering your services to the business every day. It has been the downfall of many great practitioners when they become so focused on accomplishing the mission, destroying the bad guy, driving absolute defense; they forget that their principal actions should be to enable the organization, not to reduce, restrict, or inappropriately constrain it in any way. So, to start off this conversation on how to protect, this is a reminder to be diligent and ensure you don't cause more harm by overprotecting.

Before you get all charged up and start running out to protect, you need to think about what you are protecting. When I asked some new CSOs what they thought they were protecting, I was surprised by the wide variety of answers I got but was encouraged by not only the inward look but the outward look of what they understood was at stake if they did not do their job. Broadly stated, in most cases, CSOs are focused on protecting people, assets, infrastructure, and technology. Of course, there are wide definitions associated with these. Take assets, for example. An asset can be a digital asset, such as intellectual property, or a financial instrument, such as a currency or trading document. An asset can be a building, a campus, or a supertanker. Your job is to understand which assets need protecting and exactly how to protect them.

In each of these areas—people, assets, infrastructure, and technology—the key in knowing how to protect each one is understanding the downstream residual impact of not protecting it. In one of my previous commercial jobs I worked for an electronic manufacturing company that provided storage technology for just about every Fortune 500 and government agency in the United States. At times, my decisions were not predicated on the immediateness of what would happen to the company I served, but rather what would happen if I did not successfully protect the issue, and I allowed a situation to occur that could have developed into a negative impact event affecting the technology and the structure of all of those companies and government agencies. What would that impact be? How would that affect the economies and societies we supported? These types of questions often help drive a clearer definition beyond the "what is the risk to my business?" concern and support the creation of priorities based on the downstream residual impact of your business threats.

In the end, you will find that you have many things to protect. Your programs will all line to the eventual strategy of defensive operations for the prevention of harm to your business or agency. It is up to you to create that broad picture, that canvas by which your own teams will operate. By understanding your business, the environment in which you operate, and the threats associated with it, and by prioritizing your efforts to address the most critical issues facing your business, whether external or internal, you will be well positioned to protect now and in the future.

To Respond

Preventing things before they happen is, of course, the desired outcome of anyone in our business. Bad things do happen, however, and as your company's senior-most security expert, you will be seen as the chief responder, the bad things know-it-all, and you will be held accountable for preparing your company, your organization, and yourself to lead through a crisis.

In the pure sense of the word, not everything you will respond to will be a crisis. In the eyes of those you serve, however, every issue will be a crisis. Taking away labels, frameworks, and everything else associated with business resiliency and crisis response, the point here is that you need to be (and will be expected to be) the rock of any type of crisis at your business. During critical times, businesses need an authoritative anchor to help sort out the process of responding, remediating, and moving forward. Critical incidents are so broad that when one is not strictly business-related (e.g., a product failure, a brand issue, a client support issue) the business turns toward the leader who should be most capable to manage them through the crisis. That would be you.

Don't mistake knowing how to manage a crisis with knowing how to fix everything or know everything about everything. The secret of crisis management is knowing the practitionership of crisis handling. It can be argued that the same crisis response protocol can be used just as easily for a fire in one of your buildings as for a data center outage at a third-party vendor site affecting your go to market. In fact, the most mature crisis management programs incorporated in governments follow the same standards and protocol developments formulated from a program originally designed for forest fires, now referred to as the National Incident Management System (NIMS). The figure below is an example of the NIMS crisis management architecture and associated functions. Notice that the descriptions are fairly general, and all serve specific functions. Your job is not to manage all those functions, but rather to ensure leadership is assigned and trained in each of those areas. Consider becoming certified in a national or global standard of crisis management. This way, when bad things do happen, and when the business does call, you will be prepared to execute appropriately.

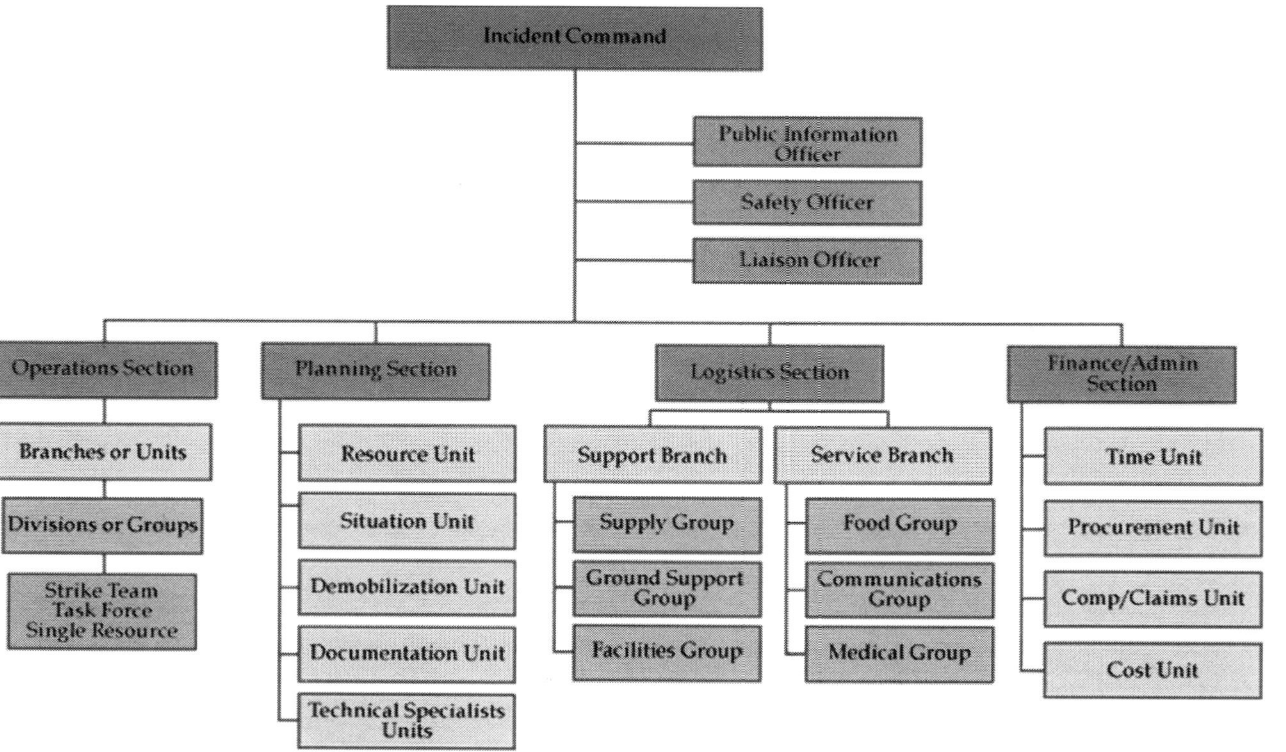
Incident Command
Public Information Officer
Safety Officer
Liaison Officer
Operations Section
Branches or Units
Divisions or Groups
Strike Team
Task Force
Single Resource
Planning Section
Resource Unit
Situation Unit
Demobilization Unit
Documentation Unit
Technical Specialists Units
Logistics Section
Support Branch
Supply Group
Ground Support Group
Facilities Group
Service Branch
Food Group
Communications Group
Medical Group
Finance/Admin Section
Time Unit
Procurement Unit
Comp/Claims Unit
Cost Unit

Inevitably, to call in a crisis, you need a 911 operator; rest assured that is you as well. Part of your crisis preparation must be understanding how to qualify issues, route issues, and escalate them as needed. The business needs you to help it solve and manage these issues, and you must be prepared to support it by doing this. Being prepared ahead of time by setting up simple processes and infrastructure to support this "911 function" puts you well on your way in meeting the business's expectations. There are three basic things to consider when preparing to be that 911 operator:

1. *Methods to Report*: The most important thing that you must be able to provide to your business is a capability to get information to you. Whether it's a centralized telephone number, a messaging service, an email address, a web portal site, or smoke signals, ensure you create a sustainable capability, inform the business of it, and train your people on how to operate it. Depending on the type and size your business, there may be multiple avenues of reporting critical incidents and issues, from automated alert notifications, to more basic technologies. By understanding your business, who needs to report, the best way for them to report, and even regional considerations, you will be better prepared to design systems, mechanisms, and processes to get information when its most critically needed.
2. *Notification and Escalation Mechanisms*: Once an emergent issue has been reported, your processes must require that you have a capability to get the word out as part of your incident and crisis managing capabilities. There is an infrastructure part to this, and there's a process development aspect. The process development requirement is understanding to whom and when to escalate. For different incidents and crisis types, different people have to be notified. In diversified businesses this often means that each one of your business units have their own requirements as well. Sometimes it's the entire company; in other types of emergencies in a single building, and during certain events may be your only way of notifying the crisis team of an escalation—that is the what. The how is a little different. Once you make certain decisions and have preplanned escalation and notification sequencing, you need a mechanism to deliver those messages. Again, these can be as simple as emails or manual telephone calls or as complex and integrated as automated messaging systems for SMS, phone, or web-based technologies.
3. *Issue Classification and Handling Index:* The last area of basic preparation for getting that "911 call" is to be prepared with a simple handling index for different types of issues. Applications and technologies that automate this for you are certainly available, but you can start simply by listing all the possible, potential, and probable types of incidents you may face based on the type of company or agency you are, prioritizing them by probability and severity, and populating them with data such as who is responsible for managing that type of incident, who needs to be notified, and other routing, notification, and escalation information. Of courses, this gets more complex as you take on the responsibility for more sites, more business units, and

more geographies, but the premise is the same. Know who will be calling, what they could potentially be calling about, and whom you have to call to get the ball rolling.

The Business Principals

The next critical attribute for the next-generation security leader is business acumen. As a business operations protection executive, you are required to understand how your business works and how it makes money, and be able to articulate how you support that business and enable it to meet its goals.

A crucial part of business knowledge is understanding profit. Another chapter discusses the general details of financial acumen, but the business principles of how profit is derived from the goods, services, or efforts of your organization are the underpinning connectors between all decisions made at your company. Is your business a revenue-focused company or a margin-focused company? If you are a margin-based company, what critical elements drive margin expansion? How is top-line revenue recognized at your company? What are the most critical times of the year around revenue development? These type of questions are minimum barriers to entry if you are truly a business operations protection executive. You cannot possibly begin to assess risk, prioritize threats, and direct your teams to protect the business if you are not even sure of how they fiscally operate.

Another aspect of basic business principles required for the next-generation security executive is to understand the concept of risk versus reward. I've mentioned it before and I will mention it again in this book: Your job as a CSO is predominantly risk management. How you identify, measure, and support the business in remediating, transferring, and accepting risk must be based on the profitability and financial implications of the business. This is not to say that risk shouldn't be addressed because it's too expensive; rather, we look at risks, their downstream impacts, probability factors, and many other measurements to create a financial risk picture. It is that financial risk picture that supports the decision-making process in context with the holistic operations and profitability of your company. Further, risk needs to be measured and evaluated across all other operations and profitability components of your company, such as research and development investments, service enhancements, workplace enhancements, and expense management initiatives. Sometimes this means that a risk that seems to be very straightforward and have an obvious resolution may not meet that risk-versus-reward threshold needed to move it forward, and you need to accept this. Security risk and privacy issues, although important, are only a component of your business's operations, and in most cases they are only a minor component in the context of the entire business go to market. Understanding all aspects and priorities of your organization will help you better provide to your leadership the information and data needed in making those risk decisions.

The final component of basic business principles for security executives is the concept that their job is actually to protect the business and not just provide security. Business executives have long lamented that the "security guy" just doesn't get it, that we are paid paranoids that are incapable of putting security issues in the context of the business they are responsible for every day. Don't be that "security guy". By converting your concept of information security, corporate security, risk operations, and the like to business operations protection programs, and by starting to use the language of your business, you will be well on the way to changing the hearts and minds of those in the business. Of course, actions speak louder than words, as discussed throughout this book, and you need to implement business-focused programs that look at the entire business process, to prioritize threat management based on business needs and criticality, and to immerse yourself into operating business units to learn how they operate and to be able to articulate the services you deliver in alignment with what they deliver every day.

Technical versus Nontechnical

There is a continuing great debate at senior levels within companies when it comes to the hiring of CSOs. This debate is focused around whether the candidates should be technical. Technical acumen can be interpreted in many different ways. Technical skills for a nurse are very different than technical skills for a computer programmer and even different still for a carpenter. For the context of this book, let's assume that the next-generation security executive has converge responsibilities and the technical skills we are talking about are relative to computer, network, infrastructure, application, and business technology.

In recent years I have seen a mass migration by non–technically competent executives into the ranks of senior security leaders. In almost every case there were very different reasons why they were put into those positions. In some cases it was because of what we just discussed, specific to an inability of the incumbent to support the business in the context of the business. In others the entity was looking for financial sanity and management in what seemed like a continuously growing monster of security necessities with limited executive financial acumen within that group. For yet another, the leadership wanted someone who truly understood their business and needed new opportunity to grow in a diversified area. Of course there are hundreds more reasons why a nontechnical leader was put into the position—many good reasons that produced great results.

As the criticality around security, risk, and privacy functions in an organization continue to increase, however, and the complexities of the integration of technology into business functions increase, we need to have reasonable discussion of how technical a security executive needs to be. Let's look at it from this perspective: If you are the chief of staff for surgical operations at a hospital, should you have medical technical acumen? Most would agree that the executive leading other surgeons and managing surgical functions should have a high degree of medical knowledge. If you are the chief financial officer of a public corporation, should you not have financial technical acumen in order to deliver on the corporate responsibilities around financial management and assurance?

I strongly believe that the same level of care and consideration should go into the development of the leadership position and the expectations for an executive accountable to lead cyber defense organizations as part of an overall business operations protection program. This does not mean that they need the capability to program applications, create Python scripts, or manage deep packet inspection devices or firewalls. What it does mean is that they have a firm grasp of the technology areas that they are responsible for through education, on-the-job training, or life experience.

How much technical knowledge does the CSO need? There is no perfect measurement, guideline, or algorithm to provide an exact answer to this. The key is that they possess the right amount of knowledge to be able to effectively discharge their duties, create and execute strategy, and provide operational leadership to their organization. Understanding the basics of networking, systems management, application architecture, information and system security, cloud computing, environmental security, defense in depth methodologies, and principles of authentication, authorization, accounting, certification and accreditation, risk management, and advanced threat management are a great start. At a high level, these skill sets enable an understanding of the large majority of business technology defense architectures, allow the right level of conversation with technical resources, and enable the translation of complex security issues in a more simplistic fashion because of an understanding of the issue and an ability to translate accordingly. If you are in a technology company, your level of technical acumen needs to be significantly higher than that of an executive in a steel manufacturing firm. If you are an executive in a financial company, then your technical risk acumen needs to be greater then that of an executive in a nonpublic consumer retail organization. The goal, of course, is to ensure you have enough acumen in the following five key areas:

1. Be confident in your ability to understand cross-discipline technical issues
2. Challenge the issue, resolutions, and solutions with technical people
3. Create and understand long-term strategies for business operations defense
4. Translate complex technical concepts into business terms
5. Evaluate, measure, and manage cross-discipline security plans

As a next-generation security executive, the bottom line is that you will be living in a technical world. The boundaries of cyber security/physical security/operational risk management in the relationship with technology are intrinsically intertwined. From what you are defending, to the resources you deploy to protect your business, to the issues and events you investigate, to how you manage your business—everything has a component of technology, and your success is codependent on your technical ability.

The Converging Paths of Disciplines

In the previous chapter we outlined what convergence is and why it is important. The fact remains, however, that only a small percentage of security executive positions are converged, and over time that percentage will increase as entities understand the business and operational imperatives for doing so.

The topic of convergence isn't limited to just cyber and physical security anymore. Some organizations are challenged with the complexity and duality of roles within the technical disciplines as well, and as a security leader you will be faced with these discussions, opinions, decisions, and political debates and need to be educated about and prepared for how to approach them.

To frame a conversation pertaining to convergence, a couple of important topics need to be addressed to understand why a change is even needed and then to execute that change effectively and successfully with a clear and shared out come. That is not to say that everyone in the conversation is going to be supportive of the direction, but as those discussions are happening, what you are changing, why you are changing it, and how it will be executed are important.

To get at the topic of what is being changed, a critical decision has to be made about what future state is hoped for. The first area to tackle is whether this group will be a policy-based or operationally focused organization. In many companies the "head of security" is relegated to policy only; however, I submit that policy authority alone does not effect change, drive action, or enable organizations to protect themselves. Policy-based security management often is out of touch with the needs of the business, is not aligned to realistic operational requirements to implement those policies, and is not motivated to ensure the success of those policies because their compensation is not aligned to operational success. With the incredible impact that cross-discipline security functions have on a business, and the constant need to adapt operational imperatives to changing technology, environment, market, and threat conditions, the reality is that the next-generation security organization needs to be operationalized and empowered to protect the business, not simply dictate rules and opine on compliance conditioning.

The concept of "operational effectiveness" is core to the discussion of why convergence matters to any given business or agency. Even more important is why a change is necessary in the first place? Does management feel that there is a gap in their security posture? Has an audit or assessment function recognized an inability to successfully implement sustainable programs and controls broadly across an organization to maintain the minimum level of security necessary for the business and markets you are in? Do the existing security leadership and security teams lack an effective ability to drive change for the company in support of their business strategy? Whatever the reason may be, it is important to understand it. Whether you are coming into a new position or you have been entrenched for many years, these simple but telling questions need to be answered, and in most cases gaps in these areas are often the result of organizations more focused on policy rather than established and empowered for operational success.

So, then, what does an operationally focused converged security organization give you? The ability to actionably drive change. Operational programs create opportunities to enable decision-making, action, and change. By providing executive security leaders with the ability to act -and -do rather then just speak and write, businesses position themselves more effectively to drive the changes necessary to successfully protect their business. The integration of functions and the operationalizing of security programs provides the security executive with the authority necessary to make decisions and put into action programs, projects, and services necessary for the protection of the business or agency. Further, from a convergence perspective, the single leadership authority over multiple disciplines enables that executive to maximize resource effectiveness, reduce complex interaction points with the business, improve metrics in the area of duplicative operations, and efficiently execute their duties by reducing complex political, emotional, and financial hang-ups.

To drive clarity and consistency around authority, responsibilities, and operational control, the use of a "responsible–accountable–consulted–informed" (RACI) matrix that defines who is responsible, accountable, consults, or simply informed is a great tool to clarify these jurisdictional, political, and operational boundaries. The important point to note is that this is simply like any other tool; it needs to be managed well and updated. As businesses change, operations change, and the needs of an organization develop, an unmanaged and out-of-date RACI can often be used as an excuse for why not to innovate, change, or otherwise improve programs and services.

Chief "Sales" Officer

Yes, you read that correctly. A CSO is accountable for protecting the organization but, with the exception of government agencies, the CSO must ensure their survival and effectiveness in the business culture. That business culture demands that every woman and man helps to drive the business forward and in effect become a "salesperson" for the goods and services they take to their markets. Businesses are quickly realizing that increased organizational capabilities in the areas of business security and privacy equate to strong market differentiators that enable client trust, drive sales, reduce sales cycles, and help when companies have bumps in the road on security and privacy matters.

This realization by the business creates new demands on the senior security leader and at the same time elevates the perception of the position within the context of the business's executive hierarchy. Of course, that elevation comes with a dual-edged sword. Not only will you be measured on your effectiveness and ability to accomplish your prime objective of protecting the business, you'll now be inducted into the core business culture of the organization, requiring you to obtain and maintain critical survival skills that demonstrate your effectiveness in supporting the business culture.

Unlike a field salesperson for your company who has only a single book of business to sell, as the "security executive sales" lead you have four distinct groups to sell to. Remember, the concept of sale isn't just about selling a product, it's also about selling your ideas. The following is a breakdown of how to think about your sales audience:

Internal (business and team): When "selling" internally, your focus is on convincing people within your business or agency of why they should invest in an idea, a solution, or a concept to help you drive your mission of business operations protection. Sometimes it is best to get leadership to buy in to a policy or standards change, make an investment in an solution set, or simply to get internal employees to "buy into" their responsibilities around security. In addition, this internal sales requirement also extends to your own team and getting them to understand concepts and operations or buying into your strategy.

External Direct Client: Your external direct clients are those entities your business sells to. In this context, typically you are a support function for your sales organization. You may be brought in to explain why your product or service is more secure than someone else's, or used to convince your company's executive team to invest in areas critical to your operation. In either case, your responsibility is typically not to "sell" the product, but, rather, to sell confidence in your company's ability to protect its business, understand the markets it serves, and show to current or prospective clients that your organization has a knowledgeable an experienced executive at the helm who is ensuring the appropriate delivery of critical security services.

Market: At times, you may be asked to represent your company to the market in general. This sales function is a mechanism to help outline and solidify the market differentiator that your company has by the way they secure the company and its products. Typically, your focus here is to talk about the markets you are in, advancements companies should be thinking about, how your company addresses emerging threats, and why you believe your company is doing it right. The overall goal in these settings is usually to help create a market-leading position for your company in the markets you serve. Most probably it is not security practitioners that you are addressing but competitors, consumers, and suppliers of your business.

Industry: The fourth major segment of your sales leadership is specific to your practitionership. It is important to represent your company to your peers in the security risk and privacy industries. Your participation in conferences, executive sharing forums, and practitioner exchanges helps to create a sense of responsibility, capability, and maturity about your company's security efforts. Speaking in public forums, introducing concepts in advanced security programs, displaying your own company's protective operation strategies, and engaging in two-way communications with your peers help to establish you as a learned and effective practitioner.

There are many ways that this helps out your business and you, but let's stick to three. First, let's look at the positive client-centric wins. When your company is known as having a good security program, it reduces complexity in the sales cycle, reduces the actual duration of the sales cycle, and often reduces friction during the contracting phase. In addition, when concerns or security issues arise, your peers who are working with you to respond or investigate these issues will have a better sense of your capabilities, programs, and ability to support their concerns, helping to drive quicker remediation.

The second important way that this type of industry participation helps your business is in the area of a resource pipeline. The truth is, practitioners want to be associated with a good brand, especially a good brand of security. By associating your business with an advanced security program for the industry, when practitioners make the decision of who they want to work for, they often migrate to the brand recognition of a great security team. The third area that this type of industry engagement helps is in your own brand. Recruiters and other businesses often turn to peer practitioners to ask who they believe are great security leaders, and the more you are involved with the industry, the more you show your skills, then the more your brand is recognized in the market of security, risk, and privacy practitioners.

Of course the key here is that you must participate and not just attend. By signing up to deliver keynote speeches, participate in roundtable discussions, and be active in security risk and privacy industry events, you not only support and advance your business's profile, you help yourself as well.

The Basics

So, now you know why you have to sell and where you have to support. Let's jump into some of the skill sets in efforts that create you as a "chief security sales executive". To start, you need to focus on a few basic skills. One of the most important is your ability to speak the language of your audience. From the executives, to the public at large, to practitioners, to investors, you need to develop the ability to speak at a level appropriate to the audience before you. I remember developing this skill most as a young police detective working health care fraud crimes for the federal government. At any given moment I could be talking to a homeless person on the street, a patient, a doctor, or a federal prosecutor and 100 different types of people in between just to solve and create a case for prosecution. In this context I quickly had to learn how to adapt, change my approach, and align to what drove the individual or group. There are five basic rules that help you obtain a skill set, which you can learn over time:

1. Speak the audience's language
2. Be direct
3. Be compelling and passionate
4. Know your information
5. Adapt to the audience

By understanding your audience and having the ability to speak (at a minimum) components of their language, you automatically create an air of equality and a basic human connection. By being direct, less wordy, and simplified, you avoid the stigma of being someone who oversells, is dishonest, or is trying to confuse a topic. This builds subconscious trust between you and your audience.

Being passionate and compelling about a topic in a balanced way serves two distinct purposes. First, it incites similar excitement among your audience, creating a subconscious positive euphoria; second, it creates the positive assumption that you believe in what you are speaking about, and as such it must be true. The next important factor is knowing your information. Nothing could be worse and more easily destroy credibility than speaking to a subject you clearly have no knowledge about. Ensure that you understand the information you are delivering, set guidelines to the parameters of the discussion in order to not set false expectations, and be honest when you don't know an answer. Not knowing everything about a topic is okay, but lying to look smart is difficult to overcome. Finally, you must be entirely prepared when you speak to a group or an individual, knowing exactly what you are going to say, and how you are going to deliver it, based on all of your planning. When dealing with people, however, things always change. Be prepared to change your method of delivery or your approach and presentation based on feedback from your audience. By just putting your head down and pushing through it, when the audience clearly isn't interested in your prepared delivery, you will quickly lose interest and opportunity, so adapt as needed.

Actions That Walk the Walk

Understanding that you need to be a productive member of your organization's sales machine is step 1. Step 2 is understanding and developing the basics mentioned above. The third step is executing and showing that you have "mad skills" and can walk the walk of supporting your business's go to market and position in those markets.

To get started you really have to learn your business. Do you know how long your company has been in business? Do you know their history? Do you know how many products or services they sell and what their market names are? Do you know revenue by business segment and geography? Do you know the products that will be discontinued and the next five products your company will take to market? Can you deliver a 30-sec elevator pitch on what your company does and why it's important for the person you're talking to?

If you don't know these answers, then set your mind to learning them. How can you be passionate and compelling when talking about your business if you don't really know it? Knowing your business helps you complete your messaging, align to the corporate brand, and instills confidence within your own business that you really understand what it does.

Another important step in showing that you're serious about your new sales title is to help your business create opportunities through client or customer interaction. Don't wait for your marketing department or sales organization to figure out how they can "use you" based on what they know because they really won't know a lot about what you do every day. Spend some time speaking with your field sales force, service specialists, implementation department, competitive intelligence teams, and anyone else with good information about what the client is asking for, in association with security and privacy concerns. Then create a list of opportunities to engage with clients in public or private settings that help demonstrate your businesses position on any given topic. Here are a few suggestions to get you started:

- Develop client-facing sales and support slicks about different aspects of your organization's security programs
- Host security education sessions on "how to" topics for your clients or, better yet, for prospective future clients
- Create standardized executive briefing opportunities for clients who want to learn more about your company's security efforts; if your operation is large enough to have a security operations center, provide tours of your operations
- Work with your company's sales effectiveness team to insert into your sales pitches language that demonstrates security as a differentiator
- Write or record blogs, participate in market periodicals, and present at industry conferences

Another important factor in many companies is proving the investment that they are making in security and the messaging associated with your go to market as an effective part of the sales machine. Spend some time reviewing your sales functions and understanding where (if any) security is an inhibitor or a road bump in the sales process. Sometimes the ambiguity of standard contract language around security lengthens the sales process. At other times, it's the terms and conditions (or lack thereof) around security that have to be renegotiated on every contract that extends the process. Whatever it is, and whatever is causing it, make an effort to help your business solve it. Perhaps it's changing policies to allow for certain types of security testing, or maybe it's allowing access and standing up new technology to provide transparency for clients into the security around their data, or maybe it's just the creation of standard language. Be a leader in helping the business solve sales issues up front and record the metrics in partnership with your sales organization. You'll be amazed at what you can solve and the amount of personal political equity you gain by optimizing your businesses ability to catch market share and revenue.

The Sexy Side of Security

The final piece of being your company's chief security executive salesperson is your ability to connect with your business and customers on the topic of security that engages and interests them, creating a memorable moment. You may be called the "security geek", "paid paranoid", or "secret squirrel" by those who like to poke fun at what you do but who most of the time have no clue of what we actually do every day. The truth is that there is a very sexy side of security; more and more, Hollywood and book authors are using corporate security, cyber security, and digital defense as a basis for some great movies and stories. Leverage that because people like it. I'm not telling you to go and disclose all of your company secrets that will get you arrested, prosecuted, or in civil litigation over disclosing government secrets or breaking a nondisclosure agreement. What I am saying is that you have an opportunity to create a story or otherwise make very human a specific security issue that otherwise would be less understood or, quite frankly, boring. Your ability to tell a good story and weave it into the point you are trying to get across is a critical skill set when you have a job that deals with areas that are difficult to explain. Concrete examples of your strategy, program, or controls in action and the resulting outcomes in the modified story format creates interest in the discussion that lasts long after your presentation. A story that starts off with, "So, we had a foreign national arrested last year by the FBI that...."is much more interesting to listen to than a story that starts with, "a negative impact event was discovered through the modification of deep packet inspection technology that reported into our security event management system and correlated against clear data provided to us via STIX integration....".

Now, go out there and sell, make it interesting, and enjoy it.

CREATING YOUR MISSION

The CSO job can be bipolar, challenging, stressful, and confusing. The secret to building the mental toughness necessary to lead through this type of emotional and intellectual challenge is the ability to create and drive toward a mission that you believe in and that will motivate others. Many great leaders have overcome incredible odds with limited resources through the inspiration of a shared mission. This mission-centric approach creates the deep emotional attachment and purpose that often connects far beyond what most people consider to be personal motivation, such as compensation or recognition. As in other parallel professions such as public safety, public service, and human services, the moral compass and value-based, humanity-based reasoning is more powerful to the human psyche than material possession, status, or self-preservation. Often, when you find mission base values in people, you find people of similar ilk. Combining people who have the same passion for a shared mission and vision creates an execution force multiplier.

Your Mission, Not Theirs

As a leader driving a mission-centric approach to creating a high-performance and optimized organization, the mission you create must be very personal to you. What does that mean? It means that this mission must evoke a deep visceral reaction within your own value chain, creating a self-inspired need to be successful in achieving the mission's goal. That mission goal must be aligned to who you are, your personal values and beliefs. It must be so powerful that it moves you in an inspiring way and becomes articulable, achievable, an inspiring to others. This is important during your job selection process because the job you choose must be capable of allowing you to create your mission from it. If not, then it is just another job, and you become just another leader.

To provide a little context, let's use me as an example. Some of the characteristics and values I deeply cherish include family, religion, and a deep love for my country. As a former federal law enforcement officer and a member of the military, I connect deeply to the sentiment of providing safety, security, and stability for our society and I believe deeply that there is a fine line between society and chaos that very well could affect those values I hold close. When I consider potential jobs, I typically seek those that have a tremendous impact in the areas of critical infrastructure, economic security, national security, or the protection of our citizenry. By working for an organization that provides services akin to those markets, it is very personally satisfying to get up every day and do my job knowing that I am making a difference based on upholding my personal values.

Creating passion from your mission does not happen by accident. It must be deeply internalized, carefully planned, and well executed. Attempting to do this by simply aligning to your business's mission is not what I mean by creating your own mission. For example, in the context of your business, its mission is to deliver that business successfully, creating a specific market thumbprint and value for their shareholders. How can that possibly be repositioned to personal values? Creating a story of why, defining your stance and why people should join you, and engraving a strategy to get there must be motivated and empowered directly from your personal values.

Mission and Motivation

When creating the mission that will be the foundational element of creating your overall security program, don't confuse it with "what our business is here to do". Your job is to inspire motivation to security, risk, and privacy practitioners to define the statement "this is what our security program is here to do". It must be motivating in an actionable way, simple to state, and connected to what your entity does. It should be articulable in a single statement and begin with "Our security mission is...." Let's look at four examples of how I might internalize my mission by different industry segments and business I could possibly work for:

1. *Health care*: Our security mission is to ensure the availability and safety of critical health services to the millions of people in our service areas through the protection of the critical technology and operation infrastructures that these services depend on, and the safety of the environments they are provided from.
2. *Oil and Gas*: Our security mission is to protect the sustainability of the energy resources we provide to the more than *X* million consumers and economies that depend on our products and to operate by continuing to provide and excel in protective and defensive programs for the structure and operations that create, deliver, and service our global customer base.
3. *Financial services*: Our security mission is ensure the sustainability of the financial economies we serve through the defense and protection of the critical financial systems and monies in our care that support the businesses, communities, and people who depend on us.
4. *Education*: Our security mission is to enable and facilitate the learning environment of our next generation of civic, business, and society leaders by creating a safe and protected learning environment and learning platform, ensuring an unobstructed educational experience for all of our current and future students.

Once a mission has been conceived, you must be able to drive your team's passion around the topic. This can be done through conversation, explanation, and discussion around downstream residual impacts if you are not able to accomplish your mission. The tangible reality of the mission is the fuel behind the passion to drive your teams. Making it real by talking about the "what if's" allows people to internalize and create the linkage between what they do every day and the mission statement. Let's consider the health care statement above as an example. How would you create a direct linkage of a downstream residual impact event that drives passion through the reality of an event? Consider the following;

> *Our mission is to ensure that the communities we serve have access to the critical health care they need. The existing gaps in our network security could have a direct impact on the availability of the networks in our emergency*

departments. In each of our five hospitals we see on average 300 patients per day, for a total 1500 per day, 20% of which are require urgent cardiac care. That is nearly 300 people who have to be treated within 60min of the onset of a critical cardiac incident in order to live. If the network that supports patient triage, patient management, cardiac monitoring, and critical communications is unavailable, how will that affect our medical practitioners' ability to quickly evaluate, prioritize, and get the right treatment for the patient? How many of those 300 won't make it home to their family after trying get treatment from us if the network isn't available?"

Driving passion is not just about storytelling; it's about attitude, commitment, and consistency. A lesson I learned early during my job as a K-9 handler for nearly 10years has never left me and it applies in many aspects of my life. The lesson is simply this: "emotions and attitudes run down leash", meaning that what the leader feels and displays is exactly what his or her followers will do. Be passionate about your job and the mission that your team is delivering. They will see that, respect that, and be passionate next to you.

Although I would like to believe that a good mission statement and a passion to achieve the mission's goal is enough to get by, unfortunately that is not reality. Having the ability to achieve the mission takes that mission statement from being just words to an actionable mantra. You are going to be the individual who makes the decision of whether your organization, your team, and you has the ability to achieve it. What are some of the abilities you need to consider? First and foremost, does the business or agency you work for want you to be successful in this mission? Do they have the organizational capability and resources to help get you there? If you are fundamentally at odds with the chief executive officer or executive committee on what protection for your entity should be, then the likelihood that they would support the implementation of the plan is not great, and your ability to execute will be greatly hampered. This will be seen by others whom you are trying to get focused on the mission, and their confidence in your ability to accomplish the mission may be questioned.

The question of ability also must be self-focused. If you are signing up to take on a significant mission in an area that you are not experienced with, do not have the knowledge that is required, or perhaps have historical deep political gaps within your organization, you may want to reconsider whether you are the right leader to execute the mission. This is not an exercise of self-doubt, but rather a discussion of capabilities to ensure that the right leadership is in place to successfully drive the mission.

The concept of the "right leadership" also extends to your direct team. A CSO does not do everything by herself or himself, and the team you put together to successfully accomplish the mission must be capable as well. Your mission focus and mission goals will change over time, and you need to continuously evaluate the leadership and the teams that you have in place to make sure that the right skills are available for the overall success of the mission.

Ensuring ability requires a multitiered life cycle approach that reviews organizational ability, resource ability, and people ability. When you consistently review your abilities, make the appropriate changes in gap areas, and make positive changes for the success of the mission, your organization will see this, believe that the mission is achievable through the abilities under your leadership, and become even more passionate in achieving the mission goals.

Creating a Compass

Earlier we touched on the effect of the mission being built on your values and principles that are relatable to others. As the CSO, you will encounter issues, incidents, events, questions, decisions, turmoil—a host of situations that require you to be well grounded and consistent in how you evaluate, engage, and respond to them. Life is about compromise and our jobs require us to understand that it is not a black-and-white world but one with many shades of gray; truly understanding your own values and operating by a set of principles that you believe in will help you create your own personal framework, thresholds, and upper and lower boundaries that allow you to make better decisions.

Values and principles combined create guardrails for you to operate by. They allow you to run fast and hard and also serve as an ever-present backstop when things get out of control. There is no list of what a CSO's values and principles "must be", for every individual has their own. Knowing what yours are is a necessity before you can lead others.

Values are simply your own personal beliefs that drive your ethical behavior. These beliefs are things such as integrity, ambition, excellence, patience, personal fulfillment, wisdom, trust, and many other things that form your basic belief structure and who you are as a person. Principles are behaviors and actions that support your values that help guide your choices. Essentially, they are your rules of personal conduct. If you've never done so, take time to evaluate your personal values. You'll be amazed at the outcome. An exercise I like to take my leadership team through on occasion is a review of all of our values because, believe it or not, they tend to be very different. But knowing the value structure of who you work with and why they make the decisions they do is a great tool in collaboration, understanding, and transparency.

Whatever your values are, one thing is certain: For your mission to be successful, the values by which you created the mission, drive the mission, and operate under must be believable to yourself and others. Consistent ethical behavior supported by the principles and values that you articulate create that believability.

Creating the Story

Communicating your mission is one of the more difficult parts of the implementation process. How and what the story communicates to others is crucial in garnering support from all of the constituents needed to make your missions possible. Communicate poorly and your leadership, justifications, and ability to execute may be questioned.

What are some of the key points that a story must have? The first is absolute alignment to the end goal of the entity you serve. Again, this does not mean that your mission statement is the mission statement of the entity; however, it must in no uncertain terms serve its end goal. Using the health care example described earlier, if the company's goal is to provide quality health care, the new story needs to tell how your mission makes that happen.

Another key point to understand and plan for is that it's not just one story, but multiple stories, depending on your audience. Understanding what is acceptable for internal audiences, clients, industry settings, or your own team will help you decide how to generate the right story at the right time. Being able to reasonably articulate your mission story in multiple settings takes practice. A good way to achieve this is to create a table or a spreadsheet with a list of audience types on one line and the components of your mission objective on another. Then, in each cell add the bullet points, facts, and story objectives that meet the need and are appropriate for each of the audience types.

Finally, the delivery of the mission story is just as important as the believability of the passion that you generate. Knowing your facts and figures and being able to answer questions at the time of delivery is critical. Make it a point to constantly reiterate the story at meetings, as part of business case delivery, and as part of public presentations. Your mission story does not happen once when you create it; rather, it is a constant and evolving process to reinforce the necessity, the significance, and the importance of the mission.

Transparency Through Facts

Another important facet of successfully developing and driving a mission is not only to ensure the believability of the mission but also to demystify it through transparency. That is, providing information and facts about the totality of your mission creates critical anchoring points, believability, and proof of the requirements of the mission's objectives. Facts, data, threat information, documented attack information, incidents, and any variety of information that points the totality of the issue, the need, and the impact helps to create that air of transparency that allows people to make their own choices based on the information. Using the example of health care earlier in this chapter, I injected data points that helped with the mission statement, such as the number of patients, the number of trips to the emergency room, the types of systems that depend on the network, along with a variety of others, in just six sentences. I could've added (depending on the audience) the number of vulnerabilities and issues on the network and a host of other information to support why I would believe that this was a critical issue.

Just as important as the data points you provide is accepting input other than your own to the mission statement and objectives. By allowing input, facts, and other relevant information into the mission process, story creation, and mission execution, you ensure that your approach is not myopically biased, and it proves to others supporting your mission that as a leader you value the input of your team and make sound decisions and choices based on facts. Absent that, especially in the area of security, leaders who act on shadowy data, stir emotions based on conjecture and not fact, and are not transparent or do not accept input are typically seen as paranoid "Chicken littles" only out to scare people into action rather than meet the need of the business or agency.

In the end, enabling your mission and succeeding in it is all about knowledge. Knowledge is power, and the more knowledge you provide to those you lead, those you impact, and those who question you, the more powerful your mission and effect become.

You Are the Expert

The success of your mission and mission objectives are in part a direct result of your ability to lead. Your ability to lead is predicated on your expertise in your job. In addition, the people who take up, support, and believe in the mission do so believing that you are the expert, and quite frankly it is your responsibility to be that expert.

But what does being an "expert" really mean? Often, people overcomplicate the term and set unrealistic expectations, making "expert" seem like an unattainable goal. The real definition of expert is a person who has a comprehensive and authoritative knowledge or skill in a particular area. That's it. Nothing more, nothing less. Your job is to obtain, optimize, and share this authoritative knowledge in the support of your mission.

Creating a foundation of knowledge of your area of responsibility occurs over time and is the combination of learned knowledge, acquired knowledge, and practical job experience, and the application of this gained knowledge that creates skill. You may want to consider a few priority areas in attaining a higher level of knowledge to ensure the authoritative part of the definition of expert.

If you are reading this book, then you have already made the decision to acquire additional knowledge about your primary objective: your job. The job of the CSO is extremely broad, requires constant education, and is based on changes in markets and changes in threats, crime, and technology; the job is constantly changing. From organizational methods to program development, if you assume the title of CSO, you should constantly work to attain new information, knowledge, methods, and skills specific to your job.

The next area you'll want to drive expertise in is specific to the industries you serve. As mentioned earlier in this book, understanding your business and what it does is critically important for you to be able to deliver the appropriate services and defend the business or agency you serve. To be an expert in creating programs that drive a specific mission, you also need to understand the entirety of the industry you operate in. Threats to your business do not happen in a vacuum; they are fairly consistent across industry segments. In fact, to properly protect your own business, you should be adept at what it takes to protect any business in your industry. Spend the time necessary to become an expert in protecting the industry you work in, and remember, as you move jobs across industries, you'll need to continue gaining industry knowledge as a life cycle approach to your professional education and expertise development.

Another pointed area for expertise development is more focused on understanding business operation environments specific to the markets you serve and the global locations your business operates in. What may be important to your business in Pittsburgh, Pennsylvania, may not apply to your manufacturing location in Manila, Philippines. The criticality of the critical infrastructure the company has in the United States may not be applicable in South Korea. The legal and regulatory constraints that affect your abilities to deliver certain services in France or Germany may not be applicable in China. Being an expert means having a firm grasp of all areas of operation where your business or agency conducts its business.

The final point in being "an expert" is an important secret and scalability of your expertise. The notion that being an expert means you know everything is entirely amiss. Being an expert does mean that you have knowledge and skills, but it also means that you know how to apply those knowledge and skills, and use the resources at hand as part of being the expert. You often hear parallels to this, that it takes "an entire village." Well, it takes your entire village to make you the expert. When you hire the right people, with diverse knowledge sets, and you know how to put them together to create the organizational skill needed to accomplish the mission, you have become an expert. Do not be afraid or concerned that others will think less of you if you use the knowledge of the organization to appropriately affect the mission. If you are not using those resources to apply situational awareness, to develop the best solution necessary, and to understand the holistic problem, then you are simply wasting resources. Use your entire village to create your expertise as a leader.

Becoming a Learned Person

Being an expert in your career lasts only as long as the next change in your career. As the saying goes, the only thing more certain than death and taxes is change. To keep up your skills, continue at a high level of effectiveness, and have the expertise necessary to lead, empower, and drive security practitioners of the future, you must become a learned person.

Learning is collecting information from a variety of means that is meant to expand and enhance the knowledge and experience you gain throughout your career. Sometimes it is technical skills, other times leadership skills, and at yet other times business or self-enhancement education. I recently spoke to a partner at a "big four" firm, and we were talking about continuous learning. He relayed a recent training that he took, as required by his employer, that had nothing to do with his job, but rather with work–life balance. His firm believed so fervently that to create the whole person's educational experience, they should require and pay for a program that ensured the quality of life of their executives. That's holistic learning, and it is something we should all strive for.

So, then, how do we get this lifelong learning? Do you have to go back to college or university? Is it professional certifications and accreditations? I can tell you that there is no single answer. A well-rounded practitioner and leader looks at the requirements and skills necessary to perform their job well, creates a scorecard of their skills and abilities and the level of each, creates a personal gap assessment, and then produces an independent development plan for themselves. Sound familiar? Perhaps you require this of all of your employees. Be sure you take the time and focus on yourself and lead by example. The following are a few areas that you may want to consider when putting together your individual development plan:

Continuing education: Continuing education at the collegiate and university level is always a good bet. Undergraduate and postgraduate degrees and certificate programs are constantly being developed under new curriculums across a broad set of industry and career topics. As a part of compensation package and normalized benefits, some amount of college reimbursement is often available from employers in both the public and private sectors. Consider educational programs outside your core skill set, such as a business program if your primary degree is in a technical specialty technology, criminal justice, or risk.

Seminars and industry forums: A less costly, and targeted learning opportunity can be found in seminars and industry forums that happen every day around the world. Typically, these are free or inexpensive, and they cover a variety of topics over the course of the week. Align your individual development plan to targeted gap areas and see whether a conference or seminar can help you fill in some of those gaps. A bit of research on the speakers and topics can go a long way.

Venture capitalists and startups: When trying to learn about rising technology, solutions, or markets I support, I often turn to venture capitalists (VCs) and small startups to give me a peek into technology yet to come. Try aligning yourself to a specific VC firm or firms that focus in your area or specialty. These firms often will invite chief security officers to one-day events where they highlight specific technology advancements based on industry problem sets that they are looking to help fund solutions to. In addition, if you visit Silicon Valley for business reasons, stay on a day or two and line up meetings across multiple VCs. You may find them to be engaging, informative, and helpful in finding technology startups or new companies that are experts in a variety of industry areas.

Publishing entities: If you are a reader, there is no lack of great publications on almost any topic you can imagine. Some publishing companies specialize in education or the advancement of security risk and privacy, often as special segments, newsletters, and additional information such as research papers in support of their publications. These tend to be informative, often technical, and great resources for knowledge development.

Security group participation: There are many groups available to security practitioners and security executives. From the Security 50 to the Corporate Executive Boards (CEB), SANS Institute, International Security Management Association, International Information System Security Certification Consortium (ISC2), Information Systems Audit and Control Association (ISACA), American Society for Industrial Security (ASIS International), among others. This is not an all-inclusive list, nor was it meant to be. In addition to an overall organization's regional council, birds-of-a-feather sessions and even government participation organizations exist around the globe. The point is there is no shortage of security groups. The key is finding the ones that are most applicable to you, that you learn from, and that help you expand your knowledge.

Executive education: As a leader and senior executive in your company, a component of your continuing learning should be focused around being an executive. Check with your company's or agency's executive development teams, if available, for programs that may be easily accessible. Use the feedback from your management as an indicator of which executive skills are important for you to continue developing.

Confident Leadership

However you develop yourself, whatever drives you, whatever mission you seek to take on, remember to believe in yourself and to be confident in your abilities. No person on earth knows everything, and the world changes every day, as will the needs of those you serve. Confident leadership means that you accept those facts, focus on your mission, and trust in your abilities and the total knowledge of those you work with every day. When you are confident, that confidence carries to those around you.

Chapter 4

Execution Assurance

As a security executive, you will be measured on many attributes by your executive leadership team. Like any executive, you will be expected to execute your responsibilities effectively and efficiently in your given area of responsibility. The complex nature of your job, the constant criticality of the decisions you make, and the significant implications of not executing well make the specific executive attribute of execution assurance more important for the security executive to deliver on. Your business will see you as the go-to person in times of crisis, and your credibility will be based on your historical ability to deliver.

Beyond the business's perception of your ability, there are three important areas that you should focus on that will serve as magnification points to help you ensure the effective execution of the roles that you fill.

TIME TO RESOLUTION

As a security executive, the criticality of the services you deliver are typically significantly more time sensitive than those of many other parts of the business operation. For instance, ensuring the safety of your workforce by solving a workplace violence issue before it becomes a workplace incident is perhaps more critical from a timeliness perspective than the delivery of a financial presentation. In the area of cyber, the timely remediation of an ongoing penetration attempt or distributed denial of a service attack is essential to ensure the continuing operations of your business and to reduce potential further exploitation of your environment from an open risk. Reduced exposure generally means reduced impact, which is an important part of any prevention program.

Although threat management is most certainly a critical consumer of the need for effective time to resolution management, it is certainly not the only one. Resolution assurance and management is also an expectation of some of your key constituents, such as your business partners, your practitioners, your clients, and even your regulators, and each has their own reasons and needs.

Let's start with your practitioners—those security risk and privacy professionals that you lead or will be leading some day. In our profession changing priorities is a daily occurrence. Whether it is a changing threat landscape, business priorities, or active incidents, security teams are required to balance heavy workloads and critical issues, all while reprioritizing to meet the needs of the mission. The only way this works is through clear and direct communication and ensuring transparent understanding of your constituents' expectations, one of which is the expected time to resolution. Their success depends on your ability to understand the situation, gain insightful input from those professionals responsible for mitigating the situation, create the prioritization for them to work with to ensure a balanced workload, and provide guidance for time to resolution in order for them to manage resources and provide you with the options necessary to make the right executive decision.

Next, let's look at your business partners, who are your internal clients. I'm sure you've realized by now that your "security" business is complex, codependent on many areas of your organization, and quite simply not always in your control. As the given expert for your company, it is your responsibility to "de-complex" the issue, the business impact, and the resolution into a digestible format that allows the company to use the information as part of its decision support platform. When you do this well, you create a double-edged sword: consistent and happy customers who believe in your ability to deliver, but often with the expectation that the resolution is simpler than it actually is. To balance this conundrum, you need to create a third leg of their expectations, which is a clear articulation of how long it will take to resolve the issue, what specific components make up that timeline, levers you and they have to adjust the timeline as necessary, and a mechanism of measurement against that expectation.

Now let's look at your external clients—those who are paying for a product, service, or deliverable that your business or agency provides. Sometimes these discussions come at the worst possible time because you are often dealing with an ongoing operational security or privacy incident that may directly affect them. Adding fuel to the fire, you may be obligated contractually only to inform them of a portion of the overall incident—that which is directly affecting them—because further disclosure of the detailed aspects of any given incident could jeopardize an ongoing investigation, be taken out of context and used in a negative manner toward your company, or, worse, inappropriately disclosed and misrepresented, exposing financial and reputable harm that may be unwarranted. It is times like these when clear articulation of cause, threat remediation, and action transparency often overcome the fact that full disclosure is simply not possible. In most cases all your client wants to know is the following:

How did you find it?
How did it happen?
Is the issue present in any other part of your business?
How are they affected?
Has it been fixed?
How are you preventing it from happening again?

Successfully answering these questions often reduces the anxiety associated with any potential impact to the client's security and data privacy interests and provides them with enough information to make decisions that they are responsible for, such as end user notification, regulatory filings, and preparedness actions for their own response, if necessary. In addition, with this type of transparency and preparation you accomplish two critical relationship necessities:

1. You create an implied impression of honesty, transparency, and trust.
2. You create an impression of professionalism, experience, job knowledge, and capability.

Whether it is your practitioners, your partners, your clients, or your regulators, the key to a successful dialogue of execution assurance is your ability to set expectations. Expectations come in all shapes and sizes, and you are responsible for understanding the critical elements of any given interaction that need to be addressed. Most will depend on the incident, and many are focused on time to resolution. For instance, in a cyber incident the common phases of detect, contain, investigate, remediate, and report all have their own processes, timeline, and outcomes and each of your participating constituents require expectations to be set based on their need or function.

Again, let's start with the practitioners. Their role in any given event is typically the operational work needed to manage any given situation. As a leader, the expectations you set are critical to their success. The decision support process is bidirectional: Like you need information from your teams to make good leadership decisions, they need good information from you to support their operational decisions. When setting expectations for or providing important context-based information to your teams, consider these five basic areas of information that will help them execute better.

Responsibilities: This may seem like an easy enough category, that your team should already understand, however, every program, incident, or significant undertaking could dramatically change their responsibility requirements and overall operational accountability. Ensure your team understands what you expect of them for their area of responsibility. Sometimes this may include all components of incident management; at others it may mean that you anticipate them bringing in third parties while they maintain a watch over standard operational work. Being clear about their responsibilities during any given work effort reduces decision complexity and enables execution excellence. Your next level of leadership will have the ability to independently plan, resource, and execute the required functions with less interaction with you if their responsibilities are clearly outlined at the beginning of the process. Expect that your teams will come back for clarification; however, those instances tend to be less frequent when you are more clear about your expectations up front.

Priority: If you have done work in this area for any amount of time, you know that prioritization of work efforts and functions are critical to maintaining operational effectiveness and resource balance. If you are in a large business or agency, having multiple ongoing incidents at any time while you continue to deliver normal business operation protection services and a myriad of project work it is expected. A common area that often reduces a person's or group's effectiveness in operational execution is when the to-do list has gotten so large, the resources and resource capacity are maxed out, and practitioners begin to flail between tasks, sometimes creating a state of ineffectiveness or operational paralysis. A great way to avoid this is to set clear expectations with regard to task priorities. By simply providing your team with a guide of what needs to be done first through last, they can reset their resource plans and in return reset expectations of their ability to execute and complete tasks.

Timing: Setting expectations often fails in all areas because of the issue of timing. For your teams there are two crucial reasons why this is important. First, "if they don't know, they won't go," meaning that if there are urgent considerations for changing a normal timetable for accomplishing a task or set of tasks, without additional information a person will continue to operate in a normal mode, utilizing the resources and processes commonly used for any given situation. By simply providing an expectation of timing, your leaders and managers can more effectively reprioritize their resources and align actions to meet the given expectation. Second, setting time expectations is a learning experience for your team. Years of obtaining knowledge, receiving on-the-job training, and learning under fire enables you to make fast, informed, and accurate decisions. The only way for your team to become as effective as you is to take them through your decision-making criteria. For instance, if you are asking for a task to be completed within 2 days, it probably isn't because the chief executive officer (CEO) is yelling at you; rather, you probably are keenly aware that there is a contractual issue or a regulatory requirement specifying completion within a 48 hour window; make sure your team understands that, so the next time a similar issue occurs they execution is more independent, driving your organizational effectiveness.

Breadth: I use the word *breadth* in place of several other possible words, such as *scope* or *area of responsibility*. The reason is these words often indicate minimizing the focus area and do not necessarily define the broader scope of any specific topic. When we are setting expectations with practitioners, we need to remember that, on a day-to-day basis, they are fulfilling job requirements within a specific job description. This often leads to tunnel vision and an inability for an organization to look broadly at the context of the issue at hand. Your job as an executive is to ensure that the totality of the issue is being managed; this often includes operating and executing outside one's normal area of responsibility. For instance, perhaps you are managing a public safety issue that includes a physical control failure at your corporate headquarters that could lead to an unsafe situation. An obvious question to you may be, "Where else do I have this issue globally?" However, your issue manager may simply be asking himself, "How do I quickly solve this local site problem?" If you do not set expectations by stating "and ensure we understand whether we have any like gaps worldwide at any of our facilities," you may be grossly disappointed when your team comes back with a remediation plan that does not fix the total risk to the business. By setting the expectation of the breadth of the task or program, you enhance your operational execution capabilities by reducing repeated and throwaway tasks.

Financial: From a financial perspective, your task is simple: Ensure your team understands the resources or constraints to allow appropriate planning and execution. Again, from an execution management standpoint, if those within your leadership control know your expectations for budgetary management up front, you can significantly reduce the back-and-forth of how they intend on tackling an issue. For instance, if a member of your management team doesn't know that additional funds are available to support a specific initiative, they may come back to you with a plan for the implementation of a program that extends many months or even years. By having transparent financial guidelines, they can adequately prepare program, project, or incident plans that properly reflect available resources and funding the first time, rather than making it an inefficient recursive financial discussion.

Another group that is important to set clear expectations with is your business and business executive teams. In the context of execution assurance, the predominant need for clarity and expectations is to reduce the complexity in action-oriented decision-making and negotiations when dealing with complex security risk and privacy issues. Expectations should not be confused with transparency, as discussed earlier in this chapter. When dealing with your internal clients (the business), think of this as a contractual clarity exercise to ensure lack of confusion, finger-pointing, or unnecessary negotiating when you could be executing to your required actions.

Policies and Standards: There is a fine line between setting expectations and creating expectations, and in the area of policy and standards that line is very thin. I offer this as one of the top five areas for setting expectations with the business because of this simple theory in modern society: *If people are not provided and educated on the rules to which they are expected to conform, how can they be expected to conform?*

Expectations can be set in many ways, the most basic of which is creating a commonly accepted documentation of appropriate behaviors and conditions. In the business sense these are set by policies that allow for governance, oversight, and management. In later chapters we will cover policies at length, but for the context of this chapter know that the basis by which you help guide your company or agency is formed by jointly established policy guidelines and standards of technology, operations, and management. Setting the rules of your corporate society, the standards by which the organization will operate, and setting expectations with your business reduces friction and other like issues that could slow you down.

Services and Capabilities: Another popular point of contention (and often confusion) is the statement, "I thought security did that." Typically, this is not meant as a malicious statement by your internal client, but rather a lack of understanding of the overall capabilities and services delivered by the security functions. The easiest way to overcome this gap is to set expectations for the baseline services that are provided in each of your functional areas using the ISO or COBIT service functionality catalog method. By stating outright, "I provide these services and I do not provide these," as well as specifying at which level they will be delivered from maturity perspective (think service maturity scale), you create an operational expectation of capabilities that reduce the need for re-explaining your decisions as you execute your program.

Responsibilities: Remember that this section is focused on driving your ability to execute, and the simple act of creating expectations with your business about not just your responsibilities but also theirs facilitates action and understanding and creates a mechanism for shared accountability. If done correctly, security risk and privacy is simply a component of your normal business operations. As you execute your job, many of the functions required for a secure business will actually be owned, managed, and executed by your partners within the business. Through the creation of responsibilities and accountability matrices (see the RACI chart below), you answer those questions early in your partnership, enabling action-orientated dialogue at decision time rather than trying to answer the question of who does what.

Sample Converged Security RACI Chart

Security Service Area	Security Org	IT	HR	Legal	Business	Partner
End Device Protection	C	A/R			I	
Vulnerability Monitoring	A/R	C/I				
Security Patching	A	R			I	
Advance Threat Technologies	A/R	I		C		
Cyber Monitoring	A/R	C/I				
Investigations	R		I	A		C
Business Continuity Planning	A / I	C			R	
Disaster Recovery Preparedness	I	A/R			C	

Responsible- Those who do the work to achieve the task. ***(The Doer)***
Accountable- The one ultimately answerable for the correct and thorough completion of the deliverable or task, and the one who delegates the work to those responsible. ***(The Buck Stops Here)***
Consulted -
Those whose opinions are sought, typically subject matter experts; and with whom there is two-way communication. ***(Kept in the loop)***

Timing and Options: When it comes to successful business relationships and the delivery of expectations set by security services, the timing of almost any issue or program can't be understated. The decisions that the business must make and the expectations they must set with their customers are based on the information you provide. Realistic calculations and transparent information with regard to knowns and unknowns help facilitate those conversations, but as a leader you need to sharpen your skills and resource estimation and process efficiency to be able to provide accurate estimations of delivery. In addition, you have to remember that these are your internal clients and they want to have choices and options as any consumer would. By approaching them with two or three options for execution timing and outcomes based on your planning, you create a strategy that allows them the flexibility they are looking for yet a controlled model that enables your ability to execute to a structured plan, reducing your time to implementation.

Finances: The last area when setting business expectations is finance. This reason is not necessarily to create and approval mechanism, but rather to set the stage for resource requirements for any given service that your team delivers. Look at it this way: If you went into a local store and there were no prices on any of the items, imagine the amount of additional time it would take you to price each of your items and negotiate if required. Your grocery store trip went from 1 hour to probably 4 hours. When talking speed and execution of your services, many times the overall organization or your business partner is funding the services you are providing. By setting expectations of costs and transparency into the method of cost development, you create a situation that makes financial business negotiations faster and easier to execute when time is of the essence.

Books could be written on the topic of setting expectations with your client base. The majority of your ability to set expectations will be negotiated beforehand within contracts or other legal documents that specify your business's responsibility to your clients. As mentioned above, it's simply a good business sense approach to ensuring a successful dialogue even in the worst of circumstances. Regulatory considerations around the globe mandate specific aspects of your security, risk, and privacy requirements to operate as a business; in some cases, however, your job as the senior-most security executive in your company or agency is to support your customer through clear expectations, including the following, which often go a long way in providing client satisfaction:

Minimum Level of Care: Through working with your business, legal, and contract partners, it is important for you to identify what your clients can expect from your business from a security perspective. The level and complexity of each program area that you outline for your clients should be based on the types of industries and markets you serve. However, every business can create a basic articulation of the minimum level of care provided specific to security and privacy issues relevant to your product or service offering.

Timing: When it comes to clients, the two areas you need to focus on when it comes to timing are specific to your control environment and incidents. Although these discussions may be more complex in practice than they seem, the results you're looking for here are a reduction in repetitive questions or dialogue as a result of a lack of expectation setting. When it comes to controls, use the method most product managers adhere to, which includes a documented and published product roadmap. From your perspective, this is a security and privacy controls roadmap, but the practice is the same. By creating a list of your committed controls, the level at which they will be implemented, and the timing thereof, you can reduce the number of questions from clients and client security practitioners who are simply seeking to understand how you are providing protection within your product sets.

Specific to incidents, the two most common conversations you will have with your clients revolve around the actual timing of the incident and the timing of remediation and/or enhancements. As a security executive you must understand that often the response of your client will be based on the facts of the incident as you provide them. For your client to make notification decisions, legal decisions, and their own action response plans, they will need the details regarding the timing of the incident. The second area, specific to remediation and enhancements, becomes a timesaver and conflict reducer for you. By setting expectations of the timing of these items, being clear and public with them, you reduce the question of whether you intend to remediate and unnecessary dialogue about the "when."

Resolution and Enhancement: The human need for a sense of resolution is ever present in the work that we do every day. Perhaps because of the personal nature and feeling that security issues drive, we must be ever more vigilant to deliver on that need to our clients in order to reduce friction and operations that impede our focus on the task at hand. By clearly articulating the expectations around the resolution of any security issue—whether it be a root cause analysis, a remediation plan, a technical resolution, or any other approach to resolution management—it is important to communicate to clients what they should expect that resolution to accomplish or not.

Second, an often positive outcome of expectation setting with clients is the inclusion of improvements that they can expect. This may be the result of ongoing product or service enhancements, infrastructure upgrades, or the outcome of the significant incident that perhaps affected them. Either way, as you increase your controls capability and your security efficacy, disclosing expectations of enhancements often improves relationships, increases satisfaction, drives a sense of trust, and elevates their opinion of your ability to execute as a security expert.

In the end it doesn't matter whether you are setting the expectations of your practitioners, your business executives, or your clients; the fact that you're setting expectations, communicating, and executing is a sign of your ability to lead, manage, and operate at a senior executive level. This book describes methods and opportunities for you to automate and make expectation setting a part of your normal everyday business process. From standard operating procedures, through special security instructions, and even operational run books, the simple act of repetitive documentation with a life cycle approach creates a certain type of expectation that in itself drives action. From a business perspective, as you learn to measure and improve your processes such as operational automation, operating procedure enhancements, and even root cause analysis investigation and mitigation, the expectations you set create perception to execute, trust, and a measurement of your ability.

REMOVING LAYERS

As a multidiscipline security executive, the number of complex security, risk, or privacy issues that you deal with on a daily basis at times may seem mind-boggling. One day it's dealing with a directed cyber attack, the next day an internal fraud issue, the day after that a travel security emergency, and on the next day maybe a product security–related client complaint. On any given day not only must you deal with ongoing urgent issues that spawn what can seem like hourly, you also must manage the normal operations of the functions you are accountable for. The only way to accomplish this is to ensure that your organization has the ability to execute at all levels including problem triage, solution design, and, most important, decision-making. Remember that your businesses executive team does not expect you personally to be doing all the work; rather, they expect you as a leader to create, manage, and operate a function that can solve these problems as a whole. Think of it this way: As a senior security executive in your company, you are the CEO of a captive security managed services and consulting business within your larger company. You are expected to run your business, not necessarily do your business.

To accomplish this you must accept that it is through your team that you will accomplish your job. To do this your team must accept and understand that they are empowered to execute on your behalf in support of the services and mission you deliver. Although this may sound simple enough, the art of team enablement through empowerment is one that is developed, not simply turned on. The three areas that garnish the most effective results when starting down the path of organizational enablement include fostering a decision-making culture, hiring the right leaders, and developing escalation paths.

The first concept, fostering a decision-making culture, means that every person in your organization feels not only empowered but also accountable for making decisions and executing to the strategy, even at the lowest levels. One of the first things you can do is to create a bidirectional mechanism of trust and evidence of an open communication strategy. One of the easiest ways to accomplish this is through an open-door policy. An open-door policy simply means this: As a leader you welcome comments, feedback, concerns, and dialogue with anyone at any level in your organization, without a complex chain of command request process or the necessity of a cumbersome scheduling process. Although no one is perfect when it comes to managing complex calendars and schedules, the fact that you welcome "drive-bys," encourage people to stop by your office, walk the floors, and make personal contact with your employees are clear indications that you mean what you say. As important as the actual act of open dialogue is the surety that employees who practice this open-door policy are not reprimanded in any way by other levels within your leadership and management group who may have yet to grasp what a true open-door policy really means. In addition to the actions mentioned above, consider a couple of the following opportunities that also echo an open-door policy program:

1. On a fairly frequent basis, reach out and call employees within your organization for absolutely no reason other than to say hello and check in. These need not be 15 or 20 min or half-hour planning meetings, but rather a surprise call that lasts 2 min and that asks about what they're working on and whether they have anything they'd like to bring up to you.
2. Host a CSO breakfast or lunch with no executive security management in attendance other than you. Make it clear that you don't have an agenda, a list of items to cover, or anything else, but the meeting is theirs to ask any question about anything. Bring a pen and some paper if you need to take notes on follow-ups items or to-do items but other than that make it as intimate as possible so your employees feel like they have direct access to you.
3. Try pulling people into your office as you see them walk by. Ask them about something they are working on or their opinion on something you are working on. The fact that you stop them just to say hello and ask questions about their work creates an important bond of trust between you and your employees. They understand that you understand that we are all practitioners trying to accomplish the same mission and we are equal in doing so.

As important as creating an open-door policy is ensuring that each member of your team knows that they have a voice. Remember that you hired each of your employees, that you pay them well to do what they do, and that they are professionals in the area of security risk and privacy, just like you. A great mechanism to show that their opinion matters pivots from item number 2 above. As a leader, try to create opportunities for all levels of employees within your organization to provide input on everything from tactical day-to-day operations, current threats, project prioritization, organizational strategy, and over-the-horizon thought leadership. The following are a few opportunities that you can create:

1. All-Hands Meetings on a quarterly basis, which include information sharing and question-and-answer sessions
2. Discipline-specific meetings (in areas such as cyber, physical security, risk, or privacy) where members of just those groups come to talk about their programs and challenges
3. "Just Do It" or Top 10 Round Table sessions where you ask your team what they believe you need to accomplish or what their top 10 list looks like
4. Attend Critical Projects Update Meetings to show your interest, learn about current statuses, and ask questions or reset direction if needed
5. Monthly manger or leadership meetings that encourage bidirectional communications as well as topical items that you can receive input on from the entire management group
6. Lunch & Learns that talk to your strategy or philosophy with opportunities for questions.

It doesn't matter whether you do one or all of these suggestions. It only matters that you engage, listen, internalize, and *act* on the input from the people you have hired to execute on your behalf. In essence, through any one of these efforts you continue establishing the idea that you encourage the ideas, inventions, and expertise of others; you encourage through practice the decision making of others; and you accept input, even if that input does not necessarily reflect your own opinions.

Another mechanism for fostering a decision-making culture is quite simply stating it. Although the proof is always in pudding, so to speak, it's important to be repetitive about your expectations of those within your team. Use terms and phrases like "I expect" and "it's your responsibility" and "I trust your judgment; that's why I hired you." This direct and open articulation of your expectations makes it clear to whomever is listening that this is the way your organization is expected to operate.

As with any decision, sometimes the wrong one is made; this is where you can truly show your leadership. Through proactive engagement, lessons learned processes, and public displays of acceptance when decisions go wrong, you provide a safety net for those who would otherwise shy away from decision-making and fear of retribution if they are wrong. We are human, mistakes happen, and they happen at all levels. To foster a decision-making culture, you must also foster a learned organization that understands that it can make mistakes, must learn from them, and be better for it.

The second pillar in removing layers stems from the layers you put in place. More specifically, make sure you are hiring the right leaders into your organization. As you drive an organization that is capable of executing at all levels, you will need other leaders that foster the same principals and ethos that you create in all levels of the organization. The following are examples of some dos and don'ts when it comes to hiring your team leaders who remove layers and enable organizational execution:

1. DO hire leaders who are aggressive in attacking problems and understand that it takes "the entire village" to solve hard problems and deliver results.
2. DO hire leaders who have a strong sense of ownership and accountability for the success of the mission and the teams they lead. Impassioned, emotionally intelligent leaders tend to create like attitudes and followers who in turn feel accountable to deliver.
3. DO hire leaders who are confident and not concerned about what their job will be tomorrow, but rather what their responsibility is today. Leaders who are confident in their capabilities are typically not bound by concerns about every decision they make and the potential impact on their next promotion. They know that if the execute well they will be reward, and success comes from their success.
4. DO hire technically competent leaders in their respective disciplines. Leadership and management are only components of their required functions. By hiring nontechnical leaders you complicate the decision-making process

because those leaders must add additional layers of technical expertise to make up for their lack of expertise.

5. Do NOT hire yes men or women. "Corporate Pleasers" are less likely to be transparent and direct to you about critical decision-making components in fear that they are not making their superiors "happy," rather than focusing on successfully accomplishing the mission. Further, senior leaders with this complex tend to cause "left side/right side" issues and unnecessarily create emergency situations when it comes to prioritization and task management, confusing the layers below and often not being transparent with their reasoning in fear they will be seen as an incompetent leader. This often causes the line-level employees to "throw their hands in the air" with the attitude of "why make decisions if my leader is just going to do what he wants anyway?"
6. Do NOT hire micromanagers. Micromanagers are not well-intentioned leaders with a strong understanding of their organizational tasks; rather, they are essentially paranoid managers with low self-esteem who are not confident in their technical job fundamentals or their ability to lead and overcompensate through overt and unnecessary petty task management of their subordinates. Although that description may be a bit direct, I cannot be direct enough about the negative outcomes as they pertain to the impact one micromanager has on the totality the organization that he or she manages. A micromanager kills productivity, adds layers of complexity, and destroys the self-empowered spirit of the engaged employee.

The third pillar in the de-layering of organizations to support effective engagement is providing a mechanism, process, or path for members within the organization to escalate concerns or issues that affect their ability to execute the plan. When things go wrong in layered organizations (whether because of size, complexity, or organizational architecture), signs that problems were brewing often happen way before an issue emerges. In many cases individual contributors, managers, and even executive leadership had advanced warning that not all was well with a given issue but failed to escalate their concerns either for fear or repercussions or a failed mechanism for them to voice their concerns. Even worse, many times critical decisions are not made because those making decisions or participating in providing input do not understand where to bring problems, conflict, or alternative perspectives and "thrash" about, wasting valuable time, often until it's too late.

As a business security executive responsible for issues that affect safety, security, and overall risks to your business, the criticality around identifying impediments that affect your ability to execute your mission early and resolve them are that much more important, and it is your responsibility to ensure that there are mechanisms within your operation to allow all members to understand that they have a ability to sound the alarm and be heard. Consider a few options to create this path that can be added as standards within your operating model:

- *Tone from the top.* First and foremost, make it a point to let everyone in your organization know that it is their responsibility to "ring the bell" and that they are expected to bring issues forward without fear of retribution or punishment. It is incredibly de-motivating and frustrating to a person when they want to be part of the solution, yet when they raise issues they are belittled, berated, or ostracized.
- *Establish project protocols.* As described later in this book, your ability to implement appropriate project management is a deciding factor in the success of your program. As part of that program, there should be well-established processes and guidelines for project reviews that provide insight into program or project status, review timelines, risks, and issues, and provide transparent views into project metrics.
- *Operation review forums.* As in project reviews, it is important to create operations reviews that cover detailed operational metrics, security program efficacy, and create a forum for all participants to be heard.
- *Be involved.* Your policy of open escalation is only as good as your willingness to participate. If your employees do not feel that you are accessible or that you do not "hear" their concerns, nor that are they being addressed, they will most certainly cease to raise their concerns.
- *Q&A.* As an extension to the open review forms mentioned above, questions and answers should be part of your normal meeting process. Whether it's setting time aside at the end of every meeting for questions or ensuring that the last 15 min of your all-hands meeting has a structured Q&A process, or you host a once a month Q&A lunch and learn, giving your employees an avenue to ask questions, get answers, and voice their concerns creates an additional path that seems less formal and very accessible to them.
- *Concerns box/anonymous messaging.* The tried-and-true method that still works in many industries and organizations today is the ability for your employees to voice their concerns without attribution to themselves. Whether it's a concerns box, anonymous messaging via an open technology platform that does not reside within your own company, or a telephone number where people can leave anonymous voicemails—the result of each effort is the same. For those associates who feel threatened by coming forward, you provide them with a mechanism for escalating concerns and questions when they may not have done otherwise. Although this may not work in all environments, depending on your leadership style, it is certainly an option to be considered.

In the end, remember that open communication, the power of personal enablement, and transparency in the decision-making process encourages, enables, and empowers your employees to think, act, and be accountable on their own, expanding and extending your ability to execute as a senior security executive.

EFFECTIVE COMMAND AND CONTROL

The final area in ensuring execution excellence is around the topic of command and control. Although not normally seen in commercial entities or explored as a portion of corporate leadership agendas, it is hard to escape the fact that to enable effective, accurate, and timely execution of your business's mission and business objectives, you must be organizationally capable of driving effective command and control within your teams. There are thousands of books about decisive organizational and militaristic command-and-control frameworks, sustainability models, and measurements of effectiveness. However, I suggest only that you take away from this book a simplistic understanding that to remain effective in your ability to execute, there is a basic understanding between executive leadership and decisive command and control. Decision evaluation, development, an execution is not a democracy. Rather, it is a purposely built taxonomy and process that avails you to the right information, by the right people; assists you in making the right (best) command decisions; and supports the execution thereof. Whether you are unilaterally inclusive, maintain an organizational leadership management chain of command, or diversify decision-making processes through subgroups within your teams, at some point you become the ultimate decision-maker as the senior-most security executive for your organization. And once that decision (whatever it may be) has been made, the process by which you drive adherence to that decisions and assure that it is being implemented is considered your command-and-control process and is key to your success.

If we take a militaristic look a command and control, we'd probably be surprised at the level of which military scholars and military executive educators teach the theory of command and control. Although often confused as a single function referred to as "C2," each function is actually independent and serves two very different purposes. At a very high level, command equals the support of the decision-making process, and control equals the support of delivery operations. In either case command and control is not indicative of the who (such as the CSO or the CEO), but rather the what. Further, even in a militaristic concept, command and control is not a singularly stacked decision concept based on a single entity; in fact it is often referenced in cross-command architectures across military services and even nation-states. For more progressive military scholars and commanders, command-and-control concepts often seem to be an ability to create shared awareness and directed self-synchronization in a supporting framework that leads to agility and effective execution of a mission. The point is, just because you have well-thought-out, indoctrinated, and established command and control does not mean that you are a mindless execution machine, but rather a well-developed, process-orientated entity that enables the use of information and operational parameters to ensure consistent and accurate delivery.

As a converged security executive for your company, another important part of your ability to execute with regard to command and control is the expectation of your ability to make good decisions during times of crisis. Let's face it—your job means crisis management as well as risk management. As a converged security executive, your broad span of controls, broad practice areas, and additive opportunities for crisis resulting from expanded operational areas means that you will be dealing with many more crisis than singularly focused peers. You need to rely on your ability to ingest information, understand the status of the crisis you are managing, make quality decisions based on the information at hand, and operationally enact services to manage those crises. If it sounds difficult and daunting, it should, because it certainly is. But taking another chapter out of the military's long history of also successfully managing through crisis, we can learn from what former scholars have developed in the way of frameworks for managing through times of crisis. In the mid-1900s US Air Force Col. John Boyd created a decision-making framework known as the OODA loop. OODA stands for observe, orient, decide, and act. It's a simplistic formula that enables decisions under crisis using a mechanism that is simple to understand and easy to implement.

The following is a brief description of how one would implement the OODA loop architecture. The observed function coalesces data—either self-collected, provided by multiple mechanisms, or simply observed within your existing environment—to be easily understood and explained in the orient phase. Within the orient phase, the implementer of the process then applies his or her previous experiences, new information at hand, analysis (if available), regional and cultural considerations, and potentially metaphysical information such as genetic heritage (if applicable) and further qualifies the observations to then be forwarded on to the decision phase. The decision phase is the initial stage for guidance to the execution phase and is where the implementer modulates their hypothesis into a decision with qualified data from the previous two stages, at which time a threshold is reached and it is time to act. Depending on the speed at which the decision must be executed, the act phase may include action quality assurance for testing of the decision hypothesis or may lead to a direct implementation of the action. Either way, as the active phase unfolds, it then becomes a new environmental feedback mechanism for the observed phase, thus completing the entire decision-making process loop.

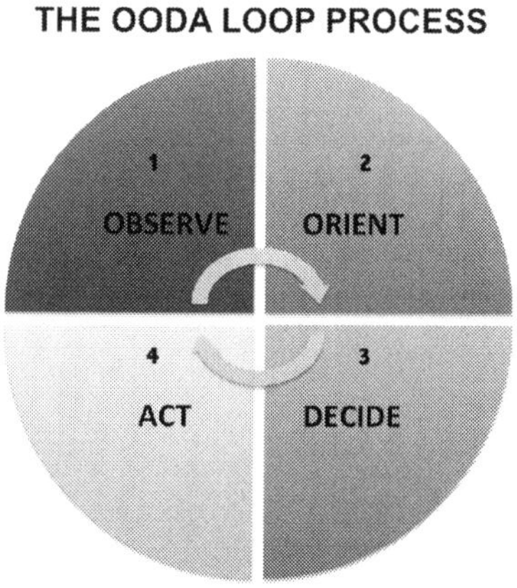

THE OODA LOOP PROCESS

No matter what framework you select to train with and use during crisis command decision-making, recognize that from both a command-and-control and a converged program perspective that an all-hazards approach must be used to ensure scalability and sustainability. Because the world is constantly changing, and your mission most certainly is as well, any attempt to create a rigid set of protocols based on known issues will most certainly fail. Utilize your own framework of common "buckets" of work, such as cyber security, business resilience, public safety, and even potentially another layer below that which supports your observe and orient phases with pre-positioned data models and data feeds. I encourage the use of standard playbooks, or special security instructions, for the top 20 most common issues responded to in each of your bucket areas, but expecting that you will have detailed plans and analytics for each potential issue that comes your way is a recipe for disaster. By using a common decision-making framework, training with it from an all-hazards functional approach, and implementing broad command-and-control functional architectures you will have a higher level of success in the effective execution of your mission and program.

Finally, a quick reminder that the old adage "don't reinvent the wheel" still applies to converged security program execution as it relates to command-and-control functionality. Through the use of well-tested and battle-proven frameworks you can quickly train your teams, organization, company, and partners to execute in a common fashion, operate on a common taxonomy, and do so across businesses, geographies, and functional disciplines. Explore systems such as the Federal Emergency Management Agency's National Incident Management System, the command-and-control crisis management system most commonly used by command staff in the military, fire services, law enforcement, health care management, and many other industries and agencies around the globe. The National Incident Management System merely creates a framework of interoperability, common command management, and mechanisms for decision success. Training is freely available on the Internet, and advanced in-person training is available for your command staff. The point is that it does not take a 20-year career as a military officer to be able to act and deliver quality command-and-control assurance in your capacity as a senior security executive in your company.

Chapter 5

Concepts of Organization

As the saying goes, Rome was not built in a day. Nor was it built without the architects considering future requirements and the underlying components necessary to enable the founders' vision. As a senior security executive, you will be tasked with architecting an organizational construct for delivering successful security services across your business. To accomplish this, you will need to understand the functional architecture options for developing security programs, important roadmap designs, and other considerations for implementing models such as a net new program or the collapse and re-architecture of a multiorganization folding into a single converged entity. As your program matures and your company's requirements change, you need to consider program advancement and new considerations to increase operational effectiveness, expand business security service maturity, and the ability to layer in advanced, integrated security capabilities for your organization.

By understanding and applying concepts of historical organizational frameworks combined with advanced organizational design for business operation protection programs, you can quickly create an organizational model for success that is expandable and predicated on the needs of your business.

ENABLING ORGANIZATIONAL SUCCESS

Before we get started on the operational construct necessary to build a security program, it is just as important to touch on philosophical imperatives that drive organizational success for security, risk, and privacy teams. Just like setting yourself up for success with a positive mind-set, it is imperative to create and maintain that same focus for your team. Basic building blocks in an organizational mind-set serve as guiding principles for delivering the required services to your business. When you build organizational frameworks with these elements as conditional ethos, you ensure directional consistency and create an integrated program across all operating areas.

Development (Individual and Organizational)

The first of these is the mind-set of the consistent development of both your people and your organization. Development accompanies change, and change is the only constant in the world. Both people and organizations need to develop continuously to meet the needs of a changing business, a changing threat landscape, changing tactics and technology, and the changing global environment. You may have heard the saying "movement is life," a popular phrase used throughout the military that teaches the discipline of never becoming complacent.

For an individual, whether a leader or an individual contributor, focusing on personal development has several positive outcomes. The most obvious, of course, is that the more trained, experienced, and broad the skill sets of an individual, the more effective and efficient they will be for an organization. The broader the knowledge, the broader the ability to deliver across multiple functions, thus reducing the resource needs of the organization. It's simple leverage.

Beyond the resource consideration, however, development is necessary for the psyche of individuals themselves. Remember, as a leader, your job is to obtain, retain, and enable the most efficient workforce possible to deliver your mission. When individuals look at what organizations they may want to join, a constant measurement that researchers indicate is important is an individual's ability to develop within that organization. If a person joins a given company and they feel they have no ability for personal development, then they will typically avoid that condition. By establishing programs, measures, and successes in the area of individual development, you create a brand and promising expectation of a place where employees can grow professionally and become valued members of the entire organization. That brand equity goes a long way in successfully recruiting and retaining the talent you want and need to drive your program forward.

When it comes to organizations, continuous development also plays a critical role in performance excellence, relevance, and effectiveness. No matter what business, agency, or industry you are in, your business changes every day, as does the world around you and the markets you serve. The services you delivered yesterday may not be necessary or relevant to the business you protect today. Two components are important to remember. First, recognize and document a multiyear strategy that drives change into your program. This sets the expectation that change is a requirement of doing business rather than a response to changing conditions that you may or may not decide to engage. The second is to create and establish an environment that rewards organizational development thinking and in fact embraces it, uses it, and displays it as a positive for others to learn by. Every organization is different, and so will be their development requirements. There is no "set schedule" that security executives should live by. Rather, they should make organizational development a component and mechanism within their organizational quality programs as well as sustainability planning.

Organizational development means many things to many people. In some cases it may mean changes or transference in service delivery. In others it may mean organizational charts and organizational structure changes. Yet in others it may mean automation and optimization through organizational process enhancements. Again, there is no checklist or certification framework for organizational development specific to security, risk, and privacy programs. It is your job to create the work, the environment, and the ability for your program to advance and move forward through change.

Instilling a Sense of Mission

The next building block that you need to master is the ability to develop and instill a sense of mission in yourself and in your organization. Although "defining a mission" seems fairly simplistic, converting a mission statement into a deep personal belief that drives human action and endurance is quite the opposite. In this context we are not defining "what you do" but rather "why" you do it that relates very deeply to yourself and to those that you lead. This "why" is the footing of an internal interpretation of each individual's purpose for believing in, and delivering, the mission requirements.

This sense of purpose is a great force multiplier. It drives action, creates consistency, and often overcomes human physiological barriers. This singular mission thread, woven throughout the higher organization, not only develops a consistent organizational approach but also creates a global bond between participants. This bond breaks down organizational, societal, and professional barriers that are normal in a larger, geographically dispersed group. People who easily identify with others often work together easily, even if that does not occur on a daily basis. Again, in the concept of a military organization, think about members of diverse military groups and entities that are put together on a moment's notice to fight a common enemy. The singular mission of defending their homeland by defeating their enemies enables them to operate as a cohesive unit wherever they are sent. This concept holds true through a mission-enabled security, risk, and privacy group that operates under the same mission parameters.

By using the skill sets and techniques discussed in the previous chapter, you can create your mission, develop the story, and use it in all aspects of organizational design. Remember, the science behind mission enablement at the individual level is the ability to deliver that story and be transparent in the individual's ability to successfully and positively affect the mission outcome. As you create an organizational structure, organizational services, and other important components of your program, you must integrate your mission ethos in every aspect of it.

A Services Philosophy

The final significant (and perhaps the most difficult) building block that you should consider is a concept of a service philosophy. Although becoming more popular with International Organization for Standardization–enabled organizations, the concept of "service delivery" in the past has not been broadly operationalized in security functions. When we speak of a service philosophy, we speak of an operational unit that provides specific offerings with specific service levels within a given scope to a specific client or set of clients.

This type of methodology enables three positive outcomes. First, it establishes a business framework that provides a foundation of measurable components necessary to manage your security business. Concepts such as the cost of goods sold, service-level costs, financial measurements, key performance indicators, and other business management tools are enabled through your ability to define what you deliver, who you deliver to, and the scope in which you deliver it. Not only does this help you successfully manage your business, it helps you successfully plan your business. Budgetary exercises by business leaders are premised on facts, in operating your security business through a measurable service model provides you with fact-based planning.

Second, it creates the transparency and expectation-setting necessary to develop good business relationships. Services enable definition, definition provides facts, and facts enable great business discussions. This type of fact-based approach delivers the "who, what, why, and where" that your internal clients expect as part of your business relationship. When expectations are aligned through documented services structures, budgets are associated and developed against those agreed-upon services, and performance is measured against those services; you provide your client with a familiar business mechanism that enables them to make business decisions based on fact rather than conjecture.

The third positive outcome is in the management of your own team. Security, risk, and privacy professionals are often "can do and will do" focused people. When they see a problem they want to fix it. By the very nature of the job, practitioners are like first responders for your business or agency. The problem becomes when that "can-do" attitude begins a pileup of the amount of work an organization is signing up for when it is not in alignment with resources or funding. When that happens, practitioners can often feel overwhelmed, disappointed in their perceived impact or lack thereof, and overstressed about the large amount of work in critical issues. The service-enabled organization understands what they will and will not deliver to the business they serve based on the agreed-upon scope, resources, and funding. This does not mean that they do not evaluate the needs of the business, create business cases for organizational development and expansion for those needs, and respond when needed to nonspecific service-related actions; rather, it provides them with a construct and a base of understanding of what is expected of them and what they can and cannot do with the resources provided. The great "stress reducer" is when your team operates under the premise of what they are committed to and what is beyond the operating commitments as agreed to by the entire business.

By using the basic building block concepts of constant development, mission enablement, and service enablement as you develop your security organization, you create and interwoven mesh of people enablement and empowerment, successful business principles, and organizational leverage and sustainability that delivers operational success.

CONCEPTS IN SECURITY ORGANIZATION

As you begin to create an organizational design to support the next-generation business you are protecting, it's important to understand the multiple concepts of organizational design both historically and, as this book suggests, the future through convergence. Whether you are a security expert who has successfully operated the physical security program and is looking to optimize your company's security effectiveness by converting to a converged organization, or you are an information technology (IT) security leader who has been tasked with creating a singular security unit to support the expanding needs of your business, a review of historical organizational concepts, the components thereof, and common misconceptions should be a part of your development process. This will help you successfully design, articulate, and defend your program design and set the expectations of your teams in the business you serve.

How We Got Here

Although I am a big believer in the old adage "look at life through the windshield not the rearview mirror," I also believe that to understand other people's perspectives, sometimes you need historical context to enrich your own. For the most part, physical security and similar programs have been a part of businesses in the formal sense since the early to mid-1900s. Although there is no one consistent historical articulation of the facts, security programs were principally formed from necessity as the economy of privatized companies began to grow after the Great Depression and then again after World War II. Since then, the industry has professionalized, created standards, and matured to the higher end of the maturity scale and in fact, has created an industry unto itself.

From physical security controls to monitoring technology, contract personnel, and even critical industry-based segments such as critical infrastructure, nuclear, maritime, transportation, and even health care, security professionals have created modernized frameworks, capabilities, and operational programs to fit the needs of the organizations and industries they serve. Although optimized for commercial use only since the mid-1900s, the skill sets associated with corporate security professionals can be linked back hundreds of years in the study of basic protection operations for civilized environments. The science around how one designs defensive programs, investigates crimes, and protects assets has been being advanced and perfected for a long time. The reapplication of that science to support industry and economies relies heavily on learning and applications dating back to the beginning of organized societies.

Many practitioners and executive leaders come from the ranks of military or law enforcement organizations; however, because of the rich maturity of the "corporate security" career field, the industry itself has created a rich and deep well of professionals, executives, and practitioners that are industrial security experts by trade, not as postgovernment careers. In either case, the typical focus of these programs has been on the protection of assets and people from a physical security perspective.

On the other hand, the information security component of the profession is in the middle of its growth cycle and has significantly less history behind it. Born from necessity after the advent of networking computing, including the ARPANET, the Internet, and enterprise computing, formalized information security programs were the result of necessary technological expertise to help secure computing infrastructures, computing systems, and information. Technology evolution has one of the fastest expansion and growth rates ever. The profession of cyber information security migrated from a handful of functional job families to dozens in the course of only 25 years. Specialties in application development, networking infrastructure, and user compute defense, data protection, analytics, and so on are continuing to be developed, modified, and formalized as necessary to support continuing global reliance on technology as an underpinning of how our civilization operates.

The preponderance of information security professionals comes from a technology background. These job families are widely considered and accepted as a technology profession; in fact, in most cases, they operate as a component of the office of chief information officer. Although some information security leaders have been acquired from the ranks of financial professionals, auditors, and even the medical field, a deep requirement of an understanding of technology and applied information management skill sets has kept this part of our profession deeply ingrained and attached to technology career fields.

Those practitioners who focus on risk management belong to a mature career field that has deep roots within the financial sector. The maturity of risk management with regard to information security management and like areas came about as a natural evolution to the critical impact that businesses saw security had on their overall operating functions. With the introduction of security-specific frameworks, risk programs became a formalized mechanism to manage priorities, establish quantifiable and quantitative analyses of security issues, and provide a mechanism for the evaluation of program effectiveness. These processes, risk mechanisms, and risk sciences were not created specific for security. Technology organizations have been using risk management concepts for a number of decades for many of the same reasons. Although the security risk programs have evolved to support measurements, algorithms, and concepts specific to security management, and threat management, the risk management profession is a well-established component of business operations in general.

In the context of privacy professionals, these programs are typically seen as compliance necessities to provide regulatory translations to business operations with regard to privacy requirements, and they often are managed under the oversight of General Counsel or a legal function. Privacy professionals are at an even earlier stage in the life cycle of maturity development than information security. Until recently, most privacy executives (chief privacy officers) were attorneys or other legal experts who supported the translation mentioned above as well as policy and controls development, and internally consulted on privacy matters for their business. Today, with the explosion of global privacy laws specific to data privacy and data protection under development or being considered, new concepts such as privacy by design, privacy engineering, and privacy controls assurance are being developed under high demand; these will not just ensure compliance with the increased regulations, but will transition from a consultant to an informative organization to an operational program that embeds privacy as an integral part of the business process.

As you can see, each component of the converged security, risk, and privacy job families comes from a very different background, and each is at a varying level of maturity in the professional life cycle. From individual contributors through the executive levels, professionals in each one of these areas tend to develop themselves to be better at the function they are in, rather then the interpretation and applicability of multiple career fields to create a better business process. Further, the complexity and "technical" requirements of each area are often limiting factors in a broad understanding of operational interests, creating a natural barrier between segments of operations.

Stigmas and Dogmas

So, if we take it at face value that convergence is the next evolution in business operations protection management, and we want to make an argument for or against it, then perhaps we should first remove some of the most common stigmas and dogmas associated with the argument of why convergence doesn't matter.

There Is No Overlap

One of the most common arguments against convergence is the theory that none of the functions overlap. Nothing could be further from the truth. Although specific service deliverables can certainly be independent, security operations management and program delivery have a lot of commonality across all security disciplines. From how we look at risk, to how we monitor it, to the infrastructures and operations that manage and process workflow for detection and response and how we respond to incidents in crisis, and many other areas, they are simply just variations or additional protocols to support each "technical" discipline.

It's a Totally Different Skill Set

It's hard to argue with the fact that executive protection is an entirely different skill set than that required to configure a firewall. It's no different than saying that an application programmer is very different from a network engineer. Every organization has different specialties. But the leveragability of converged organizational management within the realm of security is not at the functional service delivery area. The business case to be made is at the executive, management, program, and platform levels. Don't think of this as cost attribution to people only. The cost-benefit and management efficiencies you gain come from consolidated platforms, enabling a broader understanding of security relevancy to business through transparency across multiple disciplines and the effective use of management to gain a broader span of control capability. Will you be able to leverage some resources? Most definitely, especially in areas such as crisis management, program management, and project management, as well as other duplicative supporting functions. When speaking specifically about resources, most of your commonality will be at the managerial level and higher. Most of your cost benefits will come in the reduction of operating platform costs, depreciation, and like assets that are required to support multiple independent operations.

Technologists Can't Manage the Physical Side of the House

Another common misconception is that technology executives can't possibly understand areas such as public safety or criminal and civil investigations. What I find most interesting about this commentary is that those who make this argument typically leave out the idea that technology executives are often well versed in process management, financial acumen, platform efficiencies, complex people management, and business process support. Aren't these the areas that we should be concerned about? As business executives, shouldn't we be more focused on operational effectiveness and managing our business? From a pure security standpoint, security executives who come from the information security or technical side of the house are still well-versed in understanding threat discovery, threat measurement, and threat management and the application of risk management for business. Understanding the "technical" side of physical security with regard to appropriate investigations management, ethics, and facilities is a learnable skill. In addition, through the intelligent use of middle management resources, technical security executives converging into singular management positions can buy the time necessary to establish new skills and reduce the gap in specific functional areas.

Cops Can't Possibly Understand Business and Technology

If the previous argument doesn't hold much water, then this one won't either. The stereotypical picture of a cop on the beat wearing a uniform and a gun belt is not typically what we're talking about here. In the ranks of law enforcement or professional industrial security organizations, those leaders who make it to executive positions have had broad management and leadership experience and often require the addition of new skill sets in support of their positions. In larger agencies such as the FBI, Secret Service, or the military, you often find leaders who have held management positions in human resources, technical operations oversight, and administration—what are currently referred to as business operations. These positions are required to get a more well-rounded executive leadership core that could potentially run the operation as "chief" at some point. In addition, the use of technology within these types of environments is fairly common. There are several compelling aspects of why this type of experienced leader makes a great converged security leader. First, these men and woman are adept at processing a lot of information in complex and evolving situations and making solid decisions. As the saying goes, no two calls are the same in law enforcement; and one day you could be managing a rash of burglaries and the next managing a massive public safety crisis such as at a natural disaster or flooding. The ability to understand the situation, orient your charge to address it, make a decision, act quickly, and do that process again for almost any issue that arises is invaluable in our business. Another great asset that most of these executives bring to the table is their ability to work with people. In the public sector, or when dealing with the public in general, you often create a diverse set of people skills that allows you to engage people from vastly different demographics and statuses. One day you can be dealing with a mentally disturbed homeless person, the next day arresting and interrogating a doctor for a felonious crime, and the next speaking at a public event for people in your community. When you obtain leadership positions you also add in the skill of dealing with city councils, businesses within your community, and other key constituents that help you develop broad executive acumen and political vitality.

As you can see, requirements to lead a converged security organization are broad and plentiful. No one individual ever possess 100% of every component in a generic job description. If you focus on leadership principles and business principles, and create a bridge that enables you to develop a continuous skill set in gap areas, you become a valuable asset of any leadership team no matter what your background is.

Classic Organizational Design Principals

As you begin to consider how to design your security program, there are some basic design considerations that are import to consider whether you are contemplating a siloed discipline approach or a converged program. Understanding why these decisions are important and having open dialogue with other executive business leaders in your company ahead of time helps set the stage for the implementation phase. If you remove structural and political issues early, you can focus on execution and your mission rather than wasting valuable time explaining your decisions after you have already designed your program. This is why these two basic issues should be addressed before moving forward with program design.

The first area is operational segregation. Sometimes referred to as segregation of duties, the concept establishes autonomous operating structures to reduce undue overt pressure or influence that creates an ethical or mission-affecting imbalance for the decision maker. This can be an issue in any part of your organization, but it most commonly occurs in the Information/cyber security components and at times in the physical security areas. An example of this is a chief security officer (CSO) who may report to a chief information officer (CIO). If the CIO exerts financial (performance oversight) or career-affecting influence over the security executive, it is possible that the CSO may not report, escalate, or remediate security issues within a CIO-managed function if he or she believes that their boss (the CIO) may react negatively.

The CSO or chief information security officer (CISO) must be empowered to report security, risk, and privacy issues; manage standards and policy oversight; and react or respond to potential security threats without fear of reprimand or career-limiting actions. The key message here is NOT that a CSO "cannot" report into a CIO, rather that businesses should **discuss, decide, and structure** who will be accountable for security, risk, and privacy oversight and avoid situations that put leaders in awkward and contentious positions. Having the confidence to execute your mandate with the confidence and organizational support to openly discuss risk issues across the business is important for a successful security program. No two businesses are the same, and this should be determined as a critical business decision rather than a decision of convenience.

Once the decision of "where" not to put the business operations security program has been made, then you need to focus on "where" to put it; this is more formally recognized as a "reporting structure." Again, every organization is different, and the maturity of the security organization, the business's focus on security, and how the senior leadership functions operate all play into the decision. In many cases you won't have a choice and you will simply be told. In other cases you may be consulted or actually be hired into a company to rebuild a security program and will be expected to make these important organizational design decisions. Either way, there are some important reporting structure points to consider.

The first is to understand that the future of organizations that deliver business operation protection programs for a business is as an operational entity. Gone are the days when security programs were relegated to establishing a policy and measuring compliance within it. Businesses and agencies need security, risk, and privacy programs that are able to prevent, protect, and respond to the changing global operating environment and threats that every business faces today. Unless a security executive reports directly to the chief executive officer (CEO) of a business, the organization should report up through an "operations" function.

Another important consideration is "corporate versus business unit". Should a company have a centralized security function or several autonomous or loosely federated security operations? My counsel is to centralize as much as possible with a philosophy of global measured service capabilities with local support. Having a centralized security function removes the major political and segregation of duty issues, with independent business leadership executives making independent security decision on their own, enforced by a business unit security executive, with implications that could affect the entire company. In addition, a centralized security, risk, and privacy program enables a level of cross-business standards, transparency, and broad risk visibility that supports better business decision capabilities and ensures standards of care and reporting. Further, the leveragability of an integrated organizational platform paves the way for an integrated operations platform. Integrated technical architecture and operations technologies reduce costs, drive speed to defense, and increase cross-business visibility and intelligence capabilities. For instance, if each business unit or division creates its own security monitoring capability or security analytics and intelligence platforms, an independent identification of a threat actor by one business unit would not provide the context necessary to understand the totality of the risk across the entire business that the threat actor may pose. By creating operations and technology operations that take into account the entire company, security leadership can better identify, evaluate, an address threats, vulnerabilities, and other potential negative-impact events inclusive of all the factors across a business, allowing them to make better risk decisions.

Once that decision has been made, the issue then becomes to which executive leadership stack a corporate security function should report to. Again, every business is different. The makeup of your company or agency executive committee and the opinion of the Board of Directors about the criticality of security in the overall operating function of the business comes into play. A few recommendations or guidelines you may want to consider are described in the following paragraphs.

First, as mentioned previously, organizations may want to avoid conflict of interest by having security executives report to the CIO of the organization. The primary reason for this concern is the difficulty and pressure that the security executive will be under to report gaps, flaws, vulnerabilities, and critical issues within the technical space without fear of retribution or career impact. Further, because of the chain of command, critical discussion points, information, and metrics could be skewed or not properly reported in favor of driving technical decisions. The other reason, in the context of the next-generation security leader, is the fact that convergence includes security disciplines far outside the technical sphere. Technology executives often de-prioritize and negatively impact prioritization in service alignment with those functions that do not align to the core mission of the CIO's platform. This may reduce the ability of the security executive to create a comprehensive converged security, risk, and privacy program that consolidates technical, physical, and privacy security programs.

The next consideration should be around the alignment of the converged security function with the operational entity. Examples of this include an organization's chief operating officer, chief financial officer, or CEO. The focus here is to create levergeable executive oversight that understands and enhances concepts of service delivery assurance and operational excellence. Although executive leaders such as general counsel often understand, promote, and support the criticality that security, risk, and privacy functions provide, the management of these functions in an operational context is often not the strong suit of those leaders. Their focus, such as in the case of general counsel, is around discipline knowledge, consulting, advising, and strategic decision development. Depending on the sphere of responsibility and job specifications, other executives such as the chief development officer, chief technology officer, and chief strategy officer often fall into the same category.

The third and final point of consideration is around the alignment to the security function with a risk executive. As is mentioned throughout this book, the CSO does equal the chief risk execution officer. Many companies have chief risk officers, enterprise risk executives, and other aligned parallel functions that are not necessarily operational in scope, but rather focus on compliance, oversight, and reporting. Many organizations, however, use the opportunity to align risk functions broadly into the role of a senior executive such as the chief financial officer (CFO) or a similar function. Using the example of a CFO, their operating premise every day is around managing the financial risks of the business. Their ability to understand the application of risk decisions across broad spectrums such as financial risk, legal risk, tax risk, security risk, and contract risk creates an avenue by which security, privacy, and other risk issues can be evaluated in the context of the entire business rather than just a singular area like tax or law. In addition, decisions for cross-business investments and expenditures in the context of risk reduction, opportunity exploitation, and strategic investments often are made by the CFO. Transparency into critical security and privacy concerns and plans that enable opportunity, reduce risk, and deliver future strategies can be added to other similar risk concern areas, that will ensure security programs have the right level of fiscal oversight and opportunity for investment and, at a minimum, discussion.

Convergence: The Future of Your Profession

As discussed in Chapter 2, the complex requirements of the next-generation security leader demand vision, programmatic, and technology integrations across security, risk, and privacy disciplines. Simply stated, convergence is a reality for the next-generation leader. When planning your organization, considerable thought should go into what convergence may look like for your organization and what it really means for your business or agency. At a pragmatic level, strategic business alignment, span of controls management, and strategic execution of business operations protection across a broad set of security disciplines under a single leadership tier just makes sense.

Operationally, all security functions within an organization, if strategically aligned to the business, should be directionally engaged in the same mission. That mission of business defense in support of the overall business success may take on different battles, threats, and service offerings, but the battlefield is still the same. The industry, geographies, and assets that you are required to protect are all part of the same community of interest. Protecting this community means that there will be overlapping operations, opportunities for leveraging resources, and the need for a simplified view of the battlefield. Let's consider a converge security leadership program in the context of the US Armed Forces and their joint operations commands. There may be ground, air, and naval assets operating in each dedicated area, but joint situational awareness and command authority comes from a joint operations command. For example, an Army military commander may be responsible for all service entities within a particular theater of operation. The focus of the military executive leadership is mission success through leveraging the right resources at the right time for the right operation utilizing mission planning, intelligence, situational awareness, and shared assets.

Absent this critical cross-functional capability, as described above, military leaders would have continuous overlapping operations and would probably interfere in each other's success. Using the converged leadership model, however, reduces the chance of overlapping missions, finds and enforces integrated service dependencies, ensures success through oversight and management, and reduces cost through shared technologies and management platforms. How is this different in your space as a security, risk, or privacy leader? It really isn't.

Industry and Vertical Considerations

The next area of organizational design considerations should be focused on the industries and/or vertical markets that you support. Certain industries or business areas require different approaches to security, have significantly different requirements for service priorities, potentially require specific oversight, or may have specific regulatory compliancy needs. Although because of the scope of this book it is not possible to provide a detailed list of each industry and their independent prioritize requirements or necessities from a program perspective, the following are examples of specific industry vertical considerations that may require additional thought during organizational design.

Critical Infrastructure Protection

In most industrialized and developed nations it is well understood that certain industries and operating infrastructures are essential to the well-being of the given nation-state, including the safety of the citizenry, the management of society, the protection of the economy, and the resiliency of the government. After the terrorist attacks of September 11, 2001, the United States created one of the most formalized critical infrastructure protection programs in the world. Initially designed and instituted under presidential directive in 2003, then later updated in a similar directive in 2013, the United States created 16 "critical infrastructure sectors" that focused on creating government policy, public and private security cooperation, and intelligence protective operations to strengthen and secure those industries, agencies, and businesses that were deemed most critical to the United States. Examples of the sectors include the defense industrial base, energy, government facilities, finance, health care, IT, nuclear energy, communications, dams, manufacturing, first responders, agriculture, transportation, and public services.

Understanding that if you belong to one of these sectors your threat landscape may be much different than those in other industry segments is a vital part of the planning process. In addition, understanding that being part of a critical infrastructure industry segment (depending on what country or countries you operate in) may require you to add specific functionality to your security program, including policy, operations, oversight, and reporting. By belonging to or being classified as a critical infrastructure organization, certain benefits may be useful in supporting and defending your organization. Certain countries allow critical infrastructure organizations to participate in unique intelligence sharing programs, provide consultative resources for threat evaluation and risk discovery and remediation planning. In certain countries and verticals, being critical infrastructure can potentially open access to specialized technologies and services not generally available the commercial entities. Knowing the industries you serve, understanding whether you're critical to the nation state infrastructure, and spending the time to understand the resources available to you if you are, can often provide incredible resources that otherwise you would not be able to afford and a force multiplier through the use of shared industry resources or government resources not available to other commercial entities.

Of course, with the good sometimes come less desirable effects. In some countries and industries that are critical infrastructure means specific regulatory requirements and oversight. This can mean more complex reporting, prescribed baseline initiatives not imposed on other commercial sectors, or requirements to share privileged, confidential information with the government that your company may not otherwise normally share. Again, this all goes into your planning process. If you do belong to a critical infrastructure, make sure that your planning takes into account people, process, technology, oversight, and reporting necessities mandated or expected in the jurisdictions you serve. Also, for companies operating in multiple countries, remember that each country may look at your business and industry segment differently. That may mean that in the United States, where your corporate headquarters may be, you are not critical, but in the European Union, where 20% of your revenue is generated, you may very well be considered critical infrastructure.

The common thread here is to understand which industries you serve and how each international jurisdiction you operate in looks at your company, investigate requirements and opportunities across each of those operating areas, and design your program accordingly.

Multinational Organizations

Other industry-independent issues and business make-up should be considered when developing your security program. One of these includes your status as a multinational organization. A multinational organization is any company that operates, delivers products or services, or potentially uses services in more than one country. Although that may seem broad, the legal and regulatory issues associated with each of those are broader, and it often takes legal experts to provide you with a framework of understanding whether you are a multinational organization. Once you get to that determination, however, your life as a security executive changes. In fact, your entire program changes, and understanding whether you are considered a multinational organization will be a critical part of your foundational decision-making during the planning process. You will need to be concerned with many areas, especially those in defense of operations, data protection, privacy, and prohibited acts. Each one of these dictates how you position equipment, technology, people, and even decide whether you use your own personnel or contract personnel to provide the services needed to protect your business. Let's take a look a few of these critical areas.

Data Protection

Privacy and Consumer Protection

Privacy and consumer protection affect just about every part of a converged security program. Different than data protection, privacy and consumer protection focuses on ensuring the sanctity of the consumer's identity and privileged information; in fact, in many jurisdictions the requirements between data protection and privacy protection often conflict. For instance, the data protection side of the law may say that you must use minimum industry technologies to protect data, whereas the privacy side restricts the use of certain threat detection technology, even in a private setting, if it can identify personal information or a person's identity. Complex, right?

To muddle the issue even more, privacy plays a critical role internationally in the protection of physical assets and people as well. For instance, in some countries it is perfectly permissive to use closed circuit television or video monitoring of a work environment or campus to protect people and resources. In other countries the use of video technology, the monitoring thereof, and the constructs of what can and cannot be monitored can be complex. As part of a multinational organization, you need to understand what privacy laws in which countries affect your protection plan, even at a facility's security level. Simple issues such as generating reports of badge access on an individual basis may actually be unlawful in some countries. As the senior security executive for your organization, it is your job to learn and create a program specific to the laws of each jurisdiction your business operates in.

Data Movement

Like data protection, data movement is in a class all its own. Data movement refers mostly to the electronic transfer of information between entities or between the borders of different countries. Companies that are based in a single country, however, may provide services or products outside that country and quite possibly could be affected by data movement laws and requirements across the globe. All multinational corporations must pay attention to data movement as well. Most laws or regulatory requirements regarding data movement are specific to consumers or some sort of protected data; however, that is not a hard and fast rule. Some countries restrict intellectual property or any data used to process business that has an impact on revenue. Paying attention to data movement requirements is important beyond just client information, as well. Ensuring compliance around the movement of data related to your own employees or business is also required under most laws.

In the context of organizational development, you need to understand how much data your company moves, in which countries you have compliancy issues, and who is responsible and accountable within your business for the protection and assurance of that data movement. If you move very little data, it may just be an add-on service requirement for an operational privacy or information security group. If you are a multinational or consumer services entity and move a lot of data across many countries, you most likely want to develop a specialty focused on the area of data movement assurance.

From a converged perspective, businesses with crossed data movement necessities often require special programs for data security certification specific to data movement. Whether it's using existing frameworks such as safe harbor, binding corporate rules, or specific industry or government certifications, companies need to not only understand the requirements of the law, but also have frameworks set up to enable them to complete the data movement actions necessary to do their business. In some organizations the certification and registration of data protection programs is left to independent business entities; in others there is the requirement of a centralized privacy standards and compliance entity. The fact to remember here is that if you must move data across borders or legal jurisdictions to complete your business objectives, you need to know the requirements within each one of those jurisdictions for the businesses you provide, and you should be prepared both from a knowledge standpoint and an organizational development standpoint to be able to support your business for those requirements.

Data Processing

For businesses that deal with the processing of information for reasons such as finance, business services, business outsourcing, insurance, or health care, the applicability of certain laws specific to data processors are often unique and enforced. The applicability extends do not just the data owners—who may, in fact, be your clients—but to those businesses that act as data stewards or custodians and use the information to provide business value. Unique requirements may fall into categories of data protection, breach notification, data destruction, or data access. Many special requirements must be validated and interpreted by trained legal experts. Often, though, the enforcement of policy, standards, and oversight are left to operational security, risk, or privacy organizations. As in data movement and data protection, the amount of information you process dictates the level of formalized data processing protection programs you have in place, thus affecting the design of your converged security operations.

Reporting

Another important area multinational entities often face is specialized reporting, with both commercial and compliance requirements. The level of reporting is dictated by things like the type of regulated industry you are in, the countries you operate in, and the requirements of their data protection authorities. Other deciding factors include things such as the certifications and accreditations your business upholds and contractual requirements embedded within customer agreements and partnership agreements. In addition, internal reporting for things such as corporate governance, compliance, and executive oversight authorities creates the necessity to develop, maintain, and provide consistent and detailed reports around key performance indicators, program efficacy, controls assurance, program sustainability, and other similar measurements.

As part of your organizational design, the amount and necessity or criticality of reporting plays into organizational design and resource calibration. Often, reporting requires a significantly different skill set in the development, correlation, and creation of algorithms, methods, and metrics to create the reports. Also under consideration is how data sets are collected, calculated, and automated to reduce future resource needs and efforts to provide repetitive reports. For instance, within organizations that I operate, professionals in the business office or portfolio management teams with expertise in business services typically provide this type of centralized service, ensuring consistency of data and consistency of representation and the automation specific to the needs of the business.

Operational Requirements

Operationally, understanding where services can be delivered and under what type of circumstances is also important to understand the needs of organizational development. Factors such as privacy laws, financial implications, criticality and speed of delivery, threat surface, and asset size and location all play into how and where you deploy your resources and how that feeds into the overall hierarchy of the organization you create.

From a cyber perspective, typical operational issues fall into either a data privacy or language issue. For instance, in some legal jurisdictions it is unlawful to move data across judicial boundaries. Although in many countries this refers to specific protected information, in many others it includes elements of personally identifiable information, which may include things beyond a name and address or date of birth, to obscure yet articulated data elements such as Internet protocol addresses. So, although you may be able to collect data and alerts from protection technology in each one of those countries, sending the details of those alerts to centralized security-monitoring facilities outside the given region is not permissible; this may require you to instantiate specific local operations for reviewing information from security monitoring platforms.

From a language perspective, you simply may not have the skill sets available (e.g., multilanguage skills) to provide the level of service needed to protect or measure the risk of your business. English is not a required language globally for business operations, however, and if you are a US-based company you may be dealing with 5 to 15–20 different languages within the business platforms you protect. You will need to make decisions on language skills required, location requirements, and service level commitments during your organizational development phase to set expectations, appropriately design your operational delivery program, and evaluate financial requirements for global operations.

Prohibited Acts

As daunting as all of the previously listed global national requirements may seem, one of the biggest areas of concern may actually be around what you are not allowed to do internationally. These areas of concern actually fall into two very different camps. The first, prohibited acts, is just what it says. Simply, you are not allowed to do it. In some countries this may mean video recording of employees in common areas; in other countries it may be unlawful to encrypt data, whereas in others you may not be allowed to use a specific type of technology or service, such as Technical Security Counter Measures or Technical Counter Surveillance Equipment (commonly referred to as bug detection). From cyber security operations to physical security protection to intellectual property defense, when operating around the globe you must be aware of what services are legally prohibited to avoid legal actions against your business or, even worse, against the people delivering the services on your behalf.

The second camp that is often confused with prohibited acts is "restricted acts." These are services or technologies that, if not appropriately implemented, monitored, maintained, or administratively approved by appropriate authorities, would violate local law. A good example of this is in the area of cyber security and data monitoring. For example, if your program required technology that monitors for the leakage of corporate information from your network in Germany, if you did not properly document how and what you would be monitoring, what the technology does, how the alert notification and investigation processes work and you did not seek the approval of both the data protection authority and what is referred to as the "Workers Council," you could be in violation of law. If you follow the prescriptive process for approval, however, you most probably will be able to deploy the technology necessary to protect the business.

The point to remember here is that many will say something is a "prohibited act" when in fact it may not be. Do your due diligence to understand what is necessary, what requires processes to enable, and what simply is not allowed by law. As a multinational company, you need to establish processes across your functional operations to ensure compliance and adherence to these complex issues.

Governments and Government Contractors

Different than the critical infrastructures mentioned above, or the "defense industrial base," many companies from many industries outside of critical infrastructure provide products, services, or people to governments around the globe. Whether you are manufacturing company that makes hammers or you're consulting on IT services to the agricultural agency of any given country, doing business with government agencies often requires additional contractual requirements, operational considerations, reporting, and security program elements not found in commercial business operations. These requirements manifest themselves in costs through operational architecture considerations, segmentation efforts, and additive protection requirements for manufacturing, intellectual property, data, as well as a variety of other areas.

Here are some key concepts to keep in mind if you are providing services to a government:

Personnel Security

Depending on the type of product or service you are providing, governments often require that all individuals providing services to them be "citizens" of their country. From a technology perspective, sometimes this extends to anyone who "can access, modify, or otherwise view their information", which obviously has incredible implications. Many of these are negotiable, whereas others are not. Understanding what contractual requirements your business has signed up for is of vital importance to the design of the security program you put in place.

Another area of potential requirements is around government clearances. This is where individuals must obtain clearances such as secret (SEC), top-secret (TS), or top-secret with compartmented information (TS/SCI) to provide services to government agencies. In some instances the government provides the clearance processing services as a component of the work function you are providing. In others, your business will be required to become a clearance processing and holding entity, which is not a trivial process. Many countries or country group entities across the globe have programs like this, including the United States, the United Kingdom, Canada, the United Nations, and NATO. Knowing which organizations you service and their requirements will determine the establishment of critical positions to manage clearance programs, enable the use of these clearances for services, and provide adequate reporting services required by law based on the products or services you are providing to the government.

Cyber Security

Built into many contracts for companies providing a variety of services to government entities is a provision for the protection of the government information entrusted to your business. Do not confuse cyber security, information security, or privacy requirements for those businesses providing only technology or data processing services. Often, deep in government contracts are base requirements for things such as data access management, threat detection and threat monitoring, reporting, and end-user awareness and training for your employee base.

As mentioned in the previous section, in the area of personnel security, contract language such as 24 × 7 operations by "X country" citizen often is inserted into contracts. Do not underestimate the level of effort required to decipher requirements within contracting language for government entities; request additional clarity around protection requirements and develop new services with expanded scope offerings to meet the needs of your government clients. For instance, in one case, the engineering groups at a certain US-based company had to enable technology monitoring dataflow operations within its security intelligence platform to be directed toward a prescribed set of analysts who were US-based. That broke our entire follow-the-sun methodology and model, added additional costs, and required rewriting of our service documentation, special security instructions, incident response processes, and even contracts for external support for incident response.

If you are contracting with a government, ensure you partner with your procurement organization, your sales organization, your legal contracts teams, or whoever is responsible for competing for and selling government business. You may need a very specific team (if the volume of government services warrants it) to support security requirements, compliance, and contract management for your sales and delivery organizations.

Although some of these things may seem over the top, absurdly regimented, or too costly to entertain, in the end that is probably not your decision to make, even as a the most senior security executive. It is, however, your responsibility to provide interpretation of contract requirements, turn those into service-deliverable capabilities, and provide financial levers and models for business executives to make a business decision rather than a straight security decision. To do this you must have a good mechanism for understanding your costs, extrapolating additional service or scope requirements, and providing those to the business in the form of options. You may think that an additional million dollars in operational security expenditures to meet the needs of a single government contract is absolutely crazy; on a $20 million deal that your business has an 80% margin on, however, they still make a profit base of $15 million even if they have to invest the million dollars into your program to meet contractual needs and requirements.

Remember, your job is to understand the needs, enable the requirements, apply financial models, and support the business in making its decision.

Fraud Industries

Those businesses that deal in industries that are prone to fraud also have specific opportunities for organizational constructs because of the uniqueness of specific security service delivery areas necessary to prevent, detect, and respond to fraud issues. These industries include finance, credit processing, insurance, health care, payroll, retail, and any industry that moves money in any significantly transactional way or other data or processes that can be monetized by criminal elements. The two areas that make these industries so unique are the operational requirements for fraud prevention and the competing area of regulatory compliance.

From a fraud prevention standpoint, successful implementation of a fraud program include the integration of technology assets, skilled analysts, and investigative services to create a holistic approach to finding technological preventive controls through attacking fraud at the source: the criminal element. When these programs are integrated well, you create an advanced, self-correcting life cycle that continually improves on the prevention capabilities of the technical fraud program through interpretation by professional analysts who understand how the criminal elements work to the successful arrest and prosecution of the criminals perpetrating the acts. This seamless capability occurs when organizations are developed correctly, information and intelligence is broadly used and shared, and changes in indicators of fraud, tactics, and modus operandi of the criminal element are shared and tested against new fraud defense capabilities in a timely manner.

The second area that needs to be addressed by most security executives and risk practitioners in these industries is the area of fraud compliance. Fraud compliance manifests itself in different ways across the globe, but in more than 35 countries around the world, nation-states have adopted the UN convention against corruption in the recommendations of the Financial Action Task Force on Money Laundering, which has guided countries to implement programs with more than 40 recommendations for anti-money laundering and terrorist financing. If you are in a fraud-prone industry, manage or move large quantities of funds, or interact with the banking industry, chances are you have some requirements under money laundering legal constructs or antifraud laws developed in the countries you operate in. Often, the requirements for anti-money laundering programs include components of knowing your client, knowing your customer, background checks, fraud risk assessments, and reporting to government entities. Violation of these government-imposed programs can create significant legal and financial liabilities for your company and threaten your ability to operate in different jurisdictions.

Whether it is creating fraud prevention programs or complying to global anti-money laundering requirements, these type of programs require specific oversight, reporting, and operational sureties. Knowing this when building your program is critical to your success.

Retail and Supply Chain

Companies that align to the retail or supply chain industry have unique security requirements that should be considered during the process of organizational design. The hub-and-spoke business architectures, centralized processing programs, low margins, supply chain and property theft concerns, and even third-party management issues create unique security program design considerations that make retail and supply chain security programs an opportunity for unique approaches to converged security. The following sections describe a few operational service areas that deserve additional consideration in organizational design.

Remote Security Management

Remote security management—the biggest consideration of these industries—is a requirement of a full-featured security controls for remote locations in many instances around the globe. Normal businesses often have independent brick-and-mortar facilities with limited access by company employees or trusted persons. The purpose of retail itself is to draw the client into a location, reversing the thought process of how to protect the site, the people, the inventory, and even the infrastructure within a retail location. Given that businesses often operate on a technology platform such as point-of-sale devices, inventory management, and telephony operations, the significance of the severity of any negative-impact issue at the local site requires immediate direct attention, or a complete loss of revenue for the site could occur immediately.

Complicating the matter is the low margin perspective of these type of industries. To maintain profitability, retail security experts often run into significant issues such as low-bandwidth access to a site, reducing monitoring and management capabilities or even the technology they can deploy locally. Special consideration have to be given for burst utilization of bandwidth in support of physical and logical security. This type of remote security management often affects issues such as regional deployment of assets or monitoring controls and affects organizational architecture, from leadership to management to individual contributors, as well as all aspects of security operational platform delivery.

Nonpremise Security Assurance

Nonpremise security assurance is pretty much the opposite issue of dealing with hub-and-spoke retail locations that, although they may be remote, are still under your management. In this instance you may be required to provide some level of security services in an environment that is not actually owned or operated by the company you serve. These unique considerations often come into play in logistic management and delivery services of integrated partners that operate as a component of your business. In some instances it's the necessity of information security such as controls monitoring the movement of data between entities for the purpose of order management or client order process management. In other areas it may be the implementation of intellectual property or logistics security controls that monitor critical issues within the supply chain that could cause a significant dollar loss to the organization if specific controls are not in place or are abused. From shipment tracking, to radiofrequency identification tagging management, to component manufacturing monitoring, you may be required to implement security and risk services "inside" the walls of your partners or providers. How you provide that infrastructure, integrate those services into your existing monitoring and response programs, ensure segregation and abide to legal contracts and regulatory issues, all the way to reporting back to your own business on the efficacy of your program, nonpremise security adds a complex spin to an already complex job.

Converged Technology Service Leverage

One of the biggest industries promoting convergence and security programs is retail. Advancements in technical security capabilities for physical security issues such as shrinkage management, logistics crime prevention, insider loss, and a variety of other retail-specific concerns have proven the necessity of leverage in technical and management infrastructure to support new programs, services, and technologies that support both sides of the house. In some organizations information security, fraud, retail theft investigations, and public safety are all separate operating functions that often report through different executive paths.

The availability of service and technology platforms such as security intelligence analytics, video metadata, Internet security, and a host of other programs or products allow multiple uses of what predominantly were single-purpose programs in the past. For instance, video cameras today can be used for public safety concerns, shrinkage management, credit card and fraud verification defense and prevention, and even provide data to the retail business side of the house for customer counts and dwell time in analyses of product and marketing effectiveness.

The use of security data aggregation platforms and security intelligence analysis applications can be shared across groups, and resources managing those platforms can be designed for convergence use across all areas of security risk and privacy.

Organizational Design Basics

Before building your next-generation security program, there are many decisions to make. We have already covered what type of organization to create and reporting lines, and in the last section we looked at how the industries we participate in shape the services we deliver to our business. In the following sections we discuss functional elements that make up the core operating sections of your "security" business. Functions, or functional elements, help to create organizational segmentation through responsibilities and delivery requirements through roles and boundaries. This approach ensures that your direct leadership team reduces accountability overlap, scope confusion, and program redundancies that lead to internal team confusion, business confusion, and a lot of wasted energy.

Five Functional Program Elements

Organizational development is not a black-and-white science. Industry specifics, business requirements, and even less concrete issues such as workload management dictate how you continue to evolve your organization over time. In fact, the next section touches on the life cycle approach to organizational assurance, which includes a life cycle and iterative approach to organizational development to ensure the ongoing relevancy of your program. There are five basic elements to an operational security, risk, or privacy organization that should be consistent and segmented to reduce unnecessary overlap and confusion while enabling you to manage and evolve your program. These elements include the following:

1. Service delivery
2. Business alignment
3. Business operations
4. Research and development (R&D)
5. Leadership and management

As you will soon learn, each one has a specific purpose and scope that works much like any other business you would build. There are components that drive innovation and create your product, other elements that deliver the services, and yet other elements that manage the overall business. Each one plays an important part in creating your "business ecosystem" to ensure consistency, focus, and the sustainability of your operation.

Let's start with service delivery. As the name implies, these are the functions that do the "do" of your "security business." These are the operations, engineering, travel security teams, privacy engineers, internal consultants, monitoring centers, and any other function that provides a service to your company. These are the operational elements that deliver tangible security, risk, and privacy services every day. The idea to segment service delivery is based and operational excellence models that create standards of product, consistent delivery, measurable output models, and mechanisms for leveragability, replication, and optimization processes.

The expected outcome with the service delivery element is that you can easily create centralized service models that deliver consistent products across your entire business, reducing the need for replicated service teams within your business. If regional service delivery teams are required for language, legal, or volumetric issues, the same replicated service delivery model would be reused to ensure the consistency necessary to manage your security program. As an example, a typical service delivery function could be something as simple as firewall management. Within a defined scope of that service, your organization knows that your "security business" provides, moves, adds, and changes managed firewalls through a specific request, evaluation, and change processes. Further, at the leadership level, you should understand the number of resources assigned to those functions, the estimated number of changes made by any given measure, the cost of providing that service, and levers that can adjust the cost or delivery capabilities. Each one of these "services" make up your service catalog of offerings that you provide do your business. This catalog helps you set expectations, create budgets, and manage your business.

The next element is business alignment. Consider business alignment the function that creates client success. In the past I've always described business alignment functions as internal business development practitioners who ensure the success of the entire organization through internal client engagement.

Business alignment teams have for years been used to create delivery assurance and close alignment with business units or divisions that they serve, especially in large organizations and governmental entities. In traditional security roles these sometimes are called information security officers, or business security officers, who work inside a business unit as the functional head of security.

Practitioners in this functional element have three core duties. The first is to ensure that the business unit they are assigned to receive the necessary services delivered to them from the centralized delivery service entity. Second, they must provide input into the development of the centralized services on behalf of their "business unit client". They are the functional representatives of security, risk, and privacy efforts specific to their assigned business unit, and they need to ensure that any services that are being created fit the needs of that unit. Last, these business alignment teams should be accountable for helping their business unit track and reduce risk. That is not to say that they own risk reduction, but rather that they are responsible for supporting the business unit in the identification, measurement, tracking, and remediation of the risks that the business has.

These types of functions create the transparency and alignment needed to satisfy the business's need for someone who deeply understands their business. These issues predominately occur in larger organizations but can be applied to almost any size business. For instance, a large multinational company may have a chief business security officer who's assigned to a specific division, with staff below him or her to manage different product groups or operating entities. In a small organization you may task every individual on your team to create a "relationship" with a part of the business, such as sales, finance, product development, or service, whereby they become the go-to person who understands the needs of that part of the business, and your business feels that they are well represented within the security program itself.

The caution here is twofold. First, you must be careful that your business alignment teams, who are practitioners themselves, do not feel the need to create independent service delivery functions because they perceive they are not getting the services necessary to satisfy their "internal clients". In fact, this is where most security organizations begin to fall apart operationally, financially, and politically. Once business alignment teams become service delivery teams, you essentially establish segmented security programs that often voice independent accountability and eventually create replicated and unnecessary services, infrastructure, and costs. Further, because this also typically becomes a competitive political issue, intelligence, data sharing, visibility, and transparency into that portion of the business becomes reduced or nonexistent, affecting your ability as a senior security executive to fully protect that organization. The second area of caution is around the concern of segregation of duties. Often brought on by a mild form of Stockholm syndrome (a psychological phenomenon were hostages side with hostage-takers because of emphatic or sympathetic emotions mostly based on a the misperception that a lack of abuse equates to acts of kindness), practitioners assigned into the business units begin to feel autonomous and move policy, standards, and decision-making responsibilities into the business unit, where they may not belong.

The next functional element is your own business operations. This is the element that becomes your back office. As we mentioned earlier in the book, you need to think of your program as your own managed security services company within a company. To run any company, you need people who understand how that business operates and create functions that manage your "business". This falls predominantly into the areas of administrative services, financial assurance, and portfolio program management. Administrative services can support everything from administrative staff and Chief of Staff functions to functional oversight responsibilities. From a financial perspective, this element helps maintain budgetary responsibilities, planning, spending oversight, and any integration with your businesses or corporate financial partners during yearly, quarterly, or monthly planning and reporting operations. Last, the portfolio project management element should be a centralized delivery component for standardizing how your organization manages internal projects, creates sustainable programs, and measures the general effectiveness and efficacy of all the programs across security, risk, and privacy.

In this area, often these practitioners are not security experts; rather they are business experts. In some major multinational companies' security programs, total spend on operational expenses may be in the tens to hundreds of millions of dollars. That is for a medium to large business, and trying to operate without business expertise as part of your overall program management offering is a recipe for disaster. In addition, security, risk, and privacy converged security groups often have many projects going on in parallel or programs under development or management. Expecting the security experts driving these programs or delivering those services to be as well-versed in project oversight is also a recipe for disaster. Taking a cross-organizational approach to implementing services that your service delivery groups can rely on in the area of business management builds a delivery assurance capability as a native part of your program as well as creates confidence that your own practitioners can deliver the difficult things that you are asking them to deliver. Last, as a business security executive, by appropriately managing your own business, your company will see you as an effective leader.

The fourth functional element necessary in the building of a next-generation security program is research and development (R&D). The R&D function is another cross-organizational approach that provides to all portions of your organization the capability for constant innovation, ingenuity, and over-the-horizon planning. R&D—sometimes called architecture—includes those individuals who are consistently planning for the strategic needs of the business through the advanced development of technologies or services that your organization will build to meet those needs. R&D functions do not belong inside service delivery groups because by their nature they do not have a structured measurable outcome that is repeatable and made to be replicated across the business. In fact, the base assumption is that they often fail while researching the future needs of the business. These groups should be empowered to challenge concepts, test theories, and try new technologies that may never be used in the future.

This is not to say that R&D elements cannot be managed. In fact, their workload, priorities, an efforts need to be strictly in line with strategic work priorities, business strategy alignment efforts, and critical risks facing the business. In addition, R&D is not a function just for "cyber" issues. The R&D element should be a cross-utilized function that ensures that standards, technologies, and programs are developed in a way that supports the nature of your operation, reducing replicated infrastructure, technologies, and general costs. For instance, if the R&D group is researching the future of threat monitoring controls, a base requirement of that review should be defining how it assists other functions, such as corporate investigations, fraud prevention, in doing their jobs and how it provides data needed by teams such as risk, audit, or program management groups. The purpose of a cross-utilized organization is to ensure the share of future investment amounts is spent best across the entirety of the organization, not just a single function.

The final core functional element required is a leadership and management program. The ability to execute, sustain operations, and remain effective in the defense of your business or agency greatly relies on those practitioners helping you lead your organization. In fact, one of your greatest responsibilities as a business security executive is to create a leadership bench with qualified assets who can succeed you if necessary. With the continuing shortage of qualified leaders in these career fields, you need to create a cadre of individuals with supporting programs that create this "bench" of future leaders and maintains the effectiveness of your current leaders as well as develops them for optimized use.

This element includes senior leadership development and training, executive program oversight functions, converged security discipline cross-education, and functional business education. Your functional leadership and management element needs to focus on creating cross-leadership transparency to drive organizational optimization, individual development programs to create converged security leadership experts, and pipeline development programs to find the next generation of leaders within and outside of your business.

By defining these core functional elements, how they will be addressed, and which program elements fall into which functional category, you can quickly begin to create an operational delivery organization that has clear-cut responsibilities, understands its part of the mission, and is empowered to move forward.

Executing

In Chapter 1 we spent time reviewing the importance of execution excellence and the imperatives of next-generation security executive specific to their roles as a senior leader. In this chapter the applicability of executing flawlessly means the difference between a well-implemented security, risk, and privacy program versus a business investment priority that fails because of lack of foresight, capability, or, in basic terms, an inability to execute. By introducing your components to a some new checklist items, adapting to new concepts, and holding yourself accountable, you will be able to quickly get your organization off the ground and running.

Design Well

As when architecting anything, your first requirement is to design well. This means that you need to take your time, do your research, garner input, document your plan, evaluate your options, gain agreement, and create your execution plan. There is a lot to this, and it does take focus and effort. In each one of these areas you need to create a project plan that defines the goal of the effort, expected tasks, resources to support you in the effort, and timelines for getting it done. Understand that, depending on the size of your company, your overall task (e.g., to build a new security program V. optimizing an existing one), with time to implementation being critical, it is not unusual for the evaluation and planning phase to take up to a year or more to complete. Certainly, as in any other program, you can work iteratively to put in framework components and elements that are agreed to during planning, but overall, it may take you some time to get it done depending on the size of the effort and procedural considerations such as executive and board level approval processes.

The important part of designing well is that you may not be the perfect person to design the program. Perhaps your immediate focus needs to be urgent technical or business support issues, yet you still need to work on your operational design. Perhaps you don't feel this is your best skill set or you lack experience. Either way, experienced practitioners are available through consulting services or similar mechanisms who can help you get through the evaluation and design phase.

The critical point here is to ensure that you are taking the time to understand the business you are serving, the services that need to be delivered, and the financial abilities of your business to support and create a security, risk, and privacy function, and to design a program with the ability to protect the organization you serve.

Flexibility

When most people think of executing flawlessly they think of a well-disciplined, documented, regimented plan that one executes and never strays from. Unfortunately, you have to build a program based in reality, and the reality is, as the idiom goes, "the best laid plans of mice and men often go awry"; you must be prepared to alter your plan, positions, and strategy to deal with reality. I have an Albert Einstein T-shirt that says "the definition of insanity is doing the same thing over and over again and expecting different results." I find this particularly true among well-intentioned, mission-centric, and highly focused security practitioners. But as business leaders or security leaders, we know that environments change, politics change, finances change, and many other elements are continuously evolving and developing around us while we create and execute our plans.

You need to be ready to modify your program implementation, organizational design, or delivery strategy knowing that you cannot be certain of every component and influencing component of the holistic plan. In fact, part of your review process should be to review critical dependencies, assumptions, and estimated outcomes to reevaluate whether you should move forward in certain areas.

Changing your execution strategy midstream does not make you a poor leader, but rather a smart one. Knowing your options to go over the hill, through the hill, or around the hill and having plans to react to any of them prepares you for facing obstacles and adversaries in your path without slowing your pace of execution.

Build versus Operate

Another key concept is understanding that there is a key differentiator between the build phase and the operate phase, and often it takes different skill sets to deliver both. During the build phase your focus is on roadmap progression through task attainment and creating momentum through program execution. In addition, the tone and tenor of how you interact with external entities such as your business partners and your team will be more urgent and futuristic when creating a vision for others to embrace and obtain alongside you. The build phase is about getting to a committed point in obtaining an expected outcome or status necessary to move to the next phase.

As a build program switches into an operational program, the focus changes from creating the capability to deliver consistently, in a sustainable way, while adding in management practices and programs that help drive efficiencies, support key performance indicators, and deliver value to the business. Your own tone and tenor moves from aggressive progression to sustainability expectations. Those expectations include process automation, resource leverage ability, practitioner optimization, and standards or controls adherence.

The key point here is to know what triggers your program's transfer from building to operations, have a plan in place to migrate it, and ensure that you have the right leadership management team in place to do it. Nothing is more painful than when a well-designed and executed program build plan reaches the point of operational instantiation and no one is there to receive it, and it falls flat. Speaking through experience, it's embarrassing, it's irresponsible, it affects organization moral, and it's entirely avoidable.

30-60-90

Many books have been written about utilizing the approach of 30/60/90-day planning methodologies. The untold science to this effective approach is using the 30/60/90-day start→stop→evaluate→adjust→execute framework. During your planning cycle, the idea is to create a set of measurable deliverables and outcome expectations at each one of those marks. In addition, a list of risks associated with each one of those phases should be documented and managed during the course of the 30-day cycle. At the end of the 30 days you evaluate the attainment of the deliverables and expectations, the validity and residual impact of the documented risks, and the implications of those outcomes against the next set of tasks in the holistic plan; you then adjust the plan based on agreed-upon decisions, and you continue to execute.

Don't confuse the 30/60/90-day planning methodology as a 30-day re-planned approach. The framework is constructed to create focused-driven behavior; it allows for an evaluation checkpoint or milestone measurable at certain intervals. The optimum phrase here is "driven behavior." These 30-day execution cycles drive behavior, outcome, and accelerate delivery. It works with internal staff as well as third-party contracting or consulting support. Important considerations include that it has a measurable time frame, with measurable output, and has a formalized mechanism for risk monitoring adjustments as needed.

This approach is not only good for the build portions of your program; it also can be used as a framework for many other areas during normal business execution. For instance, when I set up merger and acquisition integration plans, I often implement a 0, 7, 15, 30, 90, and 180-day program. At each evaluation point, process, policy, and technology integration conditions are set in the base requirements for specific business actions. That means the business cannot do certain integrated functions unless the agreed-upon actions have been met. These have financial and operational impacts that both the acquired company and the business are keenly aware of. By creating a stepping stone mechanism, with evaluation criteria at certain points, you create that driven behavior necessary to complete actions.

Maturity and Expectations

Self- and organizational awareness are key factors in the ability to drive and execute a strategy. You have to realize that the size and maturity of your business, your organization, and your own abilities have a direct impact on your ability to execute. Setting these expectations ahead of time with yourself and your business helps in the execution cycle by reducing second-guessing and disappointment by all parties involved.

To avoid this unnecessary condition, focus on maturity as a measurement using something as simplistic as an industry-standard capabilities maturity model (CMM). The idea is to establish the expected level of maturity and future levels of maturity around your key processor programs, goals attainment over time, program features maturity, and the evaluation of key practices and programs on a standard measurement of 1 through 5 (5 being the most mature). The most important question you have to answer is, "What level of maturity should each component of my program have?" Each level of any industry CMM approach has a very specific meaning. If you use the US Department of Defense approach, level I signifies it's chaotic and undefined; level II says at least you have implemented a repeatable process; level III signifies that you've created standards and processes to improve them over time; level IV identifies that it is well-managed, has measurements, and you can identify program deviations; and level V demonstrates a maturity level that includes automated optimization of the entire process, including the ability to self-measure and improve process performance.

Let's go back to the question, "What level of maturity should each component of my program have?" That needs to be part of your detailed plan and expectation setting before you start. It is simply unrealistic to believe that each one of your program components needs to be or will ever be at the highest level of the CMM. In fact, I argue that focusing on attaining that level for each component of your program is irresponsible and immature. CMM level V capabilities as measured by external firms can be costly, labor-intensive, and take away from other priority functions you may need to defend your business.

Create a maturity chart for all of your programs based on any one of the industry CMM models and articulate for each one what you are measuring, what each level means, and what it takes to attain that level. Then, create the decision point/statement that says what maturity level you believe that program should be at for normal operations and why, and be prepared to defend it. Next, create a calendar or roadmap for your maturity model that states by quarter or by year when you expect to attain the stated level of maturity.

Remember, there is a huge difference between build and operate. Build will only get you so far, and operations enables programs to mature based on the very nature of operational management. Do not expect or set the expectation that you will obtain a high level CMM during or at the end of each build cycle for each of your programs.

Your Multiyear Plan

The discussion about a calendar/roadmap for your maturity levels brings us to our next point about creating your vision and executing against it. That vision must contain a multiyear plan for your security, risk, and privacy "business". From service maturity to service expansion, technological developments, and right through to global expansion, it is your responsibility to build and create a vision and a reasonable mechanism to obtain that vision, and to do so on a multiyear cycle aligned with your business strategy.

As CSO you are in a fight every day operationally against a multitude of issues. I often describe the technology level as the difference between a CIO and a CISO or CSO is that CIOs typically have a steady 1–3 years to solidify change management capability based on historical technology development and adoption rates, business change, and user behavior. Those of us in the security space participate in protection operations that change daily, weekly, monthly, and, depending on the issue, sometimes hourly. Malware is created at an astronomical rate, and new vulnerabilities are constantly discovered in technology and business operations, with no commercial remediation capabilities immediately at hand. Threats and threat actors are unpredictable at best and require constant adjustment to preventive controls, defensive programs, monitoring capabilities, and response plans.

That said, fundamental advancements in your program, technology stacks, and the optimization of your operations, and in alignment with your businesses or agencies go-to-market futures, takes years of planning, developing, and executing. Your strategic execution plan must include a multiyear look ahead that describes how the components you are implementing today affect or enable components necessary for tomorrow to drive the business strategy. Creating a 5-year outlook is probably not beneficial because most businesses do not necessarily plan out that far. Although financial models may project operational expense based on business ventures, advancements, and assumed markets, the reality is that a 5-year plan for security will probably be changed so much during the 1 to 3 year plan that the two additional years at the end of that model are wasted effort. Using a 1 to 3 year model, however, typically is productive and drives value. Although threats and threat actors change, technology in major business program implementations can typically take from 1–3 years to complete. This provides security leadership with concrete planning capabilities that are not likely to be as easily changed as those 4 or 5 years out. In addition, most of your own programs will take up to a year to fully implement and, assuming a max capacity deployment or funding model, some of the major programs or projects won't even be started until year 2.

As part of your planning roadmap, create alignment of your programs and projects to your documented security risk and privacy strategic initiatives that line back up to the businesses strategic pillars. Identify dependencies, parallel efforts, and levers that allow you to accelerate or back off, depending on business need. As with all of your other programs, be transparent in your equations for your risk priorities as part of your yearly life cycle approach, or as often as necessary; re-stack those priorities and move items within your roadmap based on the business and risk needs.

By showing your business that you are not trying to build Rome in a day, that you have a vision that's aligned and associated with strategic business imperatives, and that you are taking a pragmatic approach in both supporting their future and ensuring the sustainability of the programs that protect their business, you create confidence in your ability to lead and confidence in your ability to manage your part of the business.

MODELS FOR ORGANIZATIONAL ADVANCEMENT

As with any organizational model, the key to continuing success and operational sustainability is it's planning to reevaluate and change as needed. Change too fast and you risk destabilizing a working and effective program. Wait too long and you risk losing talent, trust, and the ability to effectively protect your business. Advancing your organization requires change, but how you evaluate the need for change, the changes you embark on and how often, and the implementation of those changes must be well thought out, planned, and executed.

The two tools that will help you accomplish change is the implementation of a managed life cycle organizational assurance process and a formalized Re-Planning program. Each has their own purpose and builds from the other to ensure balance, validation, and a closed-loop cycle necessary to ensure the success of the changes you make.

LIFE CYCLE ORGANIZATIONAL ASSURANCE

Life cycle organizational assurance refers to establishing a set of operations to create a programmatic and closed-loop capability for continuous quality improvements and sustainability operations for a converged security, risk, and privacy program. The extensibility and intensiveness of your implementation of these processes will be dictated by the operation's size and your responsibility, breadth of functional scope, corporate requirements, as well as the overall criticality of the mission to your business. Creating an organizational assurance program involves best practices in strategic alignment, mission effectiveness, service maturity, and organizational efficacy. These practices affect every part of your operation, and by focusing on the principals that most greatly affect your ability to successfully deliver cross-discipline and cross-business services, you create an ecosystem of sustainability processes and measures that ensures your ability to positively affect your business objectives.

Strategy Alignment

In a Chapter 1 of the book the necessity of aligning to your businesses strategy was made evident. Your ability to protect the business depends on your ability to understand the current and future direction, imperatives, and priorities of the entity you serve. As the senior security executive for your company, you need to establish routine and regular check-ins with senior leaders responsible for business strategy to monitor for changes to the strategy, priority shifts, and other issues that may require you to change the security, risk, and privacy strategies you are responsible for. The senior leaders may include your CEO or President, your Chief Operating Officer, the Chief Financial Officer, or, in many companies, the Chief Strategy Officer. Whether it is a person or a committee that creates and maintains the corporate, business, or agency strategy, getting in front of them biannually at a minimum or quarterly, your job is to listen, understand, and interpret any changes and decide whether they have been substantially modified, which in turn requires you to alter the security strategy.

As part of this process, you should regularly document those changes and update your strategy document. Remember that your strategy starts with the strategic plans of the company and flows all the way down to your services, programs, and projects. Changes at the top should force you to recalculate your priorities, evaluate financial investments, and make changes to schedules, service levels and capability maturities, and programs.

Mission Effectiveness

The next part of your life cycle organizational assurance program is your ability to measure mission effectiveness. This is your method of determining whether your operational program is effective or in need of change to meet the needs of the established mission. Different than organizational efficacy, which we will explain shortly, this measure is all about the mission effectiveness. The bottom-line question you should be asking yourself (and measuring your entire program on) is, "Are we able to successfully accomplish the commitments we made to the business?"

In mature organizations these measurements will be significantly quantitative through established key performance indicators, operational metrics, and business feedback. Mission elements should be evaluated with specific measures that establish the overall impact, progression, or program success that are agreed on by senior management. An example of this is a mission objective to reduce the effect of negative-impact events on the business. Three parts of your program that could affect this are your abilities to prevent, detect, and respond. Each one of those three points could have very specific measures.

From a prevent perspective, you could be specific about the number of specific issues or a percentage increase in preventing a specific problematic area such as malware. That measure may be a program that is focused on decreasing malware infections by 25% over the fiscal year. To accomplish that, you make investments in technology, redefine responsibilities, and create new policies. Each one of those would have a measure of effectiveness to support the overall mission objective. From a detect perspective, your mission impact measure could be the reduction of time from incident occurrence to detection by 25%, and again, you would use the existing and planned program changes for the year and their measures as a mechanism for establishing whether your program is effectively meeting the established mission criteria. See Example below as an example of a mission effectiveness matrices.

Sample Program Efficacy Measures / Scorecard

Area	Objective / Question	Measure	Q1 Actual	Q1 vs. PQ	Q2 Actual	Q2 vs. PQ	Q3 Actual	Q3 vs. PQ	Q4 Actual	Q4 vs. PQ
Business and Brand Protection	**Business Protection Operations**									
	Are we increasing incident and vulnerability detection capabilities?	Monitoring Maturity - % of Data Center Visibility								
		Threat Detect Capabilities coverage # of DCs								
	How well are we managing incidents?	Median time to close incidents								
	How are we reducing the attack surface?	Average time to discover an attack								
		# of vulnerabilities identified and remediated								
		Median time to patch								
	Financial Systems Defense									
	Are we increasing fraud detection capabilities?	# of applications/products actively monitored								
	How good are we at handling fraud cases?	% Averted Loss vs Potential Loss								
Create Value	**Enabling Innovation and Business Growth**									
	What's the value added by the Client Security Support Services	# of sales-related client engagements # of client contacts								
	Did Security Programs impact client satisfaction?	Client Satisfaction Index –Security Elements								
Resiliency	**Ensuring continuity of corporate business operations**									
	What is our BCP readiness and maturity?	# of BCP Plans completed & implemented								
	What is the adoption level of centralized BCP/DR/ Crisis management policy & standard	% of plans migrated								
Sustainability	***Sustainability and governance of Corporate Security, Op Risk & Privacy Programs***									
	Are our investments aligned with the most critical risk areas?	% of capital invested in reducing Enterprise Operational Risk Issues								
	Are standards being adhered to?	# of findings identified and remediated								
		Median time to remediate finding								

In smaller and less mature programs, measures and reports focusing on more qualitative reviews may be more effective. Formal and informal discussions, evaluations, and program testing may make more sense. Third-party assessments, business impact evaluations, and team reviews focusing on incidents, defensive operations, and program progression are all alternative mechanisms for determining mission effectiveness.

Service Maturity

Earlier in this chapter the use of a CMM was discussed for establishing, monitoring, and measuring your program's service maturity. This process is not only used to have a discussion with your business on the services that you intend to create and at which level and why, but also a management tool for you to use as part of your life cycle organization assurance tool set. Tracking and measuring your service maturity allows you to understand whether the programs you are operating and developing are positively affecting the services you are delivering to the business. If you are not making progress on your service maturity commitments or are way ahead in other areas, you can make informed evaluations and adjustments to your investments, priorities, and the effectiveness of your management team.

Organizational Efficacy

The organizational efficiency aspects of your life cycle assurance plan is all about evaluating whether you have the right pieces in place within your operation to successfully affect the mission you have embarked on. Those pieces include how the security, risk, and privacy functions are organized; how and where you deliver your services; and the effectiveness of your team, including leadership, management, and individual contributors. Just because you created an organization that was designed for the business and implemented with careful consideration, input, and buy-in doesn't mean that it will remain effective and relevant over time. Like your controls environment, you need to establish a process by which you evaluate whether your program meets the functional needs of your operation.

From a people perspective, you need to focus on current ability and futures. Both the people (individuals in positions) and the positions (job family, position descriptions, etc.) should be evaluated. This is where a documented job family and corresponding position descriptions become critical. Knowing what positions fill which need (alignment) is as important as having the right positions as part of your tool set. Also, as in risk management, where you need to define your "risk tolerance", you need to document your "human capital management gap tolerance." As management, you must come to accept that you will never have 100% of every quality, skill level, and experience level for every position staffed. Simple attrition, required skills enhancements, and changes in technical requirements create gaps against the pristine model you develop. The science is to establish an acceptable level of resource gap and in which areas, and document it against your human capital plan. When you conduct your review, use that gap analysis as the measure for the people portion of your effectiveness evaluation.

A similar evaluation can be accomplished at the leadership team design level in much the same manner. By creating the needs of each senior position and a list of necessary leadership attributes, combined with a standard set of generic skills you need in your leadership team (skills not necessarily aligned to a given position), you can establish a proper baseline and quantitative measurement of your leadership team. Some of these broader skill sets that don't align to a single position but you may want on your team are things like negotiation skills, team building skills, finance skills, and marketing skills. Once you have that list and populate your evaluation, you have a fair and unbiased look at the skills in place, gaps in necessary leadership capabilities, and a measure against your gap tolerance. If there is an imbalance, it's time to start making decisions and re-planning your team.

Consider partnering with your Human Resources organization and use tools that they may have to collect information, metrics, and measures on performance, skill, etc.

Another important component of the review should be the organization itself and how your "security business" is functionally constructed, including subcomponents. As societal humans we tend to establish lanes or natural groupings that "belong" together. For instance, in converged programs, perhaps you may naturally align components such as public safety, travel security, executive protection, and forensics under a single function. Once these structures are created we tend to leave them in their natural hierarchy. To ensure optimal performance, however, you must design optimal constructs that facilitate core operating issues like transparency, ease of decision making, access to critical information, location, and the like. In this example, perhaps you would consider moving the forensic organization to align with a Threat Management function because you plan on creating new automation and you may want to cross-train incident responders with critical forensic skills to improve evidence-handling effectiveness during cyber investigations.

There are endless mechanisms for providing organizational reviews. Whether you use an external third party or your own internal resources to deliver reviews, you should create the scope and measure of effectiveness that you are evaluating your organization against. It's actually harder than it sounds, but it is important. For instance, is the outcome of the review to assist you in migrating from a build organization to an operations organization? Is it measuring existing effectiveness in delivering your current set of services or whether you will be able to deliver on your future strategy? Maybe you are implementing a new operational framework like ISO or NIST CSF and you need to understand whether you are organized correctly to make the transition. Whatever the reason, state it at the beginning to create focus, establish boundaries, and set expectations.

RE-PLANNING

Whatever the frequency of your effectiveness reviews, there will come a time when you need to re-replan. Re-planning can and should happen on a fairly frequent basis to optimize your program's performance and align to changing business, security, threat, and industry conditions. How much is enough? There is no canned answer; it depends on your organization's structure and change tolerance, resource bandwidth, and the capabilities and criticality of your operation to the business you serve. Re-planning should typically be a "planned" event, although operational conditions may trigger the need sooner than a scheduled review. For instance, I typically hold two to three planning sessions a year with my leadership team and make adjustments as needed. The only cautionary note to consider here is that re-planning equates to change and change requires resources, time, and people effort. Constant or too frequent re-planning can cause operational resource strain and unnecessary confusion, and eventually takes away from mission effectiveness. Create a schedule, stick to it, be transparent to your organization on the decisions and how you came to them, and measure and report on whether those changes were effective.

Re-planning is different than re-design in that re-planning is adjustments to the existing design and program components to ensure the success of the committed design. A strategic redesign is essentially a new organizational or program blueprint for your business operations protection program. It is essentially a re-architecture, either partially or in whole.

Obviously, this is not necessarily an "every year" review and should be done after careful consideration. Redesign implies "re-implementation" and changes your ability execute. It does not necessarily mean the total stop of forward progression or momentum of your program, but the operational impact shifts resource capacities and focus from normal day-to-day operations until such time that the changes have been internalized, affected, and normalized.

What are some of those careful considerations and just how do you decide to commit to a strategic redesign? Again, there is no textbook or documented answer or standard that you can call on. Sometimes it is your decision based on your decision criteria and at others it may be a formalized part of your company's business reengineering life cycle and is simply a required task. There are, however, a few events, issues, or opportunities that may cause you pause and consider whether it is time to revisit your design.

Strategic Business Alignment

Simply put, sometimes the organization you are leading is not aligned to the way the business you are protecting operates. At times it may be a result of a new opportunity at a new company, at others it may because the company itself had a significant change in strategy or operations design, or perhaps your program morphed over a number of years because of critical operational issues and you didn't have the ability to adjust to changing business events. Whatever the reason, "strategically aligning" to the business isn't just adding a service or adding a new position; it involves your operations, communications, and defensive strategies, resourcing, and just about every part of your program. When you identify that your business is operating in a very different way than when you last designed your program, and you are still operating in a manner consistent with the "old business," you should consider a strategic redesign as your next step to make the appropriate program adjustments.

Over-the-Horizon Planning

As mentioned earlier in the book, to be successful in business operations protection you need to go beyond aligning the business and enable it. To do this, you need to live the US ice hockey analogy of "not skating to the puck, but rather skating to where the puck will be". In security this means implementing an over-the-horizon planning process to strategically plan for projects and programs that are needed to create barrier-busters for your business. Again, this is not an every-year item and often 2–3 years go by before any significant change is necessary to the long-term roadmap. During the over-the-horizon planning process you may uncover gaps in your organization's ability to support the long-range plan, such as operating capacity, skill sets, infrastructure, locality, and a host of other issues. Some of these may be program adjustments, whereas others truly affect the totality of the operation. It is during these times that revisiting your strategic operational design may be appropriate.

Opportunity Creation

When dealing with people, the principal elements of leveraging your human capital management assets is pretty simple. Step 1: find good people (recruit). Step 2: keep good people (retain). Both have their challenges, but over time it is always retaining your people investments that proves to be the most challenging. One of the principal issues is opportunity, or the lack thereof. Unless you are a giant multinational corporation with hundreds or thousands of resources, typically there are only so many positions to satisfy the needs and aspirations of your best talent. In many cases it is not just compensation but responsibility, span of control, growth experience, new skills development, or management growth. At times, the limited scope or size of your operation may negatively affect your talent's ability grow, or perhaps you are having difficulty creating a successor pool because there are only so many senior positions to go around. When you begin to see negative trends such as above company or industry averages in voluntary separation percentages, a high percentage of negative employee comments in employment satisfaction surveys (such as "I do not feel I have growth opportunities"), or the simple realization that you do not have the ability to create appropriate succession plans, it's time to take a look at alternate ways to create opportunity. One of those ways is by changing the design of your program. Although it may not be the only reason you complete a redesign, the answer just may be to create new opportunities to ensure operational sustainability and people retention through a redesign of your entire program.

Fiscal Considerations

Although there are hundreds of reason why fiscal positions change, there are really only two outcomes: you reduce your operations expense or you increase it. Perhaps the company or industry you are in has taken a financial hit and all departments are required to take a percentage reduction to help maintain profitability or fund growth areas within the business. This means you need to reduce staff, or cancel projects, or decommission programs with less priority. Perhaps news in the media of breaches have caused or convinced senior management that they need to address identified gaps or recognize security problems and your budget was just significantly increased. This may mean you are significantly increasing headcount, or deploying new technology, or creating new service areas. In any case, when a significant financial change occurs (large enough to affect your operational footprint), it may be time to look at your strategic design.

Services Alignment

The last trigger indicator we'll cover is service alignment. This can be internal (within your own organization) alignment based on gap or overlap discoveries, or simply the maturing of a service or function that now provides you with an opportunity to shift workloads or even improve span of controls. There can be external service alignment with other business functions, such as the IT organization; an audit; a convergence mandate; or a fraud team, where you must shed specific functions, resources, or operations. Whatever the case may be, when you are redefining the services your organization provides, substantially changing your service catalog, or optimizing operations, a strategic redesign may be in order.

The How To

Once you have made the decision to implement advanced organizational assurance components, the next obvious question must be, how exactly do you start down the path of implementing such a program? The good news is that by the time you have the operational and leadership maturity to move forward with operational assurance programs, you'll have gained significant program implementation experience, have a solid framework to launch from, and have a business that is familiar and engaged with the services you deliver to them. However, the opportunity ahead of you requires significant efforts to get you to the next level. The following should be part of the overall program implementation and considered as dependencies that will help guide you, educate you, and provide for an informed and balanced approach to enhancing your program's maturity level.

Business Input

As you did in your basic organizational development, always start with the business. It is necessary to achieve the business requirements and expectations, and to confirm the overall alignment of your service offering. Essentially nothing new here, except for one addition: involving and utilizing the expertise of your business in the implementation of advanced services. Your advanced programs equate to business process optimization and strategic change management—something most businesses have been doing operationally for a very long time and, in fact, often have full-time staff dedicated to providing those services. Seek out and engage experts who are available to help educate you and your team, potentially provide planning and implementation consulting services, or help during different components. Functions such as finance, business operations, business improvement planning, quality, human resources, and IT are likely to have people who are trained and who have "been there and done that." The simple point is you don't have to go it alone, nor must you always unnecessarily spend precious budget dollars. Using existing corporate resources ensures you have organizational knowledge and influence as part of your process, intelligently use existing company resources as a responsible leader, and create bonds with the business by allowing it to have influence and be a part of your program. As you create your advanced services project plan, identify key skills necessary and work with your human resources partners to see whether those people exist in your company.

Revisiting Service Commitments and Maturity

The next body of work is reviewing your service catalog and scope of commitment, and obtaining the necessary data points to evaluate your maturity levels. Do not confuse this with the actual advanced maturity model; rather, this is the collection of what you are doing, why you are doing it, and the data points of "how" you are doing it. Consider this a necessary data collection exercise that documents the current state.

Gap Analysis

A gap analysis is the delta between what you said you were doing for your business, what that reality really is, and future needs as identified in the business input process. Again, this is a simple data-gathering exercise that states facts. All too often, as an executive, you get busy with the day-to-day and operate under a certain set of expectations, but when you are operating in a less advanced model, you can lose the details, and sometimes the reality of where your program is at does not match your memory or expectation. You cannot waste valuable planning and program engineering cycles and resources to go back and make secondary changes because you did not have the right information and operated based on assumptions rather than facts.

Prioritization and Financial Planning

Stakeholder Buy-in

Advanced programs change the way you and your team work, the way and how often you engage your business, how your information is presented, and how your functions are perceived. For those stakeholders who are engaged in the process, including your own team and those at the receiving end of the changes, create a communications and buy-in process to explain the what and why of the changes, and, where appropriate, seek feedback and make adjustments to meet the needs of your stakeholder ecosystem. Stakeholders vary based on which advanced function you intend on implementing and can vary from individual contributors to your board of directors. This exercise should focus at what processes are changing, who is involved (either providing the service or receiving the output), and who stands to be significantly affected in either a positive or negative way, then engage, inform, and agree when possible.

OPTIMIZATION

The last section of this chapter looks at understanding how optimization is a constant role in every part of your program. It doesn't matter whether you're engaged in normal day-to-day services or creating advanced program components—as a next generation business security executive, optimization needs to become a part of how you work, not an exercise you go though on occasion. Optimization is the process of advancing the methods of how and what we do through where the outcome allows better delivery, use of resources, and business impact. There are hundreds of business optimization frameworks, process enhancements, certification programs, and methodologies for you to learn from. There are countless books and seminars and entire industries that have developed around business consulting and technologies to help you "optimize" your business. As a business executive, is import for you to gain exposure and experience in this area and know that optimization is a business requirement. The point of this section is not to outline or debate those models, but rather to suggest that you can make optimization a standard tool you use every day through making the following four principals of operation requirements for your organization to live by. By using these as checkpoints, barriers to entry, and questions or targets infused in everything you do, you create an embedded self-policing mechanism for driving optimization as an organizational imperative.

Creating Efficiencies

The concept of creating efficiencies is fairly basic: Modify one or more actions to reduce the effort necessary for an outcome. Sometimes efficiencies optimize speed, sometimes they reduce resource load, sometimes they just make something easier to understand. Whatever the reason or outcome, as business leaders we should be aware that efficiencies make better use of our resources, optimizes our spend, and are a more intelligent way of doing business. In security, risk, and privacy programs this can materialize in many ways. Perhaps it is a technology purchase, service enhancement, or organizational change. Whatever the effort, make asking yourself and you team, "How does this decision create efficiencies?" a part of every decision-making process and hold yourself accountable through measuring the outcome.

Automation

The second optimization standard that you should drive is around automation. This may seem like an obvious concept, yet it is often one of the most overlooked tools available. Automation has many incredible optimization by-products, including quality improvement, speed, resource management, transparency, and even integration enablement. Automation can be applied to processes, controls, reporting, and just about everything you do. Automation removes human error, increases the speed of throughput, and creates operational consistency. From issuing identification badges to running advanced cyber intelligence query validations, automation is a necessary and vital part of creating and enabling a next-generation converged security program. The language of your teams, your portfolio and program management ethos, and your decision support criteria should all start and end with automation as a required component. Asking simple questions: "Can this be automated? If not, why? What is the financial comparison of automation costs versus multiyear manual implementation? How would your metrics change if this were automated? How does manual deployment limit the functionality? How does automation expand the functionality?" These and similar questions help educate and inform your organization about the positive business and operational impact the effort of automation achieves and instills a standard expectation model for automation as a component of how you do business.

Outsourcing

The third principle is outsourcing. What is outsourcing to you? What does it imply? Does in conjure a negative implication in your mind? Well, it shouldn't.

Outsourcing is nothing more than having a different entity perform a service or function on your behalf. That's it. There are many reasons to consider outsourcing as a component of your operations. First and foremost, it eliminates workload, which allows you to focus on other workloads. Are you using your employees to provide non-value-add or less strategic functions that can be provided through a third party with a better financial model? Are you providing a service that duplicates a required operating infrastructure that your IT department already has in place? Are you sending employees and audit teams to the same locations, where they are just asking different questions? Are you providing an intelligence function that looks only at your set of data rather than using a third party that has the ability to see across companies, industries, and the globe? What are opportunities in your services and functions where having a different entity provide the function makes more fiscal sense, could provide better quality, and can act as an important resource recovery?

Your focus here should be how you optimize your business functions to reinvest in advancing your programs; do not get caught up in terminology and political ideology. This is about fiscal responsibility, focusing on core value-add work, not consumerized managed security elements. This is about opening up resources and maximizing your human capital by enabling them to focus on core mission requirements rather than less material elements of your overall program. This is all about smart business management.

I am not suggesting that you "outsource" security. In fact, I am a major proponent of establishing security, risk, and privacy as core internal components of business operations for any company. Three pointed questions need to be asked to elevate you to be the business leader you need to be as a security executive of the future:

1. Should we be doing this work element?
2. Can someone else do it better at a better value?
3. Is there a work element I can outsource to create capacity to focus on something more critical?

By holding yourself and your organization accountable to honestly answering those three questions, and by creating mechanisms for using outsourced service delivery partners, you create and incredible avenue for your company to optimize and leverage it's security spend and operations. This is how you create the ability to reinvest and reduce your total cost of ownership. This is smart business.

Maintenance→Not Status Quo

Think of your security programs as cars. If you perform normal maintenance such as oil changes, minor repairs, and preventive maintenance functions, your car can last for years and easily operate in good working order for hundreds of thousands of miles. Ignore the maintenance requirements and small repairs, and pretty soon you go from replacing a cracked hose to replacing the entire engine, and there is a significant cost difference. Security programs are the same. The normal maintenance processes and reviews mentioned earlier in this chapter enable you to make "adjustments" or "efficiency tweaks" to your program as needed and during the course of normal operations. Avoid, ignore, or delay necessary program, platform, or resource maintenance and the costs can be substantially different when the issue becomes an emergency.

"Maintenance" is broad term. From a technology perspective, maybe it's patching and upgrading the technical security infrastructure or facilitating security technology. Imagine the damage that can be done to your business and to you professionally if the cause of a security or public safety incident is because of the lack of care and maintenance of the technology platforms you are responsible for? The same goes for programs. Are you inefficiently managing resources by not reviewing your own program business processes and removing complexity, redundancy, or unnecessary components? How about your people? What is the cost of training, professional education, or adjusted compensation congruent with an individual's value to the business versus the cost of recruiting for a replacement of paying for services to perform the work of a vacant position.

Creating maintenance programs should be a component of every part of your operation and monitored as measurement of your operational quality program. Maintenance is not a "risk decision" it's a required element in your total cost of operation and a responsible business requirement.

Chapter 6

Advance Program Development

In the previous chapters we talked about the security function, the security executive as a part of business, and the basic foundational elements supporting the creation of a security ecosystem of business protection operation disciplines called converged security. This chapter focuses on how to do it. This chapter goes from creating a documented roadmap to executing through advanced program development, from understanding planning considerations around the threat, the industry you are in, and the role politics plays to critical planning elements of people, processes, technology, and organizational development. This chapter provides a step-by-step, function-by-function review and planning considerations that help you create, execute, and deliver a successful operational roadmap.

SITUATIONAL AWARENESS: UNDERSTANDING THE BATTLEFIELD

Good decision support methodology demands a keen understanding of the situation. As far back as Sun Tzu's *The Art of War*, military strategists and educators have been teaching situational awareness as a form of human cognitive reasoning for operational excellence. Loosely defined, situational awareness focuses on a person's ability to understand their environment, their ability to understand their position or relation to the environment, and their ability to use information, recall, and other infused information, whether provided or recalled, to project their future position within the given environment.

As a senior security executive for your business, you will be required to make decisions every day—some more urgent and tactical than others, but the fact remains that to make "good decisions," there are key elements of your decision support process that require preparation, research, and understanding in order for it to be a valid element, and situational awareness is one of those. From internal politics to advanced adversaries, this section guides you through a framework of the key components necessary to create a core situational awareness view.

The What

The "what" of situational awareness is a multiphase cognitive process with required outcomes that can be tiered by things like time. Most commonly broken down are decision-making objectives for the short term, long term, or even longer term, often referred to as tactical, strategic, and research, respectively. Earlier in this book I referred to a process designed by a US Air Force pilot named Col. John Boyd referred to as the OODA loop, which stands for "observe, orient, decide, act." The OODA loop could be considered the "process" of situational awareness. That process, as defined, comprises three components: situational assessment, sense making, and analysis. Each one of those has a specific outcome required to complete cognitive understanding and enable your ability to use the data from this concept in your decision-making. For situational assessment, the required outcome is situational awareness. When we talk about sense-making, that is simply understanding the components of your situation. The final phase, analysis, requires an outcome of prediction, which then becomes the informing fact by which you can make a decision and act.

Although that may be a long-winded way to get at the point, it is essential that you create a baseline understanding of fundamentals and very specific areas around the business you are protecting, the environment you're operating in, the threats that are at hand, and your capabilities to effect your mission, including people, process, and technology. You also need the same awareness level specific to your priorities at hand. Using the concept of military pilots, they have to understand whether their priority is self-preservation, the protection of another asset or aircraft, or their ability to drop a payload on a target on time. Those three very different priorities, interjected with whatever situation the pilot is in, dictate very different decisions and actions. This is no different than the position or predicament that you will find yourself in, and the priorities are often fluid based on the situation; they will be very different across each one of your areas of responsibility of security, risk, and privacy.

The Business

From the beginning of this book we talked about operations protection as the future of your profession. In previous chapters we learned about business process documentation, the business value chain, and the importance of each one of those processes in educating yourself on the "what" that you are protecting. But knowing your business and knowing your business well enough to have informed situational awareness are two different things. The inclusive posture of not just your business but also the market and industries you operate in, your competition and strategic inhibitors, and even your consumers are all components of your "business," and having a tangible understanding of each one of those areas is critical to establishing your situational awareness.

KNOW YOUR BUSINESS

In this section we take a look at how you can round off your existing knowledge of your business in ways that support cognitive decision-making for program design and advanced program operations. Assuming you have already studied your business's value chains and have an understanding of what you make, how you make it, and what each part of the process is, it's time to look at things like how you take that product or service to market.

Go to Market

Knowing your business's go to market is important because it answers many questions about who your business targets in its given market, what the current and future product portfolios you are responsible for protecting are, how your business interacts with clients and customers, and where and in which markets you sell, promote, and engage customers. These are all key questions necessary for you to create a security strategy for defending your business because your business is where it operates, not inside the data center or within the campus you are protecting.

Many people within your business can provide you with this type of information; depending on the size of your business, your centralized or segmented business architecture, and the numbers of products or portfolios within your business, you may need to reach out to many people to get a clear understanding of your total business go to market. Key people that you can focus on in mid-size and larger companies include the chief marketing officer, chief sales executive, senior executives for the product portfolios, and, of course, the chief strategy officer.

Functional Makeup

Another area of your business or agency you should gain more knowledge of is its actual functional makeup. Through the business process and value chain documentation efforts, you learned how your business creates and delivers the value they take the market, but it does not give you a contextual understanding of each one of those elements. The functional makeup of your business defines how planning is done, why and how your business is organized to achieve the strategic objectives of the company, how leadership is empowered and where decisions are made, and where actions are controlled.

The following are a few areas that you should dive deeply into to understand how your business truly operates, where the authority is positioned, and where you need to interact to accomplish your mission:

Executive Committee

The executive committee typically comprises the senior executives who report directly to the chief executive officer or president of the company. In some companies it includes the presidents of each division, whereas in others it is corporate executive leadership. Whatever the case, you need to know who are the most senior decision leaders in the business, how decision-making works within the executive committee, what they focus on as a group, and what they are expected to manage independently and execute to.

You also want to get a feel for how each of them think about security. You will be sometimes shockingly and sometime humorously surprised at how they interpret the different parts of security, risk, and privacy. It is your job to create a baseline of understanding, expectations, and relationships with each one of the senior executives.

Divisional and Business Unit Makeup

In smaller organizations, learning about divisions and business units (BUs) is not going to be a problem. In large multinational corporations, however, this could be a full-time job for a single person just to keep track of how the corporation is established and what divisions and BUs make up the entirety of the organization. Predominately, this is necessary to truly understand where everything is that you must protect. If you're in a large defense industrial base organization that has different divisions focusing on different markets, your protection strategy for each one will most probably be very different. In addition, you need to understand how diverse the organization is. That will help you in structuring your organization, including your business security functions and service delivery organization, and global resource positioning.

When you start the process of understanding your division and BU structure, begin with the basic concepts of hierarchy, what each component within the hierarchy does, any cross-relationships or shared responsibilities, their operation and service delivery footprints, and key leadership in each part of the overall structure. Next, collect information on products and services for each of the components. This is important because as you make decisions on what you're protecting, it provides you with a larger comprehensive calculation of the size, volume, and breadth of the services you need to implement in support of the totality of the business. Further, as part of your decision-making capabilities, having this data enables you to quickly understand the potential impact of any given situation knowing the totality of your threat surface.

Corporate Functions versus BU Ownership

As the senior business operations protection executive in your company, you are going to need to know were certain operations are performed and where decisions are made. In decentralized organizations, BUs often manage their own human resource functions, have their own general counsel, and essentially operate as an autonomous business unto themselves. In other companies, the use of shared service functions are implemented, where functions such as information technology (IT), security, legal, human resources, finance, and the like are centralized and deployed locally within the BUs.

On any given day, you need to know immediately whether you have to call the BU president, a corporate executive, or have the autonomy to make a decision or take an action yourself. During a crisis is not the right time to attempt to figure out who owns what functions, who is authorized to make what decisions, and at what level different decisions are made. By creating a functional understanding, defining who you need to interact with and for what reasons, and making that a part of your established communications and crisis management processes, you set expectations and enable your organization to be successful.

In addition, for front office and back office functions, you need to know who to go to for information during the course of investigations or in support of risk calculation and remediation issues. By working with your own team, you can create a quick decision hierarchy for access to the critical data components necessary when responding to negative-impact events.

Policy

As the most senior security executive in your company, your job, in many cases, is to essentially enforce the company policy. Using a government example, think of your job and responsibilities in the context of being the head "law enforcement" agency, like the US Marshals in their support of the Department of Justice. For the sake of argument, your general counsel would be the head of the Department of Justice, or the attorney general. But government only works when all the pieces are there, right? An important part of most governments is the legislative branch, which creates the laws. In the civilian or commercial world, those laws equate to policy. The interpretation of those laws in enforcement and oversight of that enforcement is the responsibility of general counsel. But who creates the laws—or policies? You may be surprised to learn that in many companies there is no single body assigned to this task. In fact, policies often are created and passed around as "corporate law" without the appropriate legal, human resource, or other stakeholder involvement or professional oversight and review.

As you start down the path of really getting to know your business, take the time to understand not only the critical policies that you are responsible for but also those that you are responsible for enforcing. For instance, there may be a corporate-level policy that you have no input in, such as a human resources policy, but the enforcement of it may fall to you. Also, validate any policy development and approval process that may exist and ensure you are embedded within that decision-making group. If there is no such group, take a forward leadership role and help develop one. As part of your continuing evaluation, identify areas of concern with regard to policies and standards, and add those into your program development priority efforts.

Although the inappropriate or ineffective development of policies for policy's sake adds no value and actually can potentially negatively affect your legal position, policies are important and required. Think of it from this perspective: If you drive through a stop sign and a police officer stops you, but there is no law that prohibits you from doing so, then there can be no enforcement action. The same goes for all aspects of cyber security, physical security, and privacy. If you can't articulate what the law, or the policy, is, how are you going to enforce it?

Technology

In today's highly technical world, it would be almost impossible for you to understand your business without having some basic knowledge about the technology your business uses to function. This is not a discussion about what technology you will use to protect your business (we will cover some of those important aspects in the next chapter). What we want to focus on here is exactly how your business uses technology. Maybe you're coming into a new job in a new industry, or you served a specific function in a specific BU and now you're operating at a centralized corporate level in the same business. Either way, getting to know the critical aspects of how technology is integrated into your business's ability to deliver its goods or services is a knowledge aspect that is required to create business situational awareness.

From a mom-and-pop corner store to a lumber manufacturing company to high-tech development companies, technology is in every business, with few exceptions. Whether it's money transactions and money movement for payment of services, supply chain management for ordering and receiving, intellectual property management, computer-based design and manufacturing, program logic control infrastructure for public services like water and sewer management, or any of a thousand other processes within any given industry and any given business, technology is what drives businesses today.

As a converged security executive, you will be involved in many aspects of supporting your business, depending on your size and scope: cyber and information security, crisis management, intellectual property protection, business resiliency, criminal and civil investigations, and many other services. Each one of these areas is dependent on your understanding of how your business works and how your product is delivered, which means it is dependent on your understanding of the technology that drives your business.

In this context, the use of your business process modeling comes in handy. By understanding how your products and services are researched, designed, manufactured, sold, delivered, and serviced—important technology platforms are integrated in each one of those processes—you can leverage that information across the development of security, risk, and privacy services necessary to protect the business within the context of the technology in use, as well.

Security Program

Of course, I would be remiss if I did not mention the importance of understanding the existing security organization. Predominantly, this is aimed at a business operations protection executive who is new to a company or a role with a base knowledge of available resources, operations, or abilities is in place. There are two reasons why this is important. First, it is difficult to create an organization if you do not know or understand what is in place. Although this may seem obvious, I have seen many cases where new senior security leaders enter a business with a template of how they have operated in the past and attempted to overlay that template onto or implement it in a business without understanding what was already in place. This typically ends up in a disaster, with significant employee attrition, business concerns on the new executive's ability to execute, and an elongated time frame for the executive to implement their strategy.

The second reason that this is important is because it actually takes some time to build out your security program—from the time that you enter a job to the time that your new plan is operational. In one of my large multinational positions, just the review of my organization, the business, and the planning process took nearly a year. In that time a lot can happen, and no matter whether you have implemented your program or not, you are the person responsible for responding to it, remediating it, and managing an issue within your area of responsibility. Through learning what is currently in place, who's responsible for what, and who you can call on, you are better positioned to manage security incidents while you are building your next-generation security program.

Politics

The last area in knowing your business may seem trite or something you may not want to get caught up in, but the fact is you need to at least understand the politics that exist in your business. Again, in smaller organizations this is probably not going to be a big deal, though even small offices have office politics. In large organizations the political environment can be as cumbersome as government politics, and your ability to understand them, interpret them, and make decisions with internal politics in mind will serve you well.

What I am not suggesting here in any way is to be political. In fact, being as apolitical as possible will also serve you well. As the senior security executive for the company you must appear to be, and in reality be, as neutral as possible. Whether you're supporting the interpretation of policies, providing investigative services against internal employees or executives, or creating priorities for the implementation of cyber defense of services, you must be seen as an individual who operates at the highest ethical levels, without political undercurrents, and who makes intelligent, fair, and relevant decisions based on facts, not alignments.

KNOW YOUR INDUSTRY

Knowing your business is a prerequisite to achieving the mission of business operations protection. But knowing your business must go beyond understanding the politics of your business, how executive leadership works, and what products you make. Knowing your business also means understanding the industry that you operate in. When I look back at some of the most effective security executives I've ever met during my career, their grasp on the industries in which they operated was absolutely incredible. From the basic understandings of how their market worked, how businesses succeeded and failed, through the competitive landscape, to the best ways to protect businesses specifically within the market, their learned and practiced trade and acumen of industrial expertise is truly what marked their careers.

To successfully protect your business, your focus must be very much external. You have to understand what's occurring in other parts of your market, what is happening to the other businesses that you compete with, market shifts that affect the futures of your go to market, and general threats that may be specific to just your industry. As we've mentioned before in this book, if you are too insular and myopically focused on the four walls of your business and what's inside, you will never see what is coming at you, nor will you see or understand what is needed to defend against future threats.

The following are the top five areas that you should begin your industry education with. There is nothing magic about these, other than they establish a set of fundamentals of knowledge required for any executive or business leader within an industry segment. By spending a little time engaging, asking questions, and observing the industry itself—including experts in your own business, in other businesses, or in industry-specific knowledge-sharing or education programs—you can quickly create a strong foundation of information and shared experience that can help you design and implement a world-class, industry-focused security program.

Maturity Model

In every industry, no matter how old or new, there is a life cycle maturity model for companies from the time that they are considered early-stage start-ups through the time that they become giant corporations. Depending where your business is along that path, you need to decide things like how fast you need to grow, where the financial model is at that stage of business development, how broad your competition is, the level of regulatory or governmental oversight, the risk tolerance of your company, and a host of other go-to-market and business management complexities. As a chief security executive you need to understand the basic concepts of maturity models for your industry, where your company is at, and where it wants to go. From the level of risk your business is willing to assume to the necessity of specific controls or compliance functions, all the way through to your impact on the margin, you need to plan your service delivery and overall portfolio of operations based on the size, scope, and maturity model of your business as they relate to its competitive position within the industry in which you operate. In some businesses you may operate in multiple industries, such as a large multinational company that has an aircraft division, a technology division, a consulting division, and an automotive division. All of these are very different, and each may have a different maturity level. Your business operations protection plan must account for each part of the business, the industries they operate in, and the level of protection required based on the business need.

If a maturity model for your industry doesn't exist from industry research and advisory services, firms, or publication entities, create your own. Spend some time with executives in your chief strategy group, marketing, and senior business leadership, asking questions about the industry. If you have an aversion to doing this because you think it may make you look immature or unknowledgeable, think again. Business executives think that the "security guy" is focused only on guards, guns, and hackers. Most would be impressed that you are taking the time to better understand "their" business, especially if you explain that you want to ensure that you have a competitive security framework for the markets you serve and against your competition. They will understand that if you have too much security, you are potentially overinvesting and possibly negatively affecting the financial performance of the company. If you're not prepared and underinvesting, you're potentially exposing their business to unnecessary risk and putting the business in a bad competitive light. So take the time, document your discussions, and create your own chart based on information you gain through research, interviews, and input from industry experts.

Competition

The two most formidable pieces of advice when you go to war are know yourself and know your enemy. Now, calling a competitor an enemy may be a little over the top, but you get the idea. Either they get market share or you do. That's competition and that's business. There are many reasons why understanding and getting to know your competition is important, but one of the most basic reasons is most often overlooked: it allows you to simply have additional information to understand and measure your own program as it pertains to market normalization. A CEO of a company I worked for once challenged me in a budget review meeting on the fact that our security organization had more people in it than the entire IT organization of one of its competitors. I was able to clearly articulate the comparison of our companies, their market share versus ours, the number of products and go-to-market offerings under our organization's protection versus theirs, our ratio of security full-time equivalents to employees at our business versus theirs, and the total percentage of security expense against IT spend as a comparison between both companies based on information obtained through competitive research. In all of those comparisons, our financials and use of resources were significantly better. In addition, I added the extended competitive landscape data, new markets we were entering, an estimated revenues associated with the requirements and security spent against those for the coming 2 years. Needless to say, it was a compelling response and the conversation soon focused on other areas. Your ability to rate your performance, investment, and organizational capabilities against others within the competitive market show your ability to operate as an effective business leader.

The next area of why understanding your competitive environment is important revolves around business operations protection. Remember that intellectual property theft, data theft, industrial espionage, and other similar business-based criminal activity is real and a threat to your business. You need to understand the current and future competitive environment, known behavior of executive leadership at those competitive entities, and technical information that would support you in investigations or defensive operations that could involve your competitors. Perhaps your cloud service software provider has service applications and you suspect that your competition has direct access to your platforms, from which they are stealing competitive ideas and designs. Do you know their Internet protocol address and that of the companies they have acquired to determine whether someone is directly logging in from those businesses? Perhaps you're asked to look into an advertisement or social media campaign slandering your company. Do you track and catalog intelligence on previous incidents by competitors or service bureaus, relationships, or even the Internet handles of your competition? Getting to know your competition means establishing a baseline of who the competition is, why they're competitive, and what aspects of your business they are competing with, and having knowledge of their business profile and behaviors.

"Knowing thy enemy" supports your defensive operations, your competitive effectiveness, your decision support structure for operational in service management and makes you a valued part of your business's leadership team.

Business Models

If maturity models were the 20,000-foot view of your industry, the business model is the 10,000-foot view. This is where you begin to understand the basic profitability models and go-to-market models of your industry. This becomes increasingly important in the next section, which describes when you begin to create business-specific protection models based on your industry and the type of business model you operate. You can be in a specific vertical, such as an industrial manufacturing industry, but have a very different competitive landscape because of your specific business model. Are you in the manufacturing part of the industry, technology as a service, business outsourcing, business consulting, process automation, or supply chain? What parts of these business models are subject too fraud, theft, personnel safety, or cyber interruptions? What are historical considerations for being successful in each one of these business models? Can your current operation ensure your business can be successful and competitive in that business model?

In previous chapters I covered the necessity of business process documentation and validation. To get that level of business understanding to the process level, you truly have to understand the business model your company operates under to make intelligent and informed decisions about your business, rather than about security issues. Again, this is an education and research exercise you need to complete. Interesting enough, the best resource you may have besides your chief strategy officer is your chief finance officer (CFO). CFOs must have incredible understanding about the market and the business models they operate under. There typically is no better person in your company, other than the CEO, who can articulate how your business makes money, what the different makeups of profitability and expense are, and issues and levers that most affect the model of business by which you operate.

Protection Models

Industry-specific protection models are sometimes concrete, theoretical, or a hybrid of both. In mature regulated markets, programs and practices often are well defined, designed, and tested as well as shared among the practitioners that protect a specific market segment. In other areas, the market may be new, security may be a new issue, or security is not a leading industry concern, and therefore resources and expertise haven't been spent on designing practices specific to protecting that market or industry. In any case, your job as a senior security executive for your business is to understand what protection models are necessary, what is available to replicate in order to reduce time and resources in developing a model, or what the gaps are in your industry with regard to protection models specifically designed to successfully protect your business.

Spending a lot of time here is a smart investment. Perhaps you are an experienced practitioner but new to the industry you're serving, or you are not coming from a traditional protection career field and security, risk, or privacy is new to you. Or perhaps it's just been a while since you've looked at the advancements and developments in business operations protection in your industry. Whatever the reason, by leveraging the experience, investment of resources, and research by others, you can quickly advance, alter, improve your model of protection through the collective knowledge and validation of others.

Protection models go beyond organizational development and who you report to. The elements of the services you deliver are often specific, based on generalized technologies, business operations models, and regulatory considerations necessary to operate your business. For instance, let's look at the railroad portion of the transportation industry. As a component of a critical infrastructure operation, you will most certainly have specific requirements around program validation, assessment, and reporting. From a physical perspective, multijurisdictional consideration of right-of-way ownership, track protection, and transportation security and law enforcement acts may require you to structure your public safety services in a very specific model, such as a requirement of having an actual certified law enforcement division in addition to a physical security transportation protection program. From a cyber and technology point of view, not only do you have the defense of the systems infrastructure necessary to run the business, you may also have rail operations management technology such as IP logic controllers that manage safety, monitoring, track management, and overall rail services that require specific security protocols and programs to defend them. From a privacy perspective, perhaps you support consumer rail, which means programs that support consumer sales and data management.

As you can see from this brief example, each industry and its components may have their own independent requirements and will alter the way that you design your security program. Many practitioners who have gone before you and many industry research entities have established standards boards, certifications, roadmaps, templated defense plans, and many other available components of a business operation protection model necessary for your specific business. By researching these, aligning them to the needs of your specific business, and integrating them with your thoughts and design interests, you can quickly create a well-designed, appropriately focused, and validated model that is very specific the needs of your business. This reduces program development time, implementation time, and certification or accreditation as needed through regulatory approval bodies you may be beholden to.

The final aspect of industry-specific protection models is your responsibility as a practitioner to participate in their development. As a leader for your business, you need to be a leader in your industry. One clear way to do this is to participate in developing standards, creating protection models, and educating your peers for the future protection of your industry. There is a big difference between competition and cooperation, and both can have positive outcomes for your own business. Through sharing research and advanced practitioner operations development concepts with your peers within and outside your industry, you establish a positive reputation for yourself and your business. You help to solidify and establish your business as a pillar in your industry, and you establish collaborative efforts that in turn will positively impact your business.

Senior Security Leaders

The last area in industry knowledge is that of knowing your peers. This purpose of this is not to know who your "job completion" is, but rather to establish a network of influence and cooperation necessary to successfully defend your business. Issues that affect your business are affecting others, and through information sharing, intelligence exchanges, and general knowledge sharing, industries are better situated to defend and cooperatively overcome industry-specific crime, cyber issues, or like concerns. Your ability to "pick up the phone" and have an off-the-record conversation about a pending or ongoing security issue and understanding how it is affecting others or how others in the industry are handling it is priceless when your company is in response mode.

To successful achieve a level of formal and informal relationships that positively impact your business with your peers, you need to understand and establish basic rules and guidelines to keep yourself out of trouble. The two most common problematic areas that we face are antitrust regulations that regulate competitive markets and the protection of monopolies and issues of protected information. A simple conversation with your general counsel or legal team about what you can and cannot do often sets the stage for creating these industry-specific relationships.

Additionally, there are other mechanisms to create a valuable level of industry peer interactions that are mediated and managed by third parties to reduce any perceived or real issues around competitive issues or conflicts of interests. Industry working groups, managed peer groups, and even formalized legal entities established to enable membership and participation with approved articles of operation and oversight can be created to provide a safe and fair environment to share, learn, and develop.

Whatever the mechanism you choose, be a leader, be smart, and create peer relationships that help enable ecosystems of trust, information sharing, and industry protection enhancement opportunities.

KNOW YOUR CLIENT

The next major component in driving advanced program development for yourself as well as your teams is focusing on your client. For the purposes of this chapter and section, the term *client* refers to your external clients, meeting those persons or entities that are paying for the product or services your business delivers. When I referred to knowing your client, I'm signifying the need for you to create the baseline of understanding of who purchases or utilizes what your business sells. I do not mean for you to have a list of every single one of your clients, understand who owns and manages the business, and everything about them. What we really should be focusing on are the basic classifications or types of people or entities that buy your product or services. This type of high-level approach to "bucketing" your clients in many ways enables you around program development, architectural design, technology decision-making, and even communication frameworks. For instance, if you are a business-to-consumer company, your approach to client-facing platform authentication and access will be significantly different then if you have a traditional business-to-business model. Although simplified, it demonstrates that understanding the client portion of your business value and process chain is important to every part of your business operations service delivery organization.

To get started, work with your client delivery, sales, customer service, marketing, or other client-facing groups to create basic classifications of the type of clients you business has. Supplement that information with demographics including typical profiles as well as industry alignment if applicable. Next, for each large bucket you create, begin to document specific client attributes or requirements around things like client expectations, client needs, regulatory considerations for the industries involved, and other data points that will help create a solid knowledge base of your major client segments. For instance, perhaps some of your clients are in the financial services industry and they have specific third-party oversight requirements that you may be held accountable to. That is something you want to document and understand. Or perhaps you are in the consumer technology retail space and current consumer demand for facilitated access into your e-commerce site requires connectivity with social media sites for authentication such as Facebook or Gmail. This type of basic client understanding construct serves as your sanity check when designing and evaluating solutions to support your businesses go to market, platform security advancements, or other security, risk, and privacy services that may affect your client.

Depending on the type of client base you have, another great idea is to create formal or informal client security and privacy advisory teams. These groups of peer practitioners in your clients' organizations have the responsibilities you have and are often interested in participating in these type of advisory groups to gain insight and transparency into how you ensure the protection of their interests, and often they are just as interested in learning from you. These types of groups serve many positive end goals. First, they establish a higher level of trust between your companies through simple transparency, engagement, and communications. Typically, when these type of programs are implemented, client engagement satisfaction and ease of doing business both increase. Additionally, at times of crisis or business necessity, you have created a mechanism to reach directly out to that client to talk about an incident that may have affected their business or, even further, the relationship by creating formalized intelligence- and information-sharing arrangements.

Knowing your client means understanding where your goods or services are going, their needs, and their expectations. It also means creating mechanisms of unilateral trust, communications, and access to your peers within your client's business. By advancing your understanding of the market you serve and your clients, and by creating and extending relationships, you become incredibly valuable to your own company and you demonstrate clear advanced skills as a business operations protection executive.

THE THREAT SURFACE

To protect your business, you need to understand exactly what and how much you are protecting; that is your threat surface. Whether you are protecting people, technology, or cities, your threat surface equates to the total sum of the person, the place, and the available attack vectors that they are open to. What's interesting is that many times practitioners create solution sets for protection programs without the advanced knowledge necessary to create a viable defensive or preventive architecture that can successfully be implemented over the entire threat surface. Basic critical information needs to be gathered, evaluated, and assessed, and used as part of your risk-based decision support criteria. The following are the minimum types of information and data points required to make important decisions around program development and operations, preventive and defensive architectures, and security, risk, and privacy capabilities development.

What Are You Protecting?

Although this is the most basic of questions, often it is one of the hardest to answer. How many times have you responded to an issue or incident and were surprised to find out that the issue involved an area, business, technology, asset, or whatever other component that you didn't know existed? This gets exponentially more difficult as your mission and responsibility criteria expands. Understanding what you are protecting as the director of physical security is fairly substantial. Buildings, people, and assets tend to add up. What if you are a senior security executive in a converged security operation and your responsibilities include cyber defense and data protection operations, threat management programs, operational risk management, public safety, facility security, investigations, travel and executive protection, product security, and intellectual property defense—and you could even throw in one or two more functions for good measure. For you to even define your capabilities, you must first understand the what, then provide program development based on the identified scope.

Even if you get a great baseline of what you are protecting, it'll change quickly because your operating environment is dynamic, your technology environment is always changing, and, quite simply, your business is always changing. As you start to think about what you are protecting, you must create a mechanism or process that enables you to drive a life cycle approach to answering that question of what you are protecting. Some great mechanisms to do this include integrating with repositories and asset management technologies to create a level of visibility of what you are trying to protect based on the business. For instance, from a technology perspective, IT organizations can often provide you access to one or more centralized configuration management databases, commonly referred to as CMDBs. These business information warehouses contain information about platform, system, software, and application assets that the business uses to conduct their operations and which you are probably responsible for defending. The more mature the organization, the more complete and updated the data sets are typically kept. Sometimes this includes information such as location, IP addresses, device identification, installed applications, version of software, version of operating system—and a whole host of useful information. This type of information is imperative to creating that pictorial representation and a quantitative measurement of assets under protection. Not only can this information be handy and useful for developing cyber defense and threat management monitoring programs, it can also be used in intellectual property planning and business resiliency management.

Another great mechanism for information includes your human resource information services platforms that manage human capital. These databases can often provide numbers of full-time employees and contractors. It can provide specific information that supports internal fraud defense programs and workforce protection and facilities security programs, and it can serve as the source of truth for access and access management platforms.

Your businesses facilitates the organization of platforms such as building management systems and capital asset registers. The building management systems technologies can give you detailed information about each building, computer-assisted designs to support public safety, and information about facilities technology platforms necessary to create a holistic plan that includes cyber operations. The capital asset registers can provide detailed information about the number of assets you are required to protect, where they are located, who has access to them, and a variety of other information that can support several parts of your operation.

The point that should not be missed is that you do not have to go at this alone. Often within your own company there are repositories of information and experts who can help you identify your entire threat surface, create a repeatable life cycle to ensure that you have the most current information available, and provide other information that can support your protection operations. You need to create the ability to ingest that information and analyze it, and great mechanisms for reuse and data sharing within your own operations.

Where Are You Protecting?

Another important component of the calculation of your threat surfaces is where it is located. The what and how many is important, but the where is just as critical in establishing the totality of the threat surface and the potential threat vectors. The most obvious part of this required knowledge component is that it is difficult to protect something if you don't know where it is. Additionally, considerations around costs, deployment options, and regulatory imperatives to providing certain protection functions all rely on you knowing where your threat surface is. But another important but less understood component of why the "where" is so important that, depending on location, your threat risk score may change. For instance, a technology asset that you may be required to protect will have very different threat profiles if it is located in a secured data center that is protected by an in-place physical and cyber defensive program than that same technology asset that is sitting under someone's desk in a small office at a remote site. Additionally, an executive traveling to London, England, will have a very different threat profile than one traveling in São Paulo, Brazil.

The "where" context of the threat surface adds critical information that establishes a broad set of decision attributes, from the ability to defend, cost, necessity, prioritization, regulatory impact, and others that greatly impact the decisions you make on why and how you protect your business.

Regulatory Considerations

The broad implications of regulatory issues that affect your ability to protect and defend your business can be vast and complex based on the type of business you protect and, again, grow expeditiously based on the amount of your mission criteria. Regulatory considerations in the areas of security, risk, and privacy are so broad in fact that it would take another entire book to define them; however, you should be aware of key issues in major operational areas of your converged operation.

Considerations such as data privacy requirements or restrictions can often affect almost every part of your operation. For instance, from a cyber perspective, in some jurisdictions it may be unlawful for you to monitor employee email using standard data leakage protection technology, whereas in others there is a prescribed process by which to register with authorities that would enable you to do so. Understanding what those considerations are in each operational jurisdiction takes time but is necessary.

Cyber defense and monitoring issues are not the only type of regulatory area you should focus on. Areas in facilities protection such as where, or even if, you are able to use video monitoring technology to protect your business is often affected by similar legal considerations. Regulatory issues around the arming and use of force for public safety or executive protection and private or commercial security enforcement and operational authorities are also diverse from state to state and even country to country.

In each of your business operations protection service areas it is your responsibility to work with industry sources, your general counsel, and other experts to research, define, and integrate these regulatory considerations into your program, whether they add additional requirements to protect, reduce your ability protect, or just add a new level of complication.

Threats

The final item in understanding your threat surface is understanding the threat. The measurement of threat surface as indicated previously requires that whatever you are protecting actually has a threat, meaning that there is a vector that can attack and, if a vulnerability exists, can exploit that vulnerability. If you don't have those elements then you don't have a threat surface.

There are simplistic mechanisms to help you define and understand threats associated with your mission scope, and there are massively complex and automated threat identification and definition programs necessary in large or critical infrastructure operations. Over time you can enhance your threat discovery and management program, outsource it, or maintain a simplistic level based on the size of the company, the industry/business you serve, and the real-life issues, such as a change in the verified negative impact actions against like assets. Whatever the case, the following five basic components are necessary for you to understand what the threat is and to support the overall threat classification and measurement of your business:

Threat acts: This is the understanding of the possibility and plausibility of an act against an asset that is under your protection, whether physical or technology related. For instance, if you are protecting an executive, you could easily list 1000 acts that could affect your principal. But by adding a level of plausibility and creating containers of act classifications, such as kidnapping, assault, motor vehicle accident, air transport accident, fraud, blackmail, and espionage, you can better evaluate and calculate your threats.

Threat actors: These are the people or entities that would attempt or accomplish the acts. In each act category it is necessary to identify potential threat actors or, more often, categories of actors. The focus should be on defining, interpreting, and evaluating their intent and capabilities.

Threat landscape: In this area you are focusing on where like threats are occurring or are most likely to occur, what the impact has been, and trends or issues that drive those threats closer to or further away from your business or agency. This helps define probability, timing, and impact measurements, all of which are important to your overall threat score.

Threat intelligence(TI): TI is the formalized mechanism (either internal or external) to gather and analyze fact-based threat information. This can be data-driven, human-driven, or observed facts. TI provides critical insight to all aspects of a threat.

Threat modeling: The "how" of the potential threat act involves taking all available threat data and creating a model with the known components and establishing the plausibility and probability by attempting to accomplish the threat act within the model. This process not only gives you the measurements and metrics necessary to define and measure the threat level but also provides unique perspectives that we often overlook when considering threat areas. It validates or invalidates the assumption and enhances your decisions support ability. Depending on which part of your operation you are measuring, there are many threat modeling frameworks and technologies to support you.

RESPONSIBILITIES VERSUS MISSION IMPERATIVES

Throughout this book we continuously focus on negative-impact events, defensive postures and architectures, and all the things you should be thinking about as a senior executive security leader for your company to better protect your business. In some industries, one of the biggest financial planning issues you need to deal with is the sharing of expense costs between necessary compliance programs and real protection efforts that focus on reducing the risk posture of your business through the mitigation of vulnerabilities within your environment, risk surfaces, threat avoidance, or a host of other ways to minimize bad things happening to your company. Compliance is a necessary part of doing business and, in many cases, it is a minimum program requirement to participate in a specific market or region or to serve a specific populace. But other than compliance issues for your specific industry, there are other less known areas that will affect your "total situation" and that need to be considered when developing your organization and your services and evaluating your ability to protect your business.

Contractual Considerations

The first area you need to go investigate is what you must contractually provide for those using your services? Do you have a place to go to get a list of what has been added to your company's contracts regarding security agreements? This is probably bigger than a bread box when you start to look at it, but it's a necessary exercise, since security, risk, and privacy is often negotiated as boilerplate language into product, services, and even technology contracts. Sometimes (and I know this is going to be hard for you to believe) sales executives decide what language should be used in order to help close a deal. In other situations, a demanding client gets the contract negotiation team to agree to their language, which may probably have zero implications in your environment.

One area to look out for is broad statements around policy adherence. Many companies like to throw in verbiage that forces their third parties to adhere to their own policies. Period. Although 100-pound gorilla–sized companies may want to enforce that to reduce the manual mapping of how each one of their third parties meets their policy requirements, the reality is that no company can possibly agree to each one of their clients' security policies. Remember, these are often very long and detailed documents with hundreds of policy mandates and aligning standards. Often, they are asking you to sign up for their policy, which may not makes sense for your industry or the type of business you are in. Instead, work with your customers and clients; focus on frameworks, agree to principles, and develop defined control goals that are often met within your own policy set and can be cross-referenced within other standards, such as documentation including ISO-27001, the NIST cyber security framework, the ISACA security framework, or similar policy mapping.

The next area you should pay special attention to is broad words such as *hacker-proof*, *impenetrable*, *totally secure*, *24/7 monitoring*, and other statements that are broad, beyond reality, overreaching, or simply not obtainable. Often, these can be fixed by agreeing to a measurable outcome, such as a third-party attestation of your capabilities maturity model (CMM), a specific certification level, or agreed national standard. For issues such as monitoring, you need to negotiate to the level of service you already provide; consider other options such as a tiered level of monitoring or "after-hours monitoring" by a third party, if necessary.

Another area that always seems to make it into contracts without those signing the contracts having a clear understanding of their implication are broad notification and response requirements. For instance, you may see language in a contract that says you must notify your client of "any security issue immediately upon the detection of that incident." Other times, you may see contract language that states you "must provide immediate and comprehensive containment of any security incident…" Obviously, both of these examples may be overstated, but I have seen them before. Simple questions such as, What is an incident? What if it does not implicate services I deliver to you or your information? What does *immediately* mean? Is it when we declare an incident or when we have a suspicion that something's happened? These are all real questions that you need to decide how to handle based on what your capabilities are and the cost associated with each one. Through taking contract specialists and legal teams through that, and by taking the business through the costs of each one of those decision points, you better your position as a business partner, and if you do need the support and financial commitments to increase your services to meet these needs, the business may be more apt to support that knowing the detailed needs, implications, and planning behind it.

Here are a couple approaches for getting your arms around this issue and maintaining an appropriate ecosystem of contract language, provisions, and agreements that can actually be implemented, measured, and provided as an attestation to your customers. First, spend time with your legal and contracts team to pull together a detailed review of all contracts and what security provisions have been agreed to. Next, convert provision requirements into controls or service requirements and complete a "truth in services" review of whether or not you meet those requirements for the product, service, or business in question. Be certain that you are not overly general, like "yes we have intrusion detection," when in reality the only intrusion detection system you have is in one data center location where that client is not even being serviced from. The next step is to formalize that gap assessment as a true risk analysis; provide the business with an overview of their financial liabilities created by these contractual gaps. The business will determine whether it is necessary to fill those gaps by adding additional services, renegotiating contracts, or accepting the risks associated with not being able to perform at the level agreed to within the contract.

The following six-step process is an abbreviated project plan including the steps necessary to get your arms around contracts in your company:

1. Review contracts and create a list of security/privacy agreements.
2. Convert language into controls or services requirements.
3. Complete a gap analysis of the reality of whether those provisions are being met or not (fully/partially/not at all).
4. Working with contract teams, create a financial model of gap implications based on contract gap (client can walk from contract worth $X of revenue, $X civil penalty, company has X number of days to remediate with no contract impact, and so on).
5. Based on *your* risk process, prioritize gaps and suggest remediation efforts to the business. This may be as simple as not fixing a gap but renegotiating a contract, or it could be as complex as deploying new technology or services.
6. Implement a company-wide process for evaluating security/privacy verbiage in contracts and be proactive by helping to create appropriate boilerplate language that is precertified for each one of your products or business areas.

It is guaranteed that every company is different, and certainly the larger and more diversified your business the bigger the effort this will be. But the point remains the same: How can you possibly plan a security services and delivery program in support of business operations protection program if you're not sure of the requirements committed on behalf of your business in legal binding contracts and documents that could greatly affect the financial position of your company? A final thought on this item: If your business has a reoccurring revenue model for services, and within your contracts you have specific language about security that you cannot and do not provide, and the contract provision specific to security does not allow for remediation—but, rather, allows for contract termination—what is the fiscal impact to your business? If you are a $20 million business does that mean immediately you have a potential $20 million contract liability? Think about it.

Third Parties

Another interesting consideration that will have a significant impact on how you develop your security, risk, and privacy programs is your relationship and responsibilities around third parties. In this sense I'm using the term "third party" as another entity that performs services or provides a product or any other artifact in such a way that supports your go-to-market or delivery requirements to your end customer as part of your overall business model. In the manufacturing sense, perhaps this means outsource manufacturing of some of your parts. From a services point of view, perhaps you outsource to a third party for a specific data processing aspect of your business. There could be hundreds of examples here, and even more when you look broadly across every industry. What's important for you to figure out is what your contract, legal, and regulatory requirements are with regard to the security of the third party that is providing that service on your behalf.

In the event that your business carries the responsibility of maintaining aspects of security and privacy into the third parties that are providing sub-business process or product components, your advanced program methodology needs to incorporate a third-party management program, the extent of which depends solely on the extent of your responsibilities. Third-party management programs refer to a broad set of services and functions that together create a life cycle approach to understand the threats or risks associated with using those third parties, their ability to maintain and manage the required level of protection within the business aspects they perform for you, and your ability to maintain visibility and assurance of their compliance to your agreements. In some companies, such as in the finance industry or in other very regulated industries, entire organizations of third-party professionals are dedicated solely to this function.

The following are areas that you should consider as part of your base third-party management program as you begin to outline the needs of your company.

First, it is important to create a tiered approach to who and what your third parties represent to your business. For instance, the company that delivers toilet paper to your offices will rank significantly different then perhaps those providing outsourced intellectual property management or manufacturing services. Depending on your industry and business, this tiered system should be based on a clear hierarchy, such as access to client information or funds, percentage of revenue impact, level of access to sensitive or intellectual property, and similar measurements.

Once your third parties are tiered appropriately, you can institute processes for things like evaluations, audits, assessments, and other oversight actions that provide insight, attestation, and assurance of the security components that are most important to you. There are many ways and programs available to support third parties that you deal with every day. From shared assessment services to outsourced and integrated governance risk and compliance automation to the use of international standards as a recognized oversight, and even the use of third parties to provide a service on your behalf. An important takeaway is to understand the requirements you may have from a legal and business standpoints and the general expectations your clients and your business have, and to provide a level of transparency and options available to support them.

The Adversary

The last, often overlooked area is those who wish to do harm to your business or your clients: your real adversaries. It is hard to have a discussion around the need, necessity, and perils of protecting your business and the efforts necessary to create the right business operations protection model if you don't know whom you are defending against. In your business today, can you reasonably articulate and show who or what entities are focused on doing harm to your business? Are you dealing with nation-state espionage, basement adolescents in boxer shorts, well-funded organized crime, terrorist organizations, or even internal employees with an axe to grind? Do you know whom you are defending against?

Now, some may argue that this is not a fair, realistic question, but why? I'm not speaking to the dedicated attribution of an individual or specific criminal element for every potential attack against your business, merely what type of organizations or individuals would want to do harm to your business and have the ability, means, and opportunity to do so? Are you a bank, and therefore are people after the money? Are you a bio-defense firm, and therefore people are after chemical architectures or physical access to compiled bioproducts? Are you a company that has aggregated information about the health care of millions of people, and therefore you are an interesting target for organized crime with the ability to turn that information into money, or a nation-state that is interested in who has what illness? How can you possibly defend your business if you are not sure what and who you are defending against?

Situational awareness means not just understanding where you are at, but who is coming at you. Information is widely available through a number of different means, including industry information-sharing groups, advisory councils, governments, and a variety of other means. Peer-to-peer relationships are important here; when speaking to other entities in your industries, you can begin to put together a picture of the overall adversary landscape. There is no single answer to get at this data; the important part, rather, is for you to compile an adversary landscape chart or list including a scoring system for the level of the adversary's capability maturity model and a weighted system for each measurable area that can then be combined to give a relevant and equalized prioritization score. The following is a simple-to-use scoring and weighting format that can be adjusted as needed but provides a starting point on how to grade and prioritize your efforts and focus on any given adversary.

Weight Assigned to each area in final calc	10%	SCORE	5%	SCORE	20%	SCORE	15%	SCORE	20%	SCORE	15%	SCORE	15%	SCORE	
Adversary	**Category**		**Intelligence Maturity**		**Adversary Maturity**		**Motive**		**Capabilities**		**Means**		**Attributed Acts**		**Notes**
	Nation State	5	Government or LEP Provided	5	Dedicated Government Agency	5	Espionage	5	Mastery	5	Government Funded	5	Multiple with attribution	5	
	Organized Crime	4	Well known researched/ Documented	4	Global integrated ecosystem	4	Financial Crimes	4	Competent	4	Well funded	4	Multiple assumed attribution	4	
	Terroristic/ Political	3	Internal/ Industry Intel with non-attribution	3	Loosely federated abilities	3	Emotional/ Hate Based	3	Supported	3	Shared Funded Ecosystem	3	Federated/ Affiliated Intel	3	
	Regional Crime	2	Internet Research	2	Skilled Individuals	2	General Crime	2	Basic Knowledge	2	Openly available assets	2	Social/ Internet Research	2	
	Individual Crime	1	Hearsay	1	Unskilled efforts	1	Target of opportunity	1	Unskilled	1	Individual Effort	1	Unproven	1	

How to Get That Information and Why It's Important

In this area of situational awareness, it is important to make factual distinctions based when good information, quality intelligence, and input, when consolidated, can be quantitatively and qualitatively aligned to your business and thus to the program and services you are creating. Obtaining this information is necessary to make good-quality decisions. To understand your situation, you must obtain and continue to consume over your entire career many points of data that help you observe and orient yourself to the current situation. The world changes, your business changes, technology changes, and the bad guys change every day; therefore your situational awareness needs to change every day. The detail provided in the previous paragraphs provide samples of the types of information that you should be aware of, and you should create mechanisms for data ingestion to understand your overall situation. Sometimes the life cycle around that data collection, analysis, and use can literally take years. Other times, maybe its as simple as a daily process or routine you set up to get specific information that helps you make continuing program changes in the evolution of your service delivery.

As mentioned before, there are a few processes that you absolutely need to embrace and use. The first, of course, is generalized business process mapping. By understanding where you operate, understanding what is providing services to you and where, and even interjecting where the controls are located, true situational awareness can only come when you truly understand the business you're trying to protect.

The next important area is threat mapping. Well defined in National Institute of Standards and Technology publications, the US Department of Defense rainbow series, and a host of other international protection standards, threat mapping provides you with a visual representation of your defined threats, threat vectors, probable exploitation mechanisms, and defensive capabilities. Threat mapping is an excellent exercise to confirm the validity of assumptions, create quantitative analysis, and create a mechanism for nonpractitioners to easily understand concerns of any given threat. These types of services can be provided by third parties or trained resources in your own team. Technology has also come a long way in this area; threat analysis and mapping software are becoming more commercially available in both cyber defense and physical/public safety arenas.

To make it a reality, however, you must first get your arms wrapped around your controls by using operational risk management groups, a control assurance team, or a combination of functions such as IT, audit, and your security engineering employees, greater well-documented understanding of your entire control environment, the maturity of each of those controls; while you're at it, ensure you add who is responsible for them. Often, one comes into a new position and ask, "Why are we doing that?" The reply is often, "I don't know. It's always been like that."

Collecting the data to understand the control capabilities that help you define your situational capability awareness has profound positive implications far beyond just the ability to do realistic threat modeling. Imagine having the ability to look at each one of your controls and the costs associated with it, and know why it was originally purchased and implemented, how effective it is against a known or assumed threat, and where else you could potentially leverage that control to reduce risks within your business. Also imagine that the same list provides you a look at your controls and a way to help you understand whether they are even needed anymore. Perhaps that threat or threat requirement doesn't exist anymore, or other controls at a higher level become the primary defense against a specific risk and the lower control is no longer necessary. Imagine that you can remove that control, reduce your costs, and reinvest in other gaps that have formed during this threat life cycle.

As you can see, knowing details about your control environment and the specifics around your controls, like why they were implemented, when they were implemented, and their operational costs, all contribute to an incredible opportunity for real situational awareness—not just of your defensive and threat management posture, but also your security "business" posture.

The Risk

In the context of situational awareness, the understanding of "risk" in this sense means understanding how to measure, articulate, and manage risks through current and trending risk management options. Your responsibility is to provide transparent and factual mechanisms for your business to understand potential inhibitors to their success measured in the terms of risk. To get to risk you must familiarize yourself with risk measurement mechanisms, frameworks, and processes that enable this active evaluation and ability to translate risk into business sense. There are many models and many interpretations of risk measurement models, but you need to find your own that makes sense for your business, the markets you serve, and the industries you are in. Take time to evaluate advancements in risk modeling approaches, algorithms, technology, and life cycle management processes. If your business is large enough and has an independent enterprise risk management function or other like risk groups, work with them to create a standard by which each of you understand your interrelation with each other, standard methods of measurement, and a framework or taxonomy necessary to combine outcomes for the business to ingest and digest complex risk information.

As the industry changes and the times change, so do the language of risk and risk articulation. How you described risk issues five years ago will certainly be affected by how your industry, the media, and the business looks at these issues today. As the chief security officer or most senior security executive in your company, you need to be greatly simplified, and that must be done in the language and in the context of your "client." Keeping current on risk articulation and business risk engagement is one critical factor of success because it is through risk that you engage the business. It is through risk that you drive change in the business. And it is through how you deliver that risk that the business will understand the true impact at hand. Work with your own teams on maintaining a consistent and standard taxonomy of risk terms that are appropriate for your business, industry, and market.

Finally, in the area of risk and situational awareness, remain current and understand options available in the most common areas of risk associated with your type of business. As you know, people are always inventing better ways to approach problems, and problem management (as well as risk management) is an evolving science. Stay away from the concept of "not invented here" and resist the temptation to feel like you have to do it yourself. Going it alone often means an insular look with limited data points and is inefficient and irresponsible. Look across the industry, across the organization, at who is being innovative in mechanisms for risk reduction and options for mitigating risk. The best form of flattery is often the replication of one's ideas, so go out and flatter someone and learn a new and better way to manage risk.

The Technology

Maintaining operational situational awareness within a converged security space includes the necessity of understanding the availability of not just technology to combat security issues but also technology available to help support your business. Technology is the future, and as the defender of those technology platforms, being up to date and aware of available technologies, changes in standards, and over-the-horizon technology futures is all part of your job.

Starting with standards is perhaps one of the better places to begin. Technologies come and go; however, it is shifts in standards that are often the telltale sign within the life cycle and longevity of the technology used and needed to defend or to manage a business. Look at forward-leaning industries and industry consortiums that create and publish standards. Changes or proposed changes in standards for security, risk, and privacy programs typically have a 6- to 18-month change cycle. By monitoring proposed changes and the reasons provided by experts, you can often keep ahead of technology evolutions that will impact your ability to protect your business. Additionally, by aligning to standards bodies, you can more proactively ensure that your enterprise standards continue to advance and avoid the issue of ineffective policies and standards in your own business. Having this type of situational awareness also helps to keep your team on its toes. When proposed technologies or changes come to your desk, your ability to challenge your organization, push back on lagging ideas, or challenge the viability of a new idea is supported by your understanding of the changing standards environment.

And though standards may change, technology may not. The available technologies necessary to operate your business and protect your company or agency directly reflect the decisions you make in roadmap development, architecture considerations, and your investment strategy. Situational awareness also means understanding what technology is, and is not, available in the market today, as well as what is protectable and what may not have a technology solution ready to defend. You will make decisions such as, do you invest research and development dollars to create your own capabilities, do you wait for the market to catch up to the technological need, or do you create a defense in depth perspective with reasonable protections and accept some risk based on business need and the criticality of what you are protecting? All of these decisions are less effective if you don't have a grasp on the technology available to support your mission and operations.

YOUR CAPABILITIES

As an executive, your responsibilities around leadership and management are significant, and added on to that are requirements necessary to lead a converged security program with multiple disciplines operating as a cohesive unit. As Harry Callahan (played by Clint Eastwood in *Dirty Harry*) once said, "A man's got to know his limitations." This rings true today when trying to manage a complex program in a complex profession. One of the great secrets of leadership is knowing your capabilities and your gaps, and developing a leadership team, management organization, and other resources to fill in those areas and help you drive toward a successful mission. Taking time to evaluate yourself and your team are important aspects of creating your situational awareness to design better program management and a better capability to deliver your mission.

There are four basic areas that we should all evaluate ourselves in: leadership, management, technical, and executive. All four areas are important, but the reality is that most of us have some things that we are better at doing, prefer to do, have natural abilities in, or have yet to learn or mature into as a professional. Life is a learning continuum; expecting that there is an end to learning or that there is a "max" knowledge attainable in any given area or discipline is a failed concept and restricts your ability to progress as a person and leader.

Leadership and management are two different things. Some people are very good at both, whereas the majority tend to be better at one than the other. Understanding the difference between the two is the important part, and you must ensure that either you have the right support to make up for those gap areas or you put yourself on a path of education, experience, and career development to close those gaps for yourself. The word "leadership" seems self-explanatory, but if you ask 10 people to define it you will probably get 10 very different answers. For example, a leader is often referred to as a guide, a person who guides a group or people toward an outcome. But what does that mean and how do you evaluate yourself? Think of a leader as a person who has the ability to create vision, a need, or a purpose and develop in others the wish to go effect that vision. We often talk about a successful security program as having the ability to "change the DNA" of a company and integrate security, risk, and privacy as core ethos and elements of a business's base beliefs and way of doing business. It takes leadership to create that vision, sell it, and create the path using a wide set of skills and programs to create an organizational ability to consume that vision. Leadership skills can be more loosely bucketed into two camps: one's ability to act and one's a ability to interact. When we speak of one's ability to act, we refer to leadership skills normally associated with the ability to focus, be decisive and make decisions, be confident, and execute. When we speak to a leader's ability to interact, we refer to things like soft-skills, empathy for others, creating optimism, and being honest in their intent. A leader inspires others through his or her ability to create vision and to be seen as a person who can take others to that vision.

A manager, on the other hand, is less about inspiration and more about control. In terms of people management, management is the science of process control and the judicious use of people resources to accomplish a goal. People are not a perfect science, and enabling workforces to accomplish great efforts toward a joined goal requires mechanisms, methods, and processes that create action through channeling people's activities, feelings, aspirations, and will to that common goal. Human capital management involves multiple layers of necessary formalized interactions, development efforts, coaching, counseling, behavior adjustment, and shepherding that takes a defined skill.

The third self-awareness area that helps create resource situational awareness is understanding your executive capabilities, also often described as your executive acumen. Executive acumen is a reference to one's personal abilities and qualifications to drive results in a leadership position. The purist's definition often references one's ability to make decisions as a leader, but I suggest that the skills and competencies necessary to be an "executive" and develop and deliver "acumen" has a broader context that includes the ability to lead change and lead through change, people leadership skills, ability to deliver results, business skills, and the "three Ps" of partnering, persuading, and politics—also referred to as the ability to build coalitions. These five areas of executive acumen work in concert to lead and change human action, create momentum, and deliver results. Although you may not possess all of these skills, it is important to know where you are strong, where you can develop, and where you need others to fill a known weakness. For instance, although I enjoy building coalitions to drive combined success, my personality and core values react negatively to politics within partnering and those who create partnerships for agendas and personal gain rather than a shared goal. I also know that it is a fact of doing business, leading teams, and being successful, so I position the people with that skill set on my team who can ignore or overlook that behavior in a way I can't to accomplish the mission. This ensures I have the ability to deliver that component of my required executive acumen competencies, even if it's through a proxy.

The following chart is an excerpt of the United States Office of Personnel Management evaluation for their Senior Executive Service core that I happen to think is a great measuring stick. Take the time and rate yourself and decide where you are at. Then create your improvement plan; more important, though, know what you need in place to deliver your mission now, even if that means supplementing your skill set with others' skill sets to ensure the success of your program.

Executive Core Qualifications

Leading Change	Leading People	Results Driven	Business Acumen	Building Coalitions
Definitions				
This core qualification involves the ability to bring about strategic change, both within and outside the organization, to meet organizational goals. Inherent to this ECQ is the ability to establish an organizational vision and to implement it in a continuously changing environment.	This core qualification involves the ability to lead people toward meeting the organization's vision, mission, and goals. Inherent to this ECQ is the ability to provide an inclusive workplace that fosters the development of others, facilitates cooperation and teamwork, and supports constructive resolution of conflicts.	This core qualification involves the ability to meet organizational goals and customer expectations. Inherent to this ECQ is the ability to make decisions that produce high-quality results by applying technical knowledge, analyzing problems, and calculating risks.	This core qualification involves the ability to manage human, financial, and information resources strategically.	This core qualification involves the ability to build coalitions internally and with other Federal agencies, State and local governments, nonprofit and private sector organizations, foreign governments, or international organizations to achieve common goals.
Competencies				
Creativity and Innovation External Awareness Flexibility Resilience Strategic Thinking Vision	Conflict Management Leveraging Diversity Developing Others Team Building	Accountability Customer Service Decisiveness Entrepreneurship Problem Solving Technical Credibility	Financial Management Human Capital Management Technology Management	Partnering Political Savvy Influencing/Negotiating

YOUR TEAM

Now that you have measured your skills in leading, managing, and being an executive, it's time to complete that total leadership core awareness picture by doing the same for your team. Remember, your job as a senior leader is to create the ability to accomplish the mission, while it is your leadership team that is responsible for delivering it. You create vision, remove barriers, and provide means by which they can deliver, and then they are expected to execute. But you need a team that can execute and you need a combination of skills in both leadership and management to accomplish that.

The first thing to remember when evaluating your team, depending on the size and maturity of your organization, is that you can't expect everyone to have every competency necessary. Just like you, people will have gaps, and as they progress up the leadership ladder, they will learn and obtain the skills necessary; one of your jobs is helping them get there. Let's take a quick look at the evaluation process.

They key in your evaluation is three fold. First, you need to evaluate who are the leaders and who are the managers. Many times this becomes overtly self-evident through working alongside people every day. Other times it takes months, or even years, of evaluation, education, and trial and error to learn that some individuals simply don't have the capacity or capability to lead. And this is really what you're trying to get at. You need to understand who can become leaders in your organization, because it is through the development of leaders that you create critical business imperatives such as operational sustainability, progressive mission enablement, and succession assurance.

Next, you need to create capabilities matrices that include your own evaluation to get a clear picture of your leadership's skills, gaps, attributes, and necessary development areas to help you create your game plan. Using the same evaluation mechanism and framework you used for yourself, utilize a color-code method whereby each person on your team has their own color; use red for those areas where you have little or no experience within your team. This creates a quick map of areas that you need to work on to create the total executive leadership picture necessary to drive your mission.

The third part of your evaluation process is the life cycle aspect necessary to maintain a healthy leadership organization. This includes migrating the right people into and off your leadership team as necessary if the requisite required skill sets are not available from an individual, the development necessary can't happen while they hold a specific position, or they are better suited in another organization. This is the reality of leadership—executive management—and it is your responsibility as much as it is to coach, mentor, and educate those who do have the talent to move forward. This also involves creating opportunities for leadership, making forced executive trades inside your team, or, if you have the opportunity, creating new positions that allow you to bring in new leaders while continually developing those on your team. As a converged security executive, this becomes even more important since it is difficult to find leaders with experience across multiple security, risk, or privacy disciplines. Through rotation or job swapping you can often create learning opportunities in skills expansion with a limited impact your organization or an individual while continuing to create a robust leadership team.

RELATIONSHIPS

The final area necessary for truly understanding your total situational awareness is the understanding of your relationships with people, partners, clients, and others who affect delivery, perceptions of your delivery, and your ability to obtain mission success. Relationships can make or break your career in many respects, and as part of your OODA loop, you need to understand perceptions, realities, and reliabilities of the relationships you have in place. Your ability to reach out for support, anticipate "air cover" from senior executives, or even the impact of pushback from a partner that you weren't anticipating can greatly alter the outcome of a planned action or program. The concept here is not "keep your friends close but keep your enemies closer," but rather what your inventory of relationships is, where it needs to be, and how it affects your mission.

Let's start with the concept of creating an inventory. At a high level these fall into two basic categories of inside and outside relationships. Inside relationships are necessary because, in many respects, these are the people helping you deliver your mission, as well as the people who are utilizing your services; they can be considered your "internal clients." As a chief security officer or senior security executive in your company, most days you will work with other executives within your business or leaders in different BUs where you are trying to get a resolve or service delivered into that business to ensure the protection or the quality of their overall go to market.

From an external perspective you're really focusing on three areas: partnerships, clients, and the market or industry. From a partnership standpoint, these can be peers, competitors, or your vendor community that help you deliver your mission in some way. Clients are your external constituents that your business is delivering its product and services to. Your relationships with peer practitioners, your ability to solve delivery issues, and the trust you create with your client base are all important attributes of the measurability of your external relationships. The final area is the market or industry; your relationship with the industry is very important because it sets the basis by which others evaluate the level of the relationship they may or may not want with you, provides a baseline by which clients measure your technical acumen or trustworthiness to establish relationships, and, at a personal level, it sets you up for career capital for the future. All of these are, of course, very important.

The best way to begin creating this inventory is to create in a spreadsheet or table of a set of basic needs and relationships that you believe are important to drive your mission. The following table provides a basic mechanism for creating that repository as well as a scoring mechanism to get you started. Remember, this is just like a CMM for your program. You don't necessarily need or want every relationship to score a 5, but you do want to understand where it should be and where it is. Once you have that understanding, you can create a plan for how to increase the relationships that need to be expanded or deemphasize those that are less necessary.

Example Relationship Tracking Sheet						
		Target	Current Measurement	Enhancement Plan	Relationship Scoring	
Internal						
BoD					5	Bi-directional supportive
	Director 1	4	2	• Item 1 • Item 2	4	Personally Established and productive
	Director 2	3	1	• Item 1	3	Formal but not personal
Executive					2	Cordial but not formal
Sec Leadership					1	Minimal to non-existent
Practitioners						
	Cyber					
	Risk					
	Converged					
	Client Sec					
Employee Base						
BU						
	Sales					
	R&D					
	IT					
	Finance					
	ERM					
	Audit					
External						
Partners						
Peers						
Competitors						
	Competitor 1					
	Competitor 2					
Vendors						
	Vendor 1					
	Vendor 2					
	Vendor 3					
Industry Org						
	Org 1					
	Org 2					
	Org 3					
	Org 4					
Industry Media						
	Media 1					
	Media 2					

Road Maps and Strategic Planning

In the previous chapter we covered concepts of organizations and how to create models for success. At the beginning of this chapter we took a deep dive into understanding our situational awareness from the state of existing defensive operations programs, to our leadership skills, to our teams. Now it's time to start planning. In this section we cover what *strategic* means, especially for senior security executives, and give you the tools to begin creating a long-term sustainable roadmap to formulate your business operations protection plan.

Strategic Thinking

To begin the process of developing your strategic plan, we should take a step back and talk about how to get there. Many excellent practitioners are drawn to this profession because of it's fast-paced, action-oriented, in-the-fight, and always changing challenges. Others like to solve difficult problems and are enthralled by the everyday problem-generation machine that this career field tends to be. Whatever your reason, it is hard to deny the simple fact that as a security, risk, and privacy executive you tend to be marred by the massive onslaught of tactical issues that impact and threaten the operational imperatives of the business or agency you serve. In fact, as the "chief of 911" for your company, you spend a great deal of your career responding to tactical situations that need and deserve your immediate attention and then get added to the bucket of "must find a long-term solution" as part of your overall strategic plan.

This means that when the time comes to make strategic changes, it will take a dedicated process to stand back, become intently focused on the required future state, think less urgently with more supporting data, and use a different systematic approach to create a plan to obtain the desired outcome. This is strategic thinking, and it is how you must slow down your operational clock, think broadly across multiple timelines, and create plans that have foundational footprints and hypothetical assumptions that you can well articulate and back up with attained decision support elements.

Strategic Security Planning Components

Your research is complete, you have immersed yourself is strategic thinking, and now it's time to make your plan. Strategic plans are often confused with business plans—they are not—and in the context of developing a next-generation security program, this is where you describe how business operations protection programs will support the business goal, what your program will include to get you there, what the expected outcomes are, and how you will achieve them. There must also be supporting information that provides background, decision points, and assumptions and how you as the accountable executive will successfully guide the company to the stated outcome. Let's take a closer look at some of the building blocks you may want to consider when developing your plan.

To begin, it's always a good idea to state the mission you are trying to accomplish; this may be obvious to you but is a great reminder to the business. The mission statement serves as the anchor to your plan development and should be the starting point of your organization architecture, program development, and defined efforts. It should be based on the mission of your business and the strategic pillars as identified by your CEO or executive committee, and you should be able to create a defined relationship from each part of your operation to the strategy of the company itself.

Next you need to articulate long-term strategic positioning or objectives that define your plan and that serve as the pillars of your strategy statement or mission. For instance, a future position could be that your plan will "create for the company a world-class product security capability ensuring a quality through security market position." The statement says where you heading and what the outcome will be. Another example could be to "achieve cost-effective leveragable global monitoring capability that increases the company's security posture through advanced threat defense and creates ability to implement new protection programs." From these statements you create expected objectives, including measures and outcomes; define the methods to achieve those outcomes; and articulate the framework you will develop to get the company there.

Now that you have an aligned mission, you have defined the strategic imperatives or pillars and defined objectives, it's time to talk strategy. By this I mean the general umbrella methods you will use to achieve the vision and descriptions of how and why those methods are necessary and achievable, how they are proven and sound, and expected outcomes both good and bad. Again, these umbrella methods are high-level and will be developed later into the programs, projects, and efforts that will become the roadmap to the success of your business operations protection plan. Some examples of these methods include the following:

- Creating a centralized security function
- Reorganizing into a converged security function
- Establishing global threat management centers
- Migrating to the partial use of outsourcing
- Adding new security, risk, or privacy service areas
- Deploying a new global protection architecture
- Aligning to a formalized framework or standard like ISO or NIST CSF

As you can see, these are high-level statements that then need to be supported by the "why." Think of progressive phrasing like this: "Our mission is to ensure X for the company. To do this we will establish Y. To accomplish that position we will diversify our service portfolio through the use of outsourced relationships to reduce the cost of providing specific operations, thus allowing us to reinvest in priority efforts to achieve the goal." The strategy in that example is to outsource and the why is to reduce cost to allow for reinvestment in new programs.

Now that you have set the path, it's time to add some details and timeline over the course of the strategy effort. Assuming an average of a 3-year start-to-end strategic roadmap, you need to describe the what, how, and who quarter by quarter of that time period, which will also play in to the financial costs. Like we said before, Rome wasn't built in a day, so your plan must provide high-level assumed efforts, projects, and programs that will be implemented, executed, and completed, along with key milestones that indicate measured progress toward the end goal.

That path must have a defined presence in the current time frame, meaning the existing fiscal or calendar year. This callout is necessary to provide tangibility and accountability on achieving the strategy. How you and your team are compensated, measured, and goaled will be guided by this callout and will support the believability and achievability of the plan.

The next phase of your strategic plan development is financial impact planning. At a strategy level, it is difficult to provide detailed cost analysis, but the financial impact of your plan over the 1- to 3-year horizon needs to be outlined. If the plan calls for a technology or services overhaul or increase, you have to explain how it will be paid for. Is it through expected budget increase? If so, how much? Will you optimize and reinvest and thereby expect a zero-dollar cost impact? Has the threat landscaped changed, and does your strategy call for a reduction in security programs, thus reducing your spend. The bottom line is that as a business executive you are expected to define the financial impact of your strategy to the business using historical considerations, planned program changes, and industry information that support your strategic theory.

The final part of your plan is documentation of the metrics and measures you will use to measure the success of your strategy and to keep your plan on track. Some of these include key performance indicators, whereas others are clear milestones that mark an achievement to a specific maturity or capability necessary to obtain the strategy. The use of expected established competencies, go-live operational dates with specific service level agreement, or a specific organizational ability are all considerations for how you will define and ensure progressive plan success. These should be backed up with information obtained as part of the planning process, and you should be able to articulate why these measurements are important and show plan success.

Why Tactical Can Be Strategic

At the beginning of this section we covered why it is important for practitioners to step out of their day-to-day operational craziness and take the time to think strategically and create a plan that aligns to the future of the business. But what makes strategic planning difficult for operational types often is a key ingredient in their success to achieving strategic plan implementation excellence: tactical imperatives.

The word "tactical" is often compared to "strategic" in a "very-different-things" kind of way. But if you boil it down, "tactical" is simply the how and who steps embedded inside any plan. As a security or even a public safety executive, you know that no one is going to give you the answers to fix what needs to be repaired or to react to any given situation. That's your job and that is why the company hired you. Many times there is no real answer because, frankly, most situations are very different and often the first time anyone as has ever seen it quite in that way. Being tactical means being able to quickly create your OODA loop and make decisions and take action to respond to changing situational elements, environments, politics, and many other factors. Being tactical means having a vision of achievement, of an outcome, and executing in a way that, no matter what comes at you, no matter how the world changes around you, uses your intelligence, training, experience, and resources to achieve that vision.

As you create and deliver your strategy, recognize that things can and will go wrong. Expectations will not align, complications will amass, components when implemented will uncover critical issues that you need to deal with urgently, and learnings will force adjustments. All of these are inputs to your decision support apparatus, and having the ability to tactically address them reduces the impact to your plan and continues the momentum forward. As they say, movement is life, and your tactical abilities to address critical issues, even in the delivery of a strategic plan, ensures you keep the life in the programs you deliver.

Over-the-Horizon Thinking

The concept of over-the-horizon thinking refers to the ability to imagine and envision future states based on limited tangible evidence or a lack of the now-and-here ability to achieve that future state. Think if it the context of the Internet of things (IOT). The data we have today, the technology being developed at breakneck speeds that support similar computing platforms, and the existing lack of technological protection architectures for the IOT begs the argument for a new approach to defending tomorrow's technology. Over-the-horizon thinking is applied when you take assumed information, such as how the IOT is being used and where research dollars are being applied, make a broad determination of a potential solution set that could be the answer to the issue, and create a path to get you to that vision.

Many experts believe that over-the-horizon thinking has little place in strategic plans, but I don't necessarily subscribe to that methodology. In a world where the current and known elements of defense and protection operations are well defined, things change every day that challenge assumptions and constantly lay to rest former gold standards that we held as gospel. Strategic planning means getting to a new place from where you are, and as a business protection executive, 2–5 years is a long time, and many of the issues you are trying to align to may not be in place and, in fact, solutions may not be available.

To truly enable the business you must create the road on which you can travel; that means getting out ahead and solving hard problems. To accomplish that you need to make some assumptions, think forward, and create visions not available as solutions. Part of your strategic roadmap may be true futures that you need to get to through research and development, investment, and ingenuity, and that is OK. In fact, that is a responsible approach to "skating to where the puck will be" rather then skating with everyone else to the puck. Vision means future, and future thinking drives actions.

Document

The final part of your strategic plan is getting it down in writing, on paper, on stone tablets, or however you decide to document it. There is no set standard because there are multiple aspects of a plan that need to be documented.

At a high level you need to create a plan that is made for whatever business approval process you may have. In many larger businesses there are standard templates, forms, or expectations for documentation. In others, not so much, so you have to know your audience and what the intended outcome of the presentation or document is, and create accordingly. In fact, that is rule 1: Know you audience and create the documentation for that audience.

You should, however, keep in mind a few things beyond the audience. First, make sure that you document the plan for your own reference in the way that you have created the plan components in your mind. You will need this to refer back to and avail detail that will not be in many of the different forms your plan will become. Next, remember that you lead a team that will be implementing this plan, so how you represent it to them is important. Many executives forget that component and after a plan is approved by their business, they present the same plan to their teams, which typically lacks the approach, details, or expectations necessary to convey a captivating message for the team implementation the plan.

At an executive level, remember less is always more. I teach my teams that anything more than 8–10 pages of slideware will divert the necessary attention away from the focus of the story you are trying to tell; and the plan, outcome, and path forward should be able to be told in 4 slides.

Fewer slides brings me to my next point: Visuals are important. Humans are visual interpreters. Take the time to create visuals that explain shifts, show the path to achievement, or explain difficult organizational or technical issues. Visuals often shortcut the necessity of explanations and reduce the friction associated with words that can be taken out of context and often picked apart, resulting in a loss of focus on the core message.

The next component was mentioned previously but needs to be reenforced: options. There is no such thing as all or nothing in this world. Everything is negotiable, and in business everything will be negotiated. As you create your plan, consider having three to four versions of the plan ready and documented, including differences in outcomes, cost, and implementation timelines. Use someone not close to the effort to poke and prod at it and, if possible, use an expert in program implementation to help create multiple models that align to the same vision. Typically, these additional models are necessary to address cost considerations, timelines, or, in the area of security, risk, and privacy, roadmaps that may require a different level of controls that may seem draconian to some or not nearly strong enough to others. Options show appropriate business skill, transparency to other considerations, and a willingness to be a good business partner.

In the end your strategic plan is yours. Yours to develop, yours to create excitement around, and yours to execute against. Your plan is a direct reflection of your capabilities as a practitioner and an executive, so take the time to research, partner, envision, and plan. Your plan is directly connected to the future success of the business or agency you protect everyday.

Innovation

Innovation is the lifeblood in any industry or entity. Change is the only real constant and is the hallmark of those companies that thrive and survive year after year. Sometimes innovations happen as a response to a catastrophic event or realization, whereas at others it is how companies manage their business. The ability to innovate and the infrastructure available to support innovation varies from business to business and industry to industry. As a business operations protection executive, you not only need to understand the concept of business innovation and prepare for it, but you must think of your own operations as a business and use innovation as a mechanism for enhancing your ability to protect that business.

The Importance of Innovation

We talk about innovation as the lifeblood of an organization. The familiar chant of "innovate or die" has been the rallying tool for business leaders for years, but there are some more simplistic reasons that often serve at the core of why businesses innovate and why it is so important for business sustainability and profitability. After spending much time with business leaders across the globe and attending lecture after seminar after executive education program, I can safely say that the importance of business innovation comes down to three basic issues: competition, complacency avoidance, and customers. Arguably, there are many other important reasons that drive innovation, but when it comes down to it, customer need (the people who buy your stuff), other companies attacking your market share (competition), and the need to mature your core business approach (complacency) are the roots of the innovative need. Let's take a brief look at each area.

In this book we've said it many times that complacency kills. It is the cancer of the human ego that allows assumed knowledge, previous performance, and success to be clouded with extreme bias that success should be the teacher rather than an input into the future success of the business. Complacency comes in all shapes and sizes and can impact all parts of the business. From products to financial management to IT and everything in between, when we as people become fat, dumb, and lazy, resting on our laurels and celebrating past performance, we fail to see the navigation signs, the roadside warnings, and end up missing the turn in the road and hurling ourselves off the cliff—and sometimes it is a long way down. Companies that challenge the norm, drive change, and force self-discovery often use innovation as the tool of choice to allow their business to see the curves in the road.

Competition is one of those areas that is often right in our face but we fail to recognize it or, worse, fail to believe it is even competition. There are disruptive competitive events and gradual events but, in the end, they all equal one thing: market share loss. If your customers are not buying from you, then that share of their wallet is going to your competition, and that's a slippery slope. Businesses large and small use innovation to keep ahead of the competition and to be the competitive influence in the market. As companies grow, this becomes more difficult because changing product or services direction means changing all of the underlying operations that support it, and the bigger the company, the harder it is to change. Large successful companies often create innovative initiatives and competitive opportunities internally to ensure that innovation is a part of how they operate. In some industries, companies create sequestered teams away from the influence of the existing core to "think outside the box" and compete with their own products.

Customers are the final leg of this triad of "why to innovate." Frankly, innovation must occur because customers want it and they are always right. Seriously, it's often the demanding customer base that is often the most "innovative" part of your business. They may need, want, or ask for components, services, add-ons, and so on that need to be developed. This spurns innovation on demand, and although sometimes companies go kicking and screaming, they always tend to go where the money flows; if their customers are willing to buy it, then they will continue to innovate to drive market share and revenues. Now, this doesn't mean that companies should or will do everything that their customers want, nor does it mean that business should reduce the scope of their focus from their core business just to become innovative. Innovation can happen in all parts of the business, not just the product sets themselves. An innovative business that focuses on their clients looks broadly across their business to create and capture the sentiment of the holistic customer experience.

Enabling Company Innovation

So, if a company is to be innovative, what then are the characteristics or efforts that they must put forward to enable their employees to execute to that vision. In the context of this book I'll stick with three that are most important for you to grasp to create innovative capability within your program.

To have innovation you need to have ideas. One of my favorite commercials form the early 2000s was an IBM commercial that linked the term "ideation" with "people thinking," and it still sticks with me today. They were essentially giving their employees "quiet time" to think up new ideas. Whatever the method, ideation—or concept design—is an operation that every business needs. In some companies these are "idea banks" where people submit ideas and the winners are funded as projects. In others, research and development groups are given the charge to use a percentage of their resources on innovation. Whatever the mechanism, if a company wants to be innovative—if you as a security executive want to be innovative—then you must create the opportunity through ideation enablement from the top down, including attitude, expectations, resources, and pathways to allow it to happen.

The next concept took me years to learn because it involves failure and, as a competitive and somewhat type A individual, failure is not something I embrace. But as I age, and look back at all the things that I have embarked on, I realize that not everything was as successful as I remember it. I recognize that the smart and mature leaders I was fortunate to have worked for not only accepted failure but embraced it as an expectation of growth and development. That is the second lesson here: If you are going to enable innovation, then you need to embrace failure. Innovation is the process of developing ideas, validating them, and then inventing the process to get there. If there was a rule of thumb as to how often you fail before you succeed, I think it is simply enough to say more than less. And this needs to be accepted and not managed in the same framework in which those daily operations, strategy execution, and project works are managed. Create the expectation that failure is expected and accepted as long as there is a process to learn from it, share those lessons, and reinvest them into future successes.

The final piece of the puzzle for enabling an innovative organization, especially as a career security, risk, or privacy executive, is moving from pessimist to optimist. Now, I know you may think I am painting all practitioners with a very broad brush, and in fact many of my friends and colleagues are very optimistic people. It is difficult to argue that a large component of our jobs is to be the "paid paranoid," which naturally leads to some pessimistic traits—and by the way, that is a good thing. But when it comes to innovation, we need to readdress our thought process and embrace, believe, and champion the "possibilities" that our innovators bring to us. Belief in your people is a powerful management tool, and often people work harder to earn the belief that you have in them. In addition, this leap of faith, this ability to believe an end result is possible, is at the core of innovation. Futures aren't built on 100% factual data; they are built on the intelligence and ingenuity of people. As mentioned previously in this chapter, if we are going to skate to where the puck will be rather than to where it is, then we need to exude optimism about the ideas that our people bring forth.

WHY SECURITY ORGANIZATIONS INNOVATE

Just like business have their reasons for innovating that are centered around sustainability and market defense, security, risk, and privacy executives have a distinct set of needs and causes that demand constant innovation as part of their everyday operation. We can easily bucket these into the three simple categories of business change, maturity, and threat change.

This book was written for the business operations protection executive, and two of the basic principals we continue to teach here are (1) enable the business through security program advancements by allowing the business to do whatever business they want wherever they want, and (2) protect though protecting the entire business value chain. On one hand you are helping the business change, and on the other you protect through their business model. Again, to sum it up, your job is to constantly change. And this is why we innovate—because the business we are today isn't what we were yesterday, and the business we will be tomorrow isn't the one we are protecting today. To do our jobs, we need to innovate our program to support that change. Innovating for change doesn't mean a major overhaul to the program or operation every time. Sometimes it's a process, others it's a new technology, whereas yet other times it's a simple business engagement model. The point here is to recognize that if we truly embrace the philosophy of business operations, then change becomes a part of what we deliver, and that is done through innovation.

Continuing on with the business concept, as your company's or agency's senior-most security executive, your are a business leader, which means that you are expected to deliver exceptional business results and execute as a competent business leader. One measurement that defines a great executive is his or her ability to drive maturity into the businesses he or she runs, which includes optimization efforts and cost management. As a security leader, what does this mean? What are the implications? How do you get there? All great questions for a your innovation program, which is why this area is so important. Being a good business leader means that you must find ways to support your business's margin and reduce the total cost of ownership for your programs. This doesn't mean do more with less; it means do what needs to be done intelligently through innovation and being mindful of cost implications. Simple uses of automation or process reengineering can often drive incredible resource leveragability through increases in output and service delivery. New technology can remove the need for manual activities that drive cost and reduce accuracy. Whatever the opportunity is, innovation programs can help you get there.

The changing threat landscape is perhaps one of the most uncontrollable of the elements that mandate innovation within security programs. From changes in terrorist targets to new technological threat vectors, converged security programs are one of the most dynamic organizations inside companies today. In a business, competitors do enter the market, but it's typically not a daily market shift. Changes in the global threat landscape *do* happen everyday as criminals, nation-states, and terrorists advance their techniques, tactics, and protocols with regard for only one outcome: their success in overcoming your defenses. Billions of pieces of malware are created to overcome cyber defenses, and ecosystems of criminal organizations are created to exchange intelligence and operational components used to facilitate their trade. Innovative approaches to modular defensive postures, including adaptive controls architectures, transcending perimeters technology, and even virtualized cyber defensives, offer flexibility and buffers for preventative, defensive, and monitoring controls. Continuing innovation is necessary to afford practitioners the tools required to respond to these changing threats. Because each business or agency is different, so is the diversity of their threat landscape and the needs specific to their environment for innovation. As they say, necessity is the mother of innovation; if you want to be an executive security leader of the future and survive the constant and coming onslaught of threats to the businesses you protect, necessity is calling your name.

Chapter 7

Your Five-Step Section to Operational Execution

If you were to convene a study on successful security programs and how they were architected organizationally, one thing would become immediately self evident: No two are exactly alike. Sure, you'll see some similarities, like engineering and operations functions. Some have security operations centers (SOCs), whereas others have critical incident response centers (CIRCs). Some have malware engineers, whereas others need more cloud security engineers. In converged entities, your protective security agents may double as investigators, whereas in others, fraud teams may be the lead investigative body.

The point is that it is not the organizational chart or the titles or the number of engineers they have that make security programs successful; it's their ability to construct a program that is operationally focused to deliver the services their business needs to protect them. It's the architecture of the sustainable attributes of an organization that is able to execute well, designed in such a way that creates an ecosystem of services ready to be consumed by the business, and formulated in a way that ensures the resilience of the operation.

In this chapter we take a look at a five-step program architecture that will help you create a *functional* service catalog with elements to enable a holistic converged security, risk, and privacy program. Specifically, these include information security, corporate security, operational risk management, controls assurance, and client focus. We take a detailed look at key functions and services within each one of these areas that should be developed and delivered at any given maturity level to provide the necessary ecosystem for next-generation business operation protection programs.

INFORMATION SECURITY AND CYBER

Certainly, one of the most fast-paced, rapidly developing, and broadest functions within our practitionership is the information security and cyber discipline. It has been called "information security" by some and "information technology (IT) security," "information assurance," "data security," "cyber security," "technical security," or "geeks with guns" by others. For the creative individual there surely is no limit to what this function could be called, but when it comes down to the job, the function of information and cyber security is to ensure the confidentiality, availability, and integrity of the technical and information infrastructure and assets that support the business. Of course, that is easier said than done, and as a security executive it will be your job to figure out what that means for your business and to create the services necessary to protect your company's specific needs.

The purpose of this chapter is not to take you through a definitive framework, as prescribed in many industry-standard models of security program architecture; rather, it is to provide you with realistic set of consolidated program needs that go beyond the basics. Every program needs an operations function, monitoring function, and awareness of the end user. These are integrated services that should come stock with every service catalog you create and have been well defined and proven as effective components of a multilayered, in-depth defense approach. The concepts and programs in the following sections represent the collection of practices, processes, and operational functions that together advance information security from an adjunct IT protection function to an advanced business operation protection platform.

Prevent, Deter, Detect, and Respond

One of the most difficult mind shifts you will have to overcome is moving from "I can defend" against bad guys to "I must be prepared to accept that I may not be able to stop all of them." As so many industry experts and security technology vendors have exclaimed, "it's not the *if*, it's the *when*" you will be breached; there is some truth to that, but I argue that it certainly should not be your operating model. Although advancing your capabilities to determine whether intrusions have occurred, create flexible control architectures that enable you to shift controls, and have better response protocols in place are absolutely necessary in today's day and age, the primary focus of your programs should always be prevention. Think of it this way: Agencies or entities that provide protective services details spend an inordinate amount of time on "advances" of the locations where they will be providing protective services. Although many things are accomplished during these advances, one of the primary outcomes is to create a protective plan that ensures the dignitary or principal is never put into harm's way. Of course, they plan for armed response, medical actions, and a host of other negative-impact response requirements, but the focus is always on prevention. They know that it will be a very bad day when they have to pull a service firearm in defense of their principal. By changing routes, repositioning stages and room setups, using deceptive location techniques, and implementing multilevel perimeter monitoring, professional agencies like the US Secret Service do an amazing job of not having to do what the rest of the world believes their job is: shooting would-be assassins.

So what does prevention mean other than stopping bad things from happening? How exactly do you accomplish this from a cyber standpoint? At a high level, prevention should be considered basic technology hygiene and basic security technology implementation. Reports such as the Verizon Data Breach Report (VDBR) often reference research on known breaches, stating that ~80% of all breaches could have been prevented if basic blocking and tackling and IT hygiene had been implemented. Most of these hygiene considerations are typical issues such as patch management, access management, implementation of least privilege, implementation of secure life cycle development controls, and a multitiered data architecture. Basic security controls that are often disregarded include network and routing configuration management, firewalls, and intrusion prevention technology. These items are basic security architectures necessary to defend industry-specific or business-specific security issues. Advanced technologies like deep packet inspection, sticky honey pots, or virtualized network obfuscation are not what we're talking about here.

Prevention also must include visibility into and transparency of your current defensive posture. Concepts such as red teaming that willfully and purposely allow white-hat hacking-like activity inside and outside your network(s) are necessary to understand were gaps are and the validity of your current control posture. Next-generation concepts such as virtualized data centers that can migrate resources from one physical location to another while enabling a secondary set of controls to confuse the attacker also focus on prevention. Is part of your advanced planning to ensure that you include the right number of resources necessary to develop processes and engage your partners in IT and other areas of the business to do those things that steal from the adversary the opportunity to do harm?

In the context of a holistic approach to prevent, deter, detect, and respond, we must not lose sight that this is not just a technology problem. Prevention must be evaluated and planned for—from the people using the technology to the machines that run the technology and the business processes in between that require the technology. End-user education and end-user awareness help to educate and modify behaviors that reduce risk by modifying risky human behavior. Review of business process documentation and controls help identify gaps in those processes that allow early intervention, reducing your overall threat surface. Although technology will continue to be the preponderance of the cost, effort, and attack surface, the end-to-end life cycle of your business, from people to machines, are equally important when designing your overall approach.

In every part of this book we focus on business operations protection and in understanding the overall business process. This is especially important in the area of prevent, deter, detect, and respond because your ability to scale broadly across your business and protect multiple business processes, and the fact that adversaries are utilizing new attack vectors that use or mimic good credentials within good business processes to do their ill will, necessitate advancing your understanding of exactly what is a good process and what is a bad process within your own environment. Technology and analytical enablement are necessary to decide "good use" or "bad use" of any given business system, application, or technology asset. No longer can you depend on "that came from a good IP address or bad IP address" or "that was a known bad request." It is the totality of the end-to-end action or set of actions within any given process that will help you isolate problematic issues and enhance your time to detection and response.

As you're developing your cyber business operations protection program, remember that cyber includes all three of the areas of confidentiality, integrity, and availability. When considering where to prioritize, be sure to include an all-hazards approach to the defendability of your company. Utilize your risk management processes and protection reviews to identify potential issues that can cause incredible availability disruptions, data integrity attacks, and even kinetic attacks against your hosting sites that could potentially disrupt operations. Do not overwhelm yourself or your team with generalized what-if scenarios; rather, exercise good risk management tools and techniques that identify probability, capability, and impact scenarios. We all know what could happen in our environments; by aligning that with the measured risk outcome you can create your top 20 issues and create run books and plans for each of those. When you're done with those 20, move onto the next 20, and so on. Before you know it, you'll have an all-hazards run book and planning process that takes into account the majority of known and discovered risks, driving your team's confidence in their ability not only to develop preventative processes but also to feel confident in their ability to respond if a negative-impact event were to occur.

Security Ecosystem

The next concept that is critically relevant to creating a world-class cyber security program is that of the engineered and managed security ecosystem. Although most definitions require the word *ecosystem* to be used in the sense of a biological grouping, in the context of the next-generation security organization we use the word *ecosystem* as a group of integrated services working together as a single unit. In fact, beyond the information security and cyber defense area, this integrated security ecosystem that we speak of is almost the definition of a converged security program. The idea of implementing the security ecosystem is to enable the maximum total use of all parts of the preventive process through response services, including people, process, and technology, to ensure the success of the overall mission.

The focus of this ecosystem needs to be both the total use and the concept of separate items working together as a grouping or a single unit. For instance, when we speak of total use, we can look at it in a couple different ways. First, perhaps we purchased the technology to implement a control standard for a very specific issue. Let's use data leakage prevention (DLP) technology as an example. Imagine you implemented DLP technology to prevent the exfiltration of regulatory protected information, such as Health Insurance Portability and Accountability Act information, credit card numbers, national identifiers, or

Social Security numbers, from your environment to a known gap, audit finding, or legal implication. Now that you've implemented it and it's working, you're done, right? Absolutely not. Your next questions should be, "How do I utilize this technology to extend its capabilities across other threat areas?" and "What else can I do with this technology?" Can you use it to protect other information such as sensitive mergers and acquisition information? Can you use it for workforce protection in identifying potential violent behaviors by searching for specific terms and conditions? Can you use it as part of your controls assurance audit process to provide factual evidentiary material to supplement or automate reports necessary to prove controls effectiveness? The point here is to recognize that total use really means leveraged asset. It doesn't matter if it's used in information security, corporate security, audit programs, or even as the manufacturer or product description intended it. You are limited only by your imagination and the maximum capacity of the resource you are targeting. During my career I have successfully cross-utilized people, process, and technology to support converged operations and even programs outside my area of operations. By creating and mandating a process and environment that demands the responsible and extended use of all resources for the betterment of the business, you show your leadership, ingenuity, and extreme business management skills.

The second part of the security ecosystem is that of collective resources acting as a single unit. From a technology perspective this has to be one of your critical design components and standards for technology evaluation an acquisition. Technical security requirements will always change, vendors will build multiple products and continuously consolidate them, then they start the life cycle all over again. The reality is that cyber threats and issues evolve so quickly that we will continue be required to have multiple technology sets in order to defend our business. Of course, the problem this creates is how to manage, monitor, and maintain all of these platforms while responsibly managing the human capital resources necessary to manage the overall protection infrastructure. More concerning is the fact that you may have a specific technology in place, but if it is not monitored then how do you know that something actually occurred? Most vendors create technology with a structure that includes its own management console, monitoring console, ticket management system, and so on. By creating base requirements or technology and vendor selection, such as application programming interface extensibility, bidirectional event flow, common platform technology (such as operating system/database), and virtualization assurance, you can develop an overall security ecosystem that invites the development of an integrated ecosystem. These standards allow for the use of different controls, monitoring, and management technologies in an integrated platform that reduces overlap, rework, unnecessary actions, and repetitive or redundant tasks. A good example of this is event or incident queue management of generalized security alerts across multiple platforms. Your security event management system, intrusion detection system (IDS), deep-packet inspection system, data leakage prevention system, indication of compromise alerting platform, and just about every other enterprise security system you deploy has its own incident creation, alerting, and workflow engine built in. The complexities of overlap requiring an individual analyst to go into each one of these functions to track any given incident is unfathomable. Perhaps a better way to approach it is to implement or utilize the most robust workflow engine available within your environment, such as through governance risk and compliance (GRC) technology or an integrated ticketing system attached to another technology such as your security event management system. Or, better yet, perhaps your IT organization already has a powerful workflow engine that you can use in a multitenant mode or integrated queue specific for security. Whatever is created as the standard, require vendors that want your business to integrate to it. Imagine the efficiencies and resource reutilization you gain by simply requiring this one simple process in one of the many areas of your responsibility.

So, how do you create this approach and consistency within your organization? One method you may want to consider is the use of a converged security architecture function. Converged security architecture simply means that you use a single set of architects as the sole entity responsible for creating an end-to-end architecture of technology components that supports all parts of your security, risk, and privacy program. In many programs each area such as cyber, corporate security, and privacy operations have their own architects who design for their specific function. However, if the end result is a great technology stack with multiple use assurance, an integrated ecosystem for increased utilization, performance, and efficiency, then you must reduce independent architecture functions into a single stack following basic guiding principles that affect your vision. These converged architects must ensure that technology being developed, and considered for use, must support not just the function for which it is being evaluated, but that they are leveraged and leveragable across the entire operating environment. Additionally, they must enforce the requirements that the technology adheres to the concepts of ecosystem interoperability, as previously mentioned. In sticking with our earlier example of DLP, when architects evaluate a similar technology, they should be able to answer the questions, "Where in other parts of my area of responsibility can this be utilized, such as physical security, investigations, audit support?" "How will alerts be provided and ingested into the ecosystem?" "How will workflow management between the centralized infrastructure and that specific technology work together?" prior to technology being selected.

This brings me to my next point around the selection, procurement, and management of centralized technology. In smaller entities this is really not a large concern. Typically, as companies grow, independent security groups are established, and intercompany communications dwindle, grossly different technology stacks emerge, reducing the ability to enforce and create an integrated ecosystem of security technologies and programs. To solve this, you should establish a centralized process for technology evaluation, selection, purchase, implementation, and management. Purchasing control should be implemented with your purchasing department, requiring purchases within the technology of security areas be routed through a review process that ensures consistency with standards.

Centralized or regionally centralized implementation programs reduced the time needed to deploy complex technology through shared knowledge and repetitive configuration assurance. It also reduces unnecessary overtraining of multiple engineers to be able to support independent deployments globally using a core-trained team that is not only specifically trained for the technology but has implementation experience across a broader set of environments.

From a management perspective, centralized technology management just makes plain sense. The ability to standardize rule sets, environmental changes, and upgrades using a single management platform (including resources) reduces misconfiguration, mismanagement, and potential orphaning components of your security architecture. It also guarantees transparency and visibility into the operating environment to reduce any issues with segregation of duties or business politics.

In larger multinational organizations that have business units (BUs) with independent organizational structures, which can make creating a single-stack technology defense architecture and integrated management platform nearly impossible, you can still enable an ecosystem for intelligence sharing, incident sharing, and any other BU-to-BU integrated service, offering arrangements that makes sense for your business. Through the use of shared standards and operating agreements you can create the beginnings of a shared operations portfolio, with the end result driving an ecosystem enablement platform. Over time, as you prove the use and the success of the positive financial outcomes, you can use that shared operations portfolio to expand the ecosystem. To do this effectively, you should make a multiyear plan that sets reasonable targets for integrated efforts, including clear metrics and desired outcomes for all parties involved. Often, as you offload unnecessary repeatable programs that can be integrated into a centralized management platform, you reduce the stress on decentralized teams or independent BUs to focus on business operations protection enhancement rather than day-to-day incident response or platform management, which often drags them down and takes them away from their core mission. By using this as an anchored selling point, over time you can expand the ecosystem considerably.

But—and there's always a but—to accomplish any ecosystem, you must provide a transparent set of standards that provides guidelines, parameters, and expectations for ecosystem enablement. Standards regarding technology purchases, deployment standards, monitoring, logging, and so on are the baseline by which you build an ecosystem. You can "mandate" until you are blue in the face, but until standards are created, ratified by all stakeholders, and posted as the "law of the land," progress to an integrated ecosystem will be slow—and not just in your area of operation. Remember that strategic ecosystem enablement means that BUs, IT, another entities are going to have to change their systems, applications, platforms, and operations to enable different components of your ecosystem. Without the ability to point to a standard, you often waste more time arguing the need rather than enforcing the requirement.

Authentication, Authorization, and Audit

The next integrated focus area that is a key part of your overall program is the focus on authentication, authorization, and audit, commonly referred to as AAA. One of the most fundamental necessities is the ability to understand who is in your operating environment, what they have access to, in the infrastructure to manage that broadly cross your business platforms. *Identity and access management* is a broad term used for this area and is a required component of any mature IT service delivery organization. In the context of your security organization responsibilities, let's take a look at why this area is so incredibly important and how, if instantiated correctly, it can reduce the overall cyber threat level of your business.

As a practitioner, think back to the types of security issues and events that occurred over the years that you had to respond to and how many of them involved some sort of access to technology or data that enabled the negative-impact event that occurred. Now think about why that individual had or gained access, how well-maintained your identity environment was, and whether that could have been prevented or was it something more simple like a good person going rogue? It is amazing when we think about it and do the research, which shows that the way we credential people into our environment, the way we manage access into infrastructure applications, and the effort we put into least privilege management all have a massive impact on the number and the extent of security incidents in our businesses. By focusing our efforts in this area, we can greatly reduce common events that happen in an automated, premeditated, or accidental process simply by denying logical access to any given technology set.

First and foremost, let's look at why centralized authentication mechanisms and authoritative identity repositories are so important. With regard to bifurcated identity collaboration, once an authoritative identity technology is integrated into a business process it is very difficult to unwind. When I spoke to some of the most seasoned technology experts in large, multinational organizations and asked them about one of the most difficult technology programs that they managed over their careers, many speak to architecting and solving identity integration issues. It is so important because over time the inefficiencies, security and compliance issues, and threat enablement that multiple repositories an unmanaged identities cause, truly affects an organization's ability to deliver products and services, and is extremely costly. I once worked for an organization that was in the services space where their number 1 most costly customer service issue wasn't anything about their product; it was password resets across multiple product lines. Imagine that you are a multibillion-dollar business and your number 1 most costly customer-affecting process is in the identity space. How does a company get to that point? Predominately, it's the instantiation and mismanagement of multiple authentication and authorization environments over years and even decades.

The easiest way to implement centralized mechanisms is to create a single-service bus methodology with specific authoritative identity platforms for your enterprise as well as your customer environment, if applicable. The service methodology must allow for whatever mechanisms of authentication and authorization are necessary, as well as advanced service functionalities within the identity space, such as single sign-on, security assertion markup language, adaptive authentication, certificate integration, mobility, and any other authentication service function necessary to operate your business. The concept of the service bus is to code once and reuse many, with the ability to update and add with incredible flexibility and speed.

Additionally, during the development of any identity assurance program, you have to ask yourself what business do you want to be in—or need to be in, for that matter. For example, there is a big difference between authentication and authorization, and you don't necessarily have to be in both. Authentication is the action by which an individual or identity is verified to a particular level as being authentic. That is, we establish a specific level of " I know who is requesting that service or action." Authorization is the act of allowing that individual or identity access to a group-specific service, asset, or function. You don't necessarily have to do both, or you may want to do everything. For instance, in your customer environment perhaps you are okay with users providing their own integrated identity from another company or authentication provider, such as Google, Facebook, LinkedIn, their own business, or those companies that are starting to provide identity verification services. All you simply want to do is give that identity access to a specific asset such as an application or technology resource. Whatever services you plan on delivering, either internally or externally, you must start by addressing the basic questions as to which services you intend on delivering as a company, and architect from there.

As you focus on developing your overall cyber security prevention and detection program, you must also use this area of authentication and authorization as probable components of the overall prevention and advanced detection capabilities when integrated with other parts of your portfolio. The future of authentication will change. Today, organizations predominantly use usernames and passwords as the principal mechanism to perform authentication. Newer approaches and technologies that focus on identity accretion and password atrophy avoidance using new multipoint techniques such as adaptive and advanced authentication provide not only better mechanisms for authentication, but also invaluable information artifacts; as part of the AAA process they can be used in a broad set of detective and preventive technologies across multiple areas such as cyber defense and fraud management. These technologies look at multiple logical attributes about the user—where the user is coming from, what technology they are using—and a host of other information, including user behavior patterns and even biometrics, create a mathematical algorithm that equates to a known pattern or behavior matched to the individual. As an example, the technology sold by RSA, the security division of EMC Corporation, uses information collected about the user's geolocation, computer fingerprinting, operating system, browser, IP address, and a host of other identifiable attributes that represent the user. So instead of just getting a "username and password" you can get 10, 20, or even 50 attributes about the user to make a mathematically sound decision about whether it is or is not that individual at the other end of the keyboard. By integrating that technology with risk-based authentication and similar technologies, you form a higher level of identity accretion.

What else does this type of technology give you? First, it provides a lot of data. The detailed information about the user (e.g., where they come from and their usage patterns) are inclusive of the platforms providing this type of authentication and are often available for exportation into other analytical or security management technologies. For instance, if an authentication is denied access because of a high probability that is not the user attempting access, the data associated with that attempt could be provided to a security analytics or event management platform or can be used by a fraud prevention technology. Other security analytic products can use that information and other similar historical data sets to create trend and algorithmic calculations that can be turned into newer detection capabilities that identify like attempts across the whole of the infrastructure in the future. The levereagability of those consolidated authentication data sets across a platform that supports the entire operating environment is very powerful.

Authentication and authorization, or what is referred to mostly as the identity components, are only two-thirds of your AAA function. The final A, or "audit," typically refers to the ability to log information about a platform, system, application, transaction, or, in general, any technology asset. The audit ability is critical to almost every part of your program, from prevention to detection to response. Your company's policies and standards must make this a priority requirement, and your teams must know how to leverage that data in all aspects of their service areas. Further, the speed at which you are able to design a preventive, detective, or monitoring control to adjust to changing threat conditions depends on your understanding and mapping of your business and enterprise system logging taxonomy and your ability to keep that mapping up to date. The use of audit information can be used by nearly every function of your organization within security, risk, and privacy. Even before automated analysis through protective technology applications, practitioners can use business intelligence, like tools to query, inspect, and interrogate data sets, in the support of issue discovery, investigation, and response.

In future sections we cover your ability to ingest this information, but for now remember that it is important to have the data, not how you get it. Remember that your IT partners or business intelligence teams may already log and collect a large amount of information or have the tool sets necessary to extract the information necessary to meet whatever standards you design. Most of the issue with audit data use is creating parsing capabilities to make structured use. In some environments, platforms and legacy applications that are critical to protect may not have the ability to log information at all without costly and business-impacting rewrites, in which case you may need to work with specialty network logging technologies that enable you to extract data from the networking infrastructure to provide information needed. Whatever the path, use what is available and build from that. Leverage existing mechanisms to consume the data and focus on formalizing your approach to the advancement of your program through the use of this type of information.

Critical Asset Protection Program (CAPP)

Listen to any information security speech long enough and you'll probably hear reference to "protecting" the crown jewels. It's a reference to the inability to protect everything in the environment and to focus on those assets most impactful to your business or agency. There is a lot of truth in that concept. No environment can be protected 100%, and not everything needs to be protected to the same level. The intellectual property that is your "business" needs to be protected differently than the expense management platform. Although both are important, one system affects your company far more.

The critical asset protection program (CAPP) helps you identify what assets need to be protected at which level and takes the business through a formalized approach to critical component defense. Through the utilization of existing services or process you probably already have or provide in a particular order, you can provide a greater level of protection and response simply by implementing a rigorous approach to a defined process for specific asset classes. This gives you a risk-based approach necessary to determine resource utilization and expenditures, a measurable mechanism for the protection level before and after, a managed implementation of advanced protection controls, and a focused approach to incident detection and response necessary to support any given critical asset. Let's look at how all of these components work together to cerate the CAPP.

The first area necessary is to understand what an "asset" is and to create that definition for your own business. Broadly applied, in the context of the CAPP an asset is any business asset, technology, platform, data, or infrastructure, either independent or as a collection, that form in whole or in part a business process. For instance, sticking with the intellectual property example used before, what would that "asset" look like? Is it just the piece of data itself or the server it's hosted on? Or is it the network filer that allows access to it and the server, the storage array, and the networking components that create the mechanisms to access it. How about automated applications used in the manufacturing process that utilize the information? There is no hard or fast rule here; in fact it is your job to help your business define the asset. A good rule of thumb is to loosely apply the aggregate of the systems and services that together, as a singular conjoined asset, make up the process that "is" the critical asset.

Now that you are getting the idea, the next question you have to answer is, How do I decide what to protect first and prioritize my efforts? This is not an insular effort within your security program and must involve a defined risk process and input from the business. Whichever risk actuation process you use is immaterial, only that each asset is evaluated against the same set of criteria. In fact, you may use a standardized day-to-day risk measurement process as part of your overall operations and use a totally separate one for evaluating the criticality of assets to the business. To start, use the business to define what is critical and why. The why is important because it provides the necessary data to enter into your evaluation model. Use quantifiable measurements where possible, such as total impact to revenue dollars if affected, impact to total percentage of customers if affected, and total compulsory statutory impact (fine etc) liability if an incident were to occur. Complete the risk scoring and ranking with data infused from what your organization knows about those platforms, including vulnerability data, known risk issues, external intelligence on exploitation abilities, and so on. Once the scoring and stack ranking is complete, sit with senior members of your company's leadership team to ask them to weigh in on the prioritization. Often the prioritization is affected by business issues that you may not be aware of but have a material impact on the overall prioritization effort.

Now that you have your prioritized approach, it's time to get it into the process. The CAPP process you develop will be unique for your business but needs to contain some basic elements that gather the right information and actions the right efforts to create a measurable and appreciative prevention, detection, and response capability for any given asset that goes through the program. To begin, your process should have a data collection effort that includes the collection, review, and validation of technical documentation, including physical and logical diagrams, business process flow, data flow diagrams, and run books if applicable. In larger, more mature organizations these may be formalized in a configuration management database or document repository. However, in many years of doing this job I have never seen a full set of documentation available for any given CAPP. This means that your teams will most probably have to work with the business or your IT counterparts to complete many if not all of the required document set.

The next effort is to complete a controls review. In this part of the process, you utilize the documents collected in the previous set to document what controls are in place from a data protection and privacy assurance standpoint. AAA, data protection, monitoring, and so on should all be included. Validation of those controls through a controls assurance process, such as testing the controls, gathering evidentiary data points of their effectiveness, and creating gap reports, provide the data necessary to perform the next phase: the risk assessment.

The risk assessment is important for two reasons. First, it creates a remediation path necessary to obtain a baseline against the rest of your environment and a measuring capability for future enhancements. Second, it provides relevant factual data for the business in a format that gives them a clear understanding of the critical assets' real issues, the expected loss calculation based on previous information provided if that asset were to be affected, and a documented mechanism with good data for them to make important decisions. This risk process should include basic vulnerability testing, detailed platform technical security assessment, and red teaming. Although you will validate new and augmented security controls and processes as the final phase of any CAPP, the testing quells discussions focused on the "reality" of the claims asserted by the risk assessment. In several mission-critical CAPP assessments I have performed in the past, I asked the testing team to record their work and used that when meeting with the business to give it a view into the reality of the situation.

Once the risk assessment is completed, your next step is to address control gaps and the risk decision outcomes by adding advanced controls into the critical asset as necessary. These can be as simple as advanced authentication controls, to necessary encryption platforms, to an entire data center review. There is no "list" of controls for you to check against in this context. It is the experience and knowledge of those involved, in conjunction with the business, that defines what the additional required controls are. When making these decisions you should have specific required outcomes that the controls will support, such as a reduction in their risk score, an improvement in the loss expectation score, or the removal of a threat vector discovered during the review. The effort is not to "add" more controls into your environment, but rather to wrap the right controls around the assets necessary to increase the preventive posture to an agreed-upon level. The hope is always to reuse controls that are already available in your service repository rather than go out and "buy" yet another tool, although sometimes that may be what is required. Sometimes, because of to the uniqueness of an asset, the criticality of the protection needs, or the newness of the threat, you may not have a control or the experience in house to support the gap. In those cases follow your normal testing and procurement process to ensure that whatever control is selected is available to the whole organization to address other similar gaps.

Before you get to the phase of testing your new control architecture, you must address the issue of visibility. Even if they get the right controls around their CAPP, many practitioners fail to design the appropriate level of monitoring to ensure that when an issue or incident involving that CAPP asset occurs, it is detected and responded to in a prioritized fashion. This is because most monitoring programs are based on standard ingestion and alerting work flows. When you establish a CAPP program, this means that you need to re-architect your security monitoring and response program as well to accommodate for it. Special monitoring queues that prioritize alerting and escalation based on asset classification need to be created, and a workflow that may include broad alerting, faster escalation thresholds, and additional team notifications (such as investigations and forensics), may need to be considered. Special security instructions for handling incident with CAPP assets should be added to playbooks, including dedicated response procedures. For instance, perhaps the asset you have deemed a CAPP asset has to do with a command and control infrastructure for programmable logic controllers (PLCs) in your environment. A new automated or specialized response requirement may be the validation of

PLC commands for the past 24 h, the validation of the PLC code on every controller, and the validation of all network traffic to and from every controller for a set period of time. The more specialized "what should we do if" examples aligned to a specific asset you can come up with, the more they can be documented, automated, and made available during an incident, and the more effectively you will be able to reduce the downstream impact in the event of an attack or event associated with the asset.

The final step in the CAPP is the testing and validation process. Just like you did as part of the initial risk assessment, the new controls and monitoring processes needs to be validated to solidify the expectations of their effectiveness. This process not only validates the control objectives, it prepares your team operationally, confirming whether controls operate as expected, whether monitoring capabilities are effective and operational, and whether newly defined response thresholds are factual. There should be two distinct process that happen here. First, the individuals who support your controls effectiveness program need to test the gap remediation and prevention metrics created to establish a good baseline. Questions like "has that gap been remediated?" and "did that new control prevent X from happening?" should all be tested and documented. The second test should be a heavy-handed red team. In this effort, no notice of full exploitation (with a mandate of do no harm) should occur. This is where you test the preventive and deterrence capabilities as well as the monitoring controls. In the same way that you showed the business that the system was exploitable, you want to be able to prove that you are now successfully prevented from exploiting the CAPP asset and that you know when attempts are made. If there are failures within the testing, be transparent about it, fix them, and retest. Complete this process until you have the confidence in your program and are able to sleep soundly at night.

Intelligence-Led Security

The concept of intelligence-led security (ILS) is certainly not a new one, and in recent years it has moved from a framework approach to a consumerized set of products within the industry. But what does an ILS program even mean and why is it necessary? In Chapter 1 we focused on the use of intelligence as a part of your decision support platform. In the operational context, that same thought process carries over to an action-enabled operational program that uses collected, analyzed, and interpreted data to make decisions, act, and defend the business. In a sense it's establishing an operational platform of data collection, analytics, and results-actionable output that feeds decision makers, command and control platforms, and defensive and reactive technology assets.

Let's start with a few examples that will help solidify the concept. Without using ILS, a normal security process may look something like this: (1) A bad guy establishes a wedge in your network through malware and moves laterally to another machine using credentials stolen from the first machine. (2) The bad guy connects using an authenticated connection to a dump site and starts transferring collected data available from each machine he accesses. (3) Company financials or trade secrets are released and you get the call to investigate. In this scenario, what could you expect a singular traditional security platform to notify you of? What would it have looked like to a practitioner monitoring the platform? After step 1, the initial intrusion, what would serve as a trigger point? In this example malware alerts may have triggered, but by the time you got there, the bad guys were already masquerading as a "good" user in your environment and probably had several to chose from. If an analyst got the alert and didn't have good systems, research, and business process intelligence available to them, the original machine would probably be cleaned and no further review may happen until you respond to the call.

Let's look at how this may have occurred with an intelligence-led program. (1) A bad guy establishes a wedge in your network through malware and moves laterally to another machine. (2) Indicators of the Zero Day malware and IPs of the attackers were previously loaded into an analytics platform looking for corroborated events. (3) Automated alerts indicating probable intrusion are sent to the Security Operations Center (SOC). (4) Automated event collection scripts, utilizing that alert, immediately collect log data, net flow, user actions, application data, and other pertinent information and provide it to the analysts' queue. (5) The analysts use available tools to run a report and confirm suspected compromised user credentials and access is cut off, denying access through the proxies outbound. (6) The analysts use their big data set to cross-query any action associated with the user activity or like indicators of compromise (IOC) and IP addresses across the enterprise to ensure with high confidence that no exfiltration has occurred. (7) Immediate validation of application and controls across affected systems and networks is in place. The incident is over in a matter of minutes.

Although a simplistic view of the use of intelligence, it underscores the power of having both internal and external information available to make good decisions, to use during the course of an incident, and to be able to have that information in a managed and contained setting that enables the use of other automation such as scripts, analytics, and multiprocess procedures as events happen. Access and use to this level of intelligence, and creating your run-time operations around the use of this type of data, creates scale and provides transparency and speed to your operations. So, then, what are some of the components you should be thinking of when developing this type of operational framework?

As you begin to build your next-generation security intelligence program think "multiuse platform." Even if you are not a converged security program yet, the data that can be collected can be broadly used and shared across multiple programs, from security to risk to privacy to audit, and even corporate security. Much of the data around users, business processes, hierarchy, transactions, computing environments, personal computers, alert data, environmental states, and facility access can all be used for multiple reasons. Ensure you create your intelligence platform with expansion, analytics, and multiple uses in mind. For instance, if you want to be able to run concurrent analytics such as cyber defense, fraud prevention, and privilege account analytics at the same time, you need to plan how you will develop your architecture to support these types of operations. By planning up front or recognizing that your intelligence platform efforts will be used in many ways by many teams, you reduce the operational impact of making changes in the future by building for it now.

The next area is data aggregation: exactly how you get all of this data, what exactly you are collecting, where it goes, how long you keep it, and how you process it. The types of information you collect are limited only by your imagination. Basics in cyber defense programs such as normal authentication and authorization logs, Dynamic Host Configuration Protocol (DHCP), Domain Name System (DNS), and transaction logs abound and should be collected. External information such as fraud defense intelligence providers and cyber-sharing groups should also be collected. By working with experienced peers in the industry who have developed similar programs, sitting with your business and IT groups to see what is available, and preparing analytical wish lists on your own with your team and teasing out the type of data you would need are all great steps in capturing some of what you want to collect. The two most important parts in all of this are the following: (1) Make sure you create a data architecture framework/taxonomy that is based on standards, uses simple language, and serves as the bible of how you will collect and process data into your intelligence collection platform. (2) Become experts at capacity planning for data ingestion and use planning. The level of data that you "can" get is greatly limited by what you can receive, store, and process. The reality is normally vastly different than the expectations in our minds and can quickly turn your efforts into an inability to execute because of system restrictions and overload. Spend the time planning for capacity and understanding how to get at and use the data in your intelligence platform before you start building it.

When thinking about the maturity cycle and capability maturity timeline for your intelligence program, remember that the use of the data does not have to wait until the analytics are in place and operational to make this capability productive in your environment. In fact, a great way to get your team up to speed on how to use the information and utilize the tools available to support analytics is to first use the platform as a data interrogation platform. The availability of the information can serve as a great tool for your SOC/CIRC or investigators when investigating or researching issues with your environment. This provides the power to query cross-platform, cross-business, global data sets, answering questions such as:

Where else has that IP address accessed my network?
What assets has that user accessed in the past 30 days?
Where else do we have that same configuration?
What is the average number of transactions that happens every day?

The question list is limitless and can support everything from operational and engineering planning to active event investigations. Even fishing expeditions for proactive analysis of your environment or hunting functions for known behaviors can be done without major implementations of advanced analytics in place. Don't wait until you have the optimum state to utilize the power of the data and intelligence you collect.

The next big step in your program is automated analytics technologies to help you make sense of the information. In some cases you may have to create your own; however, as the market matures and the purchasing base expands as companies build out collection platforms, more and more new analytic platforms are becoming commercially available. Your focus should be on creating a road map of the needs of your business operations protection program in alignment with the information available, and the ability to ingest and interpret the results. The short way of saying that is to build only to what your company is capable of collecting, processing, and using, and create a stepping mechanism to get you to the next level as your abilities mature. Some of us have learned the hard way by setting overreaching goals and then losing millions in investments because the organization and the technology simply did not align. Create the operational and human capital capability mapping in association with your planning. When possible, use purpose built analytic packages that map to your data sets and can use limited subsets of information necessary for the specific problem the tool is trying to solve. Avoid large, broad-based tools that search across multiple data sets, consume critical intelligence system resources, and provide limited output. Create a tiered platform ability that moves the necessary data components into a segregated platform that is specific to the reporting or analytical function you have chosen that does not affect the security intelligence platform's overall resource sustainability capabilities.

Take a progressive approach to crawl, walk, run into analytics. Big successes come in small packages and help build confidence in your team and the platform and help you work out issues that you may not have encountered before or expected. Start with collecting the data and understanding how to use it. Then add on automated application with mature commercial history that solves a critical issue. As you mature, add more automated analytic components across multiple service areas; finally, advance into mature concepts like machine-learning algorithm development technologies and artificial intelligence programs to help you find those needles in the haystack.

Finally, although it goes without saying, this type of data aggregation platform with critical cross-business intelligence is very powerful, and your adversaries know this as well. Protecting the systems that protect your business must be at the forefront of your mind and engineered into your program. Create defense protection operations and err on the side of caution and restricted use to ensure the integrity and the availability of your next-generation security intelligence platform.

Critical Incident Analysis and Response

Another key attribute in developing an advanced cyber and information security program is the implementation of services that can monitor, analyze, and respond to security-related issues across your enterprise. This incident analysis and response team, sometimes called a computer incident response center,

CIRC, emergency computer response center, advanced security operations center, or cyber defense center, is the tip of your spear when identifying and responding to potential threats against your organization and will be used to "hunt" for malicious activity—all in an effort to reduce the duration of exposure and the extent of impact, and to prevent negative-impact events from occurring. For the purposes of this section we stick with the term CIRC.

To explain better what a CIRC is, we should start with what it is not. A CIRC is not an SOC in the traditional sense, meaning the functions discussed in this section are not meant to support the ongoing operations of the security infrastructure, technology, or day-to-day management of security services to a company's end user. Although most SOCs have responsibilities for cyber monitoring, the sheer volume of operational services that goes along with maintain an SOC precludes the implementation of advanced analytic and response functions as defined in traditional roles.

So, if day-to-day operations of security is not the function, what is? The CIRC is a dedicated, advanced set of people, process, and technology that understands the business and business context and provides cyber and converged intelligence, analytical, discovery, investigative, and technical response services in an effort to further prevent, deter, detect, respond, and reduce the effect of negative-impact events in any given organization. Although there are many maturity levels of CIRC-like programs, the intended purpose is to have a higher-skilled organization that can operate quickly across boundaries with the autonomy to discover anomalies, analyze threat and alert data, react with authority, and improve the technical security infrastructure through automation, tuning, and input to the security engineering and operations programs.

The terms *analyst* and *analytical* are key to a CIRC program. The skills necessary to look at cross-discipline data streams and understand and discern good actions from bad actions takes an individual with technical *and* analytical skills. These specialists must have the ability to think broadly about their environment, threat actors, Techniques, Tactics and Procedures (TTPs), and general technology; create theories; and investigate massive amounts of evidentiary data to reach definitive conclusions.

The CIRC function looks at indicators, alerts, and reports from practitioners and the business to evaluate potential threats, then launch investigations to understand root cause, incident scope, and potential impact. They are responsible for developing response protocols, creating urgent action teams, and managing through a security-related event.

Mature programs have additional services that further the mission through unique capabilities that enhance other functions within the overall service. For instance, the term *hunters* is applied to specially trained analysts who spend their days utilizing advanced intelligence from the industry to look across the environment of indications of attempted compromise, compromise, fraud, policy violations, illicit or illegal activities, and a host of other potential issues. They spot-check CAPP assets, know weak spots, gap areas, and other potential "hang outs" of malicious activity and investigate hunches, clues, or potential targets of interest. Often these teams use "undercover" methods and further utilize specialized technology such as honey pots to uncover would-be wrongdoers. As threat actors continue to hone their trade, masquerading as good users, it is the responsibility of the hunters to hone their own trade to quickly find problems and issues within the environment before they turn disastrous.

Another critical function that CIRCs provide is advanced technical forensics services. In many companies, eDiscovery and forensics have been limited to disk duplication and analysis, data retrieval, messaging platform discovery, among others; however, the need for cross-enterprise data collection, device inspection, memory analysis, and multipath evidentiary analysis and collection are new skills that are necessary for today's type of converged investigations that happen inside companies every day. From at-state memory dumps to the global extraction of specific user-based actions from multijurisdictional proxy architectures, today's investigations demand the detailed technical understanding of networking, memory analysis, unstructured and structured data organization and management, storage architectures, mass data collection techniques, deep-packet inspection/verification/analysis, malware analysis, and a host of other very technical actions that have become a part of almost every type of investigation. Those who perform that level of analytical and technical evaluation and investigations every day and, with some additional forensics and evidence management training, can often be leveraged from your existing resource pool to best provide these services.

When considering the CIRC as a core part of your new program, a required mandated outcome of that team should be the enhancement of repeatable and automated functions. CIRC experts create investigative, research, and response methods every day for new issues or problems they work on. Those efforts need to be documented, automated, and shared as part of a larger optimization effort across your groups. Those lessons learned and developed can be repackaged and distributed to engineering and operations teams, into platform ecosystem operations, and across converged security, risk, and privacy teams to support detective operations and response to day-to-day efforts. This type of resource reuse is an incredible force multiplier that leads to incredible organizational speed and effectiveness.

Platform Sustainability

In the area of information security and cyber programs you will always find the functional components of engineering and operations. Sometimes larger programs often separate these conjoined operations. Although at the beginning of this section I mentioned this was not to review baseline aspects of building a security program, my experiences lead me to provide advice based on the issues surrounding platform sustainability and the services necessary to ensure operational uptime to the extended security, risk, and privacy technology ecosystem platform.

Security technologists are typically great at managing security technologies and applications such as firewalls, IDS, DPI, DLP, RMS, and any other of a host of security technologies provided by a variety of vendors. The addition of rule sets, the management of workflow, the instantiation of advanced detection techniques, the use of tools for discovery, and so on are the lifeblood of what our operations and engineering teams develop, bring to the fight, and manage every day. Where security platforms normally develop weaknesses is in the basic and routine care and feeding of the underlying operating systems, as well as the maintenance and monitoring of normal device and application functionality, which often are not managed well. Now, I say that not to cast a broad brush, but I have consulted for hundreds of companies, taken over the executive management of several, and built several more, and the one consistent thing that I find is that security operators tend to migrate toward, and excel, at operating the security and not the base operating functions. Additionally, because of those types of program gaps and the busyness of these types of functions in general, the underlying architecture (such as AAA) also suffers and potentially exposes gaps in the security of the security infrastructure itself.

To avoid this and ensure the operating integrity and sustainability of the platform, here are a few suggestions to create a more comprehensive life cycle approach to platform management. First, consider outsourcing to IT. Yes, you read that right. Outsource to IT. The management of base operating systems, their ability to monitor uptime/downtime and green-yellow-red functionality is what their profession has done for more years than security has been a mainstream profession, and most do it well. This may make necessary some additional actions to invoke changes and make your team slightly less nimble, but it will force the ISO-like rigor that most IT functions are capable of delivering to maintain a technology platform far larger than our ecosystem of security devices. Additionally, those skill sets necessary to manage databases, platform operating systems, networks, and so on are becoming more and more difficult to find and maintain as the security industry is changing and security, risk, and privacy engineers focus more on core operations, analytics, and applications management than on IT subfunctions. By utilizing your peers in IT as service providers, you relieve resource constraints, add depth of knowledge, and integrate sustainability operations with the rest of your business.

If outsourcing to IT doesn't work, then you may have to build that in as a required deliverable of your security engineering and operations teams with appropriate service level agreements, monthly key performance indicators, and resources dedicated to the function. Areas to look out for are device health and uptime, configuration and access assurance, and ecosystem participation monitoring. Just because your security infrastructure is feeding alerts and processing risks doesn't mean it is operating as intended. How does your team know that the right information is flowing from end devices? How are you sure that the correct analytic applications are firing? How do you know that specific sensors are inspecting the correct traffic in other parts of the world? All of these questions need to be asked and measurements and monitoring tables implemented to ensure the consistency and availability of the cyber defense platform.

An alternative to both of those options is the use of third-party managed security services (MSS) vendors to provide that functionality on your behalf. Although you will need to do a full cost analysis, outsourcing to a third party the management of your technical infrastructure is not a new thing. In fact, many large and small companies have been successfully utilizing well-established providers for many years. A collaborative relationship that creates a co-delivery model between the advanced institutional knowledge that your team provides and the experience platform machine of an experience MSS provider is often a cost-efficient mechanism to deploy and manage your security infrastructure. Unique financing options such as leasing often reduce your capital expense exposure of a long financial tail and limited ability to replace devices, through built-in replacement periods and full options for mandated device management. Additionally, long gone are the days of "all or nothing" MSS companies that require that they provide the monitoring service as well. Today, lease programs from some of the largest technology providers in the world partnering with MSS vendors give you unlimited and flexible options for platform management and often can be leveraged through existing IT spending, again making it a more affordable option.

Whether you outscore to IT, a third party, or manage it yourself, the security and defense posture of that platform cannot be overlooked. Security technology platforms and ecosystems need to be treated as CAPP assets and managed accordingly. From platform monitoring to red teaming to risk assessments, the security of the protective architecture of your company must not be a victim of the "cobbler's children syndrome" and should be prioritized as a base program cost. From an optics perspective, if your organization is out "judging and enforcing" corporate requirement for business protection assurance and your own program doesn't follow the standards, how then can you act as an authoritative figure? Second, if your job is to defend the company and you cannot defend or prove the defensibility of the platform you are charged to maintain, then are you really doing your job? Make sure that you have the right programs to document, assess, and protect your security program. Make it a part of your project deployment life cycle that requires a sign-off from you on every single security project before it is considered "go-live" to reduce the temptation for your own teams to bypass these types of programmatic operations assurance work streams. Remember, at the end of the day, if those responsible for defending the business are incapable of defending themselves, maybe your business has the wrong people defending it.

CORPORATE SECURITY

As a converged security executive, the functional requirements beyond the cyber aspects of your job can be just as broad and diverse, and depending on the size of the company or agency you are employed by, these programs can be not only very large but also significantly different by country of operation and jurisdictions as a result of legal and cultural issues. The broad aspects of the corporate security components of your job are necessary to ensure the physical safety of your workforce and the protection of the physical infrastructure and property, to help manage your company through critical issues, and to provide governance and enforcement services when the rules and norms of the policies that govern your business are violated.

In some companies this may mean actually having your own police force to protect a large population, such as a campus environment, whereas in others this may mean the use of a multitude of partners and vendors to support a distributed workforce among hundreds of locations. The size and scope of your corporate security program should be based on the size of your business, the type of facilities and work environments your company uses, the industries you operate in, threats against your company or people, and a multitude of other considerations that help determine the need, size, and scope of the services you deliver. In this section I highlight the common programs that you should consider as foundational services necessary to protect an average company. These can be provided by handful of people or by thousands, depending on the scope of your operation. The important point is to understand the major responsibilities from an operations perspective to assist you in designing your corporate security service delivery platform.

This section is designed to give you a high-level conceptual understanding of each required functional area as well as suggested program attributes that will provide you with a general idea of service requirements and the businesses expectations.

Public and Workforce Protection

The terms *public protection* and *workforce protection* are broadly used to describe laws, policies, procedures, and services that are implemented to ensure the security, safety and health of employees and visitors within a workplace. These programs, often required by law, involve a life cycle of defining and identifying hazards or safety concerns, the implementation of programs and practices to protect from those hazards, and ongoing safety training and awareness education for employees. From the guards at the gates to the individuals tasked with site risk assessments to the individual employee who serves as a fire warden for their work area to support their fellow employees in an emergency—there are many components to an operational workforce protection program. In many companies there are separate functions that manage specialty areas such as health safety and industrial safety. The following section describes the most common components of an operational program that should be in place when architecting a holistic converged workforce protection security program.

Facilities Security

Facility security is the service function that maintains the environmental security necessities of your business. From how we secure our buildings, property, and assets to how we manage and control access, as well as credential people into our sites, the facilities security component is what most people refer to as "physical security." The polices you develop will dictate the rules and standards to guide the service levels you deliver. Organizations such as ASIS and similar professional security certification bodies provide prescriptive architectures that can be used as a road map for accreditation and expected industrial service levels. The following are base program attributes that you will need to implement no matter what size your organization is.

Credentialing: Credentialing includes the process and services used to determine the identity, background, and need for access levels into the company's facilities. This includes badge and ID management of employees and visitors.

Site Security: Site security is the program that evaluates the needs of the entire property from a security perspective. This includes the risk assessment processes such as the Homeland Security Common Assessment model or similar processes that evaluate the threat to and needs of the entire property. Decisions such as fences, barriers, gates, lighting, and even parking are contained within this function.

Building Physical and Electronic Security: From the types of doors and locks to the use of electronic access systems and security control systems, this function addresses the next tier after site security of the actual building. Key management, electronic access control, video security systems, physical intrusion security systems, panic alarms, gunshot detection systems, and all other process and systems used to control access and security of the building itself fall into this category. Practitioners need to ensure a life cycle approach to design, implement, monitor, and manage all control systems and processes implemented in any category, but especially this one because of the implications of failed access control or security monitoring platforms. Local laws often dictate additional requirements or restrictions, including worker safety laws, privacy laws, and, depending on your industry, industrial security laws. Ensure that your program takes into account not just the needs of your business based on risk, social acceptance, and the ability to enforce, but also the laws applicable to your operating locations.

Monitoring: Sometimes an area often overlooked is the monitoring of your facilities security platforms. Where do your alarms systems alert? What operating playbooks and special security instructions are provided if something is discovered? Do you have 24/7 monitoring or only during peak or off hours? Are these services provided internally by full-time employees, by contract employees, or do you use a managed security service as the basis of your monitoring program?

Alarms and video systems are only as good as the processes implemented to monitor them, yet not all instances require around-the-clock monitoring. By creating a tiered approach based on risk and need, you can develop your framework for enabling action based on the output of the systems you have implemented to protect your workforce.

Guards and Patrols: Depending on your business's type, location, and size, you may or may not need a physical security presence. A food retail location in the middle of New York City may have a very different need that the same retail store in the middle of Idaho. A site containing your primary data center may need something different than your small sales office in South America. Considerations such as uniforms, plain clothes, and armed or not armed are all components of the overall function that you must create as part of your program. Do your security officers act as a deterrence and alert authorities only, or are they expected to identify, engage, and perform first responder–like duties? Determining the need and the type of physical presence is a major project and decision for your company. Once these decisions have been made, whether you perform the function internally or contract with a professional security services firm is your next step. Components such as contract management to training oversight, post orders on a location-by-location basis, and security vehicle fleet management, guards, and patrols add an incredible level of capability to your program but also significantly increase your executive management function.

Emergency Response Processes: The development, documentation, and training of responders and your employees is incredibly important and should be considered a dedicated function. If there is a fire, shooting, medical emergency, or a weather-related issue, what should your employees and visitors do? Who is responsible for managing the issue? To add to the complexity, you may not have security personnel at all sites; therefore you must develop your program to account for volunteers or assigned duties by job function at a local site, such as a facilities manager, general manager, or others who act as an extended part of your organization in emergency situations. Simple decisions—such as who can make decisions during times of crisis, who can declare emergencies, or who should be notified—should all be made ahead of time and trained to ensure everyone knows their jobs. Further, interaction with local government public safety officials such as police, fire, and medical response personnel should be addressed as part of this process.

Training and Awareness: The final functional requirement in this service area to be mentioned here is training and awareness. If we expect our employees and visitors to act in a certain way, then we need to communicate and make them aware of the expectations, policies, and behaviors that the company requires in order to protect them and the interests of the business while they are at work.

Fire Protection

Although not always thought of as a core part of "security, risk, and privacy", fire safety services responsibilities often fall on the shoulders of a company's security programs through the public and workforce protection programs. In industries that have large campuses, chemical operations, or full-service public safety organizations, fire prevention and response services may be managed through another function. In fact, some large companies have their own fire response personnel and equipment to act as their first responders. In most cases, however, you need to account for the safety of your personnel during fire emergencies through a managed fire protection program. You need to consider three major services when developing worksite fire protection plans.

Fire Safety Assessments: This is the ongoing evaluation of your environment based on local fire codes and visual inspections of fire hazards within your business's physical locations. Assessment should be documented and gaps or issues evaluated and remediated, with specific accountability being assigned to trained personnel.

Fire Response Processes: Training first responders and employees how to respond to or evacuate from a fire emergency is a critical component of this service. The assignment and use of fire marshals in each physical working location and the training of first responder personnel on the use of fire suppression equipment such as fire extinguishers or built-in fire suppression equipment all come into play here. As the head of the organization that is responsible for protecting your employees and visitors, you need to create the policies and programs on how to respond to fire alarms and actual fires across your entire company and at every location. The speed with which people respond to fires and the training they have to effect that response could mean the difference between life and death in an actual emergency.

Fire Systems Monitoring: The final area in the fire protection service security in systems monitoring. Just like the other portions of your facility safety monitoring, local building codes and laws dictate what type of systems you implement, and most probably how they are monitored and dispatched. However, whether or not your fire alarm system is centrally monitored directly by the local fire department or uses a third party that then automatically dispatches fire personnel, you need to establish a plan for local monitoring and response to help during necessary evacuations and to communicate with fire department first responders.

Active Shooter Protection

In the United States and across the world, workplace shootings and homicides are a fact of life, and although the numbers are not at the level that most believe (in the United States, of an average of 9000 firearm murders per year, approximately 500 involve the workplace), this does not remove our responsibilities as employers and security executives to protect the workplace. Of the 518 workplace homicides that occurred in 2013, 77 were multiple-victim homicides, meaning that if horrific events like these were to occur in the environments you protect, there is strong statistical data that show it could involve multiple employees or visitors.

As the senior executive responsible for business operations protection, with or without regulatory compulsion, our jobs are to provide a safe and protected work environment for our business's employees to feel free from harm and to make their work environment someplace they want to be. The work environment is an incredible component of an employee's holistic satisfaction with their job, as well as a major component in creativity and work output. Your ability to provide a safe work environment directly contributes to your company's goals of employee retention and productivity management.

Workplace violence is not an easy issue to understand. Although the preponderance of US data shows that the majority of the attackers are either current or former employees of the business that is affected, and that most shooters are male, there are still many that involve domestic violence issues spilling over to the worksite. Another great statistical indicator is that the retail sector seems to have the largest number of incidents by industry, but government, hospitality, finance, and transportation also rank high. The fact is that those seeking to commit criminal activities with firearms or mentally disturbed persons are not easily bucketed into a clear profile that we can all see coming from a mile away. Different cultures, social issues, national policies, and the work environments themselves play into this horrible type of crime, but this doesn't make us helpless to prevent similar actions or reducing the impact if one were to happen. The following are the five components of an active shooter management plan that could help you save lives at your business.

People Prevention: In too many cases of workplace violence the same facts unroll at the end: (1) Everyone knew that the eventual shooter had people issues. (2) No one reported them or they were not acted on. (3) The individual spoke of violence or the use of weapons. (4) A workplace incident occurred and the appropriate intervention did not happen.

These are all solvable, starting with policy and right through how we manage our employees when they are in crisis. The first step is to set a firm and well-documented policy about workplace violence that clearly articulates zero tolerance for violent speech or actions. This must be a concept that the entire leadership teams buys into and must be enforced, meaning that Human Resources (HR) and the business takes proactive and definitive steps when acts of violence or threats of violence occur, every time, and without prejudice to position or level in the company.

The next part of your people approach must be to have a mechanism for your managers and HR professionals to report suspicious or concerning behavior and to have a team or a person responsible and trained to evaluate the potential threatening behavior. This mechanism must include communications, personnel issue evaluation protocols, site safety and security evaluations, behavior tracking, and intervention services for the employee in crisis if necessary.

Once you have these mechanisms in place, you must train your managers and HR team on the process to set clear expectations; they then are accountable for reporting behaviors that threaten the safety of the work environment. It is these early intervention programs that seek a resolution by supporting an employee through a crisis or removing a threat in a professional and well-thought-out way that often reduces the chances of workplace violence occurring.

Environmental Defense: As a security practitioner there are things that you can do to limit the opportunity of events happening and, if they do occur, to limit their impact. How we design access to our facilities, whether we require inspection of hand-carried items of our employees or visitors, and even what technologies we use to detect or alert of certain situations, such as a person with a gun or gunshots, are all pieces that equate to an environmental defense position that helps deter and prevent workplace shootings.

As in any other environmental security architecture review, the opportunity to manage the paths of people's movement to managed entries and exits force assailants to entry points that are often secured, monitored, and or staffed, allowing an early warning to happen. The use of locked doors, protected entry area lobbies and enclaves, and mantraps further reduce access to the main portion of a building; even if an individual makes it into a lobby area, it will take force, and the sound of an attack will provide an early warning to the remainder of the facility.

The use of technology can also come into play. For instance, newer camera and video analytics technology can use image recognition to determine that someone has a firearm (either a handgun or rifle). By adding these types of capabilities to only entrance locations or on your facility's perimeter, such as in approaches from parking areas, early detection can trigger proactive alerts that force a facility lockdown and automatically notify law enforcement. New technology such as shot detection that understands flash and sound waves can be deployed in critical areas or high-threat target areas such as lobbies, HR, and cafeterias and can alert security, law enforcement, and site personnel of an active issue. By speaking with your service providers or vendors, you can develop a proactive and pragmatic approach to a tiered, active shooter defense program.

These are not-all-or-nothing situations. Remember, you can create escalation protocols that implement certain procedures during credible threats or at sites with higher possibilities of violence resulting from the numbers of people or types of demographics or previous site history. Working with your HR and leadership organization is important because these types of plans and protocols need to be supported as an entire company effort, not cast as the singular efforts of a paranoid security expert. Through the use of data points including national statistics, internal personnel issues, investigative information, and gap assessment data about the location or sites themselves, normal prudent and responsible executives often come to the same conclusions and will work to ensure the protection of their employee base.

Employee Response: In the unlikely event that a shooting occurs, employees must be aware of what they need to do. There is a lot of discussion and questions around this: How do you train an entire workforce? At what level of detail should they be trained? Should the use of multimedia and videos be used? How effective is the training? These are all good questions, and it is an internal people-and-policy decision that your executive leadership and HR executive teams should be a part of and support. At the very minimum, however, people should know the simple basics of escape/hide out/take action. In fact, these are the same three basic principals that most professional and governmental trainers use when teaching how to survive an active shooter situation in the workplace or even at educational institutions. The first is to escape if you can do so safely. If you know the direction in which the shooting is occurring and can get out the building without crossing the path of the shooter, do so, and take as many people as you can with you. If you are not sure where the shooter is, or if he or she is in close proximity, hide. Get under or behind something that offers cover and concealment if possible. If it can be locked, even better. Always stay away from a window the shooter can look through. Be quiet and calm and wait for law enforcement to respond. Finally, take action if necessary. If your employee can't escape or has been found by the shooter, they have to know that it is OK to fight back. Their only choices at that point are to get shot or to fight; they need to fight and often attackers do not expect that. The more nonstop fight they bring to the attacker, using anything they have—from chairs to scissors to staplers—the more ability they have to survive.

Armed Security Response: An internal armed response is also an option, but should not be taken lightly. Untrained security guards or security personnel with a "carry license" is not a valid option. It often introduces more risk of an untrained person bringing another gun into the situation, potentially shooting innocent victims, and potential additional liability by setting an unrealistic expectation of being able to defend against something they are not trained for. Organizations that seek to have their own internal response capability are those mature organizations that already have an armed security program. Strict policies around who is armed and for what reasons, their initial and continuing training, use of force standards, and health and weapons proficiency requirements all need to be identified, managed, and enforced. If you do extend a standard armed security program into an active shooter response program, then your armed security personnel and even onsite law enforcement personnel should be trained in active shooter response. These are specialized certified programs that teach responders what to expect, how to engage shooters, and how to work with multiple agencies on a response. Again, this does not need to be an all-or-nothing protocol. Perhaps you have a higher threat at your site because of terminations or a mentally disturbed person who has recently threatened the site; by working with your business and legal executives, you can use trained and armed third partiers or law enforcement personnel to protect the facility until that threat subsides.

Partnering with Law Enforcement: Whether or not you have an onsite armed protocol, you need to partner with law enforcement. Local law enforcement will always be the first to respond to an active shooter situation, and the more they know about your business, your facility, and your capabilities, the better chance you will have to limit the impact of an active shooter incident. Through early planning and partnership you can work through issues such as how law enforcement will enter the building. Do they get their own key card or keys through a lock box on site, or do you fail doors open (the automated mechanism of unlocking doors after a triggered event like a power failure or alarm activation) during an active shooter situation? How big is the location? Do the responding offers on the day shift understand the layout of the site? If you have a mass causality incident, where can they set up a command post and get infrastructure quickly to respond? There are 100 more questions that you or your local chief law enforcement executive may want to ask each other, and the closer you partner, the better the outcome if you have an active shooter incident.

Criminal and Civil Investigations

If you think of your business as its own small city, you'll understand the concept that even the perfect city has its share of problems. Sometimes its citizens doing things they shouldn't and sometimes it acts of outsiders that cause problems. In any case it's the responsibility of the city's police department to investigate crimes or other issues, and in the context of a business, you are by default that police department. This doesn't mean you are the "law"; you are simply the agency that supports the investigation of negative-impact issues, matters, and activities that require investigation. In most cases it is the head attorney, or general counsel, for a company who serves as the company's "law."

From a segregation of duties standpoint, think of him or her as the US Attorney and you as a US Marshal. You are an extension of their authority within a company as they are charged with the responsibility to interpret policy, law, and other considerations with regard to what extent the business should or should not investigate and the outcomes of those matters. Although lawyers litigate and investigators investigate, it is, and always will be, your partners in the general counsel's office who provide the investigative oversight and legal guidance necessary to ensure an appropriate and legal service is being delivered. Significant criminal action has occurred against practitioners in our profession in major international companies that conducted internal investigations that crossed the boundary of criminal law, and they were charged accordingly in criminal courts. Creating the right framework of investigation approval and oversight, scope of authority, evidentiary management, forensic support, and interrogation or interview processes is critical to ensuring the successful outcome of any investigation.

Providing these services is critical, and like any other service you have to determine what type of investigations your business may need, who will provide those services, and what level of service you can provide internally or externally. Remember that it will not always be "you" providing those services. If the number of investigations that you support or have supported in the past in association with the number of external investigative supports includes utilization metrics that show that an internal full-time employee would be fully utilized, you may want to consider hiring a full-time investigator. The historical and institutional knowledge of a company often helps resolve many aspects of cases, such as who to contact, known problem areas, and how to work within the system. Additionally, from a converged perspective, experienced investigators can also be cross-trained to support other service areas such as event protection, executive security, and fraud prevention programs, as well as intelligence operations. If the metrics don't add up, make sure you establish vendors in each global region of operation and have pre-executed nondisclosure agreements and contract terms completed so when you need to call them, you do not waste any additional time finding a competent vendor or negotiating.

Typical investigative services include the following:

- Individual or entity background checks necessary in employment, due diligence, or in the support of general legal matters.
- Internal employment law matters such as misconduct and policy violations of employees and executives
- Theft (physical and technology-based)
- Economic diversion and sales crimes
- Theft of intellectual property such as corporate secrets, client lists, or sensitive business information
- Sexual harassment
- Workplace violence and threats of violence
- Potential violations of business and regulatory laws such as Office of Foreign Assets Control, International Traffic in Arms Regulations, and The Foreign Corrupt Practices Act
- Logistic and supply chain matters

This is just a sample of some of the most common issues you will be responsible for investigating. By spending time with experienced litigation, employment, or general practice attorneys at your business or firms that support your business, you can get a better historical perspective on what type of investigations you may be called on to support for your specific industry or business.

When developing an investigation services program, there are several import procedural and support elements that should be established to ensure that investigations are conducted, managed, and processed in such a way that protects the integrity of the investigation and associated processes. The most important is to establish the investigative approval process.

Who Investigates What: Believe it or not, one of the biggest issues in large organizations tends to be who does what when it comes to the word *investigation*. Investigations can happen in the area of HR, policy violations, contract issues—the list goes on and on. As the chief security officer you typically will not have the bandwidth or resources to manage every type of investigation, and often, some are better handled in specialty areas. Working with your partners in legal, establish the guidelines and framework for what issues or incidents are to be investigated by which organization and at what level. Have your legal teams manage that authoritative policy and ensure that all accountable and involved parties are educated. When deciding what your investigations group should focus on, start with a criminal act or an act that could potentially become a criminal act, or any issue that could result in a legal proceeding. Use the input from your legal partners regarding other issues they believe fall with in your sphere of responsibility. Make sure your investigators or vendors are experienced in the areas that you are accountable to investigate.

Investigative Approval Process: The investigative approval process should be a formal mechanism whereby policy or practice, the necessity, legalities, and corporate issues surrounding the need for a formal investigation should be reviewed and approved by the appropriate person or persons, who in most cases is an attorney. This formalized process protects the integrity of the investigation from claims of, for example, the misuse of power and ensures that the investigation is in line with local jurisdictional considerations. The use of a form or application that outlines the investigation, assumed targets, probable cause or initial report or statement, the extent to which the investigators can operate without receiving additional approval, and the types of evidence that are allowed to be collected should all bc documented.

Interview and Interrogation Process: The interview and interrogation process is sometimes one of the most useful tools in an investigative tool kit. In civilian and commercial settings, however, their use must be well managed to avoid civil tort actions or legal liability from local employment or privacy law. As in the investigation, approval of the use of the interview or interrogation process should be obtained and a standard applied to its use and who will participate. Often, if a company employee is to be questioned then a supervisor or a HR representative should be present. Also, who will be asking the questions and what their training and experience must be in order to conduct an interview should be determined. Trained interviewers with prepared questions and investigative purposes should be the foundation of the policy or standard you create around conducting interviews and interrogations.

Investigative Documentation: The use of applications, forms, or other methods to maintain overall organizational case management and the direct management of any given investigation is a necessity. Information, interviews, and data collected in support of an investigation need to be well documented in order to provide to attorneys, judicial systems, and law enforcement reports that can be used in official proceedings. Just like in public safety and law enforcement, reports of the investigative matter are critical when making cases and ensuring the integrity of a case as it goes through internal or external proceedings.

Many vendors offer applications that manage investigative processes and reporting. The use of a technical solution is important because it allows for cross-case intelligence development, historical reporting, case analytics and reporting, report change management and validation, and many other operational and management functions that increase the value of the data, reduce integrity concerns, and leverage processes to reduce resource issues.

Evidence Management: Following the rule of court in the management of evidence is crucial to establishing the integrity of that evidence as well as its admissibility during legal proceedings. Whether it is digital or physical evidence, the processes that manage chain of custody, evidence handling, and evidence interrogation should apply for every type of case, even if you believe it will never enter the judicial system. Many cases start out as an internal matter then turn into a case processed in a public venue where the initial evidence was critical in defending the business's position. From evidence logs to tagging to monthly evidence audit processes, establishing an evidence management program is essential to your investigations services framework.

Fraud Prevention

Depending on what type of industry or business you protect, fraud prevention is often an important part of defending it. Many different types of fraud affect businesses, from internal fraud to external fraud. Sometimes the fraudsters are after money, whereas other times they are after information. Sometimes they target your company; sometimes they target your customers or partners through you or vice versa. Investigate the types of fraud that affect or have affected your company in the past or similar companies in your industry. Work with your business to determine the probability and document a risk assessment that articulates the potential downstream results if fraud were to occur, then determine whether a fraud prevention program is necessary.

If a you and your business determine that the company is at risk, the two major functions within a fraud service that need to be established are fraud monitoring and fraud investigations. Fraud monitoring is the ability to look at specific types of data and, through an applied process of risk analysis, determine whether that operation or transaction was in someway fraudulent. Of course, the financial services industries have been doing this for decades, as have the insurance and, in more recent years, the health care industries. An entire technology industry has been established around fraud prevention and detection, and it has had great success in defending against fraudulent activity. But in order for your business to take advantage of these technologies, you must understand how fraud occurs or could occur in your business process. As we discussed in earlier chapters, in cyber defensive operations programs, you needed to use your business process workflow and identify controls and areas of opportunity for bad things to happen. In the context of fraud, that same process must occur, and you need to map those "indicators of fraud" and create real or probable fraud schemes specific for that business process. Once those fraud schemes are developed, you can evaluate what data components are necessary to automate the identification of that fraud and, if that data is not available, work with your business to create it. Once you understand how fraud could happen in your business, you have created probable fraud schemes, mapped out what would be indicators of those schemes, and instrumented your environment to collect that data, then you are ready to begin the prevention and detection process.

The other major area in fraud prevention operations is the investigation of fraud. Fraud investigations are considered a specialty area, and there are practitioners and vendors that are very experienced, even to the industry-specific level. Depending on the number and type of frauds you need to investigate, you may need to establish an investigative protocol in the investigative area specific to frauds, as mentioned above. Further, the importance of participating in industry and government fraud data-sharing programs cannot be overstated here. Many times fraudsters go from one victim company to another in the same industry or across several, and often those other victim companies are already investigating these crimes and can provide insight into TTP's and methods used by the fraudster. Specialty law enforcement organizations around the world also have fraud specialists who can be great partners in combating fraud.

Travel Security

As a business operations protection executive, your mission is to ensure the business can operate anywhere it needs to at any time. For many businesses, accomplishing the "anywhere" part often involves employees of the company traveling in support of the business, commonly referred to as business travel. A travel security program commits to providing a level of "protection" for employees when they travel, either in their own countries or broad. This doesn't mean having 24/7 protective agents surrounding them, but rather the ability to enable a basic five-step program that sets guidelines about business policy, enables effective risk management processes for travelers, and is able to react on behalf of your employee and in support of their protection when things go awry. The following are the basic five points needed to enable an effective business travel protection program:

Policy and Standards: These establish what is business travel and what is not and what is permissible to do while on business travel. This should be done in conjunction with your procurement, travel, HR, and finance teams and should cover approved travel methods and vendors. Additionally, the policy must indicate who can approve travel, how security standards will be set, and the responsibilities of management, the business, and the employee.

Travel Risk Management: In travel risk management you establish the framework and process for how travel security ratings are evaluated, assessed, and established. A commonly accepted method is to use a governmental model that establishes a color code based on the risk to any given region, country, or location. The color code should indicate the risk level, the reason, and what precautions or processes must be adhered to based on the risk level. For instance, if the travel code is orange, perhaps all travel to that location must be for important business only and must be approved by a BU executive in conjunction with the chief security officer. By being open about the evaluation process, providing clear guidance, and offering services to ensure the success of the process, your travelers will often be more accepting and cooperative when managing through travel protection issues.

Traveler Tracking: When bad things happen they typically are not announced beforehand and happen fast. In the terrorist attacks on the Mumbai Hotel in 2008 I was responsible for travel security in large, multinational organization that had six travelers in the direct vicinity. Within in 30 min of the attack we knew where each employee was and had made contact. In the following 90 min we had four contract armed security response teams en route to the area to collect our associates, and within 4 h of the attacks unfolding we had exfiltrated all employees from the area of operation. That was not luck or happenstance. The integration of our risk monitoring service with our global travel database enabled a quick view of any traveling employee associated with any geolocated issue. From there the mandated traveler information database that integrated with our employee directory and could be manually and directly updated by the employee allowed for quick access via multiple communication methods.

These types of traveler monitoring services are important to establish. If there are travel accidents with aircraft or trains, or political or criminal activity in any given area, time is of the essence when locating your travelers and making them safe. Additionally, preestablishing agreements for security, transportation, and emergency services during travel needs to be contracted ahead of time. Many risk and insurance organizations within companies can assist in purchasing addendum traveler protection in association with existing corporate policies; travel-specific assistance services are also available form companies that specialize in this area.

Traveler Communications: As mentioned above, communicating with your travelers is important when bad things happen, but communicating with them before and after is just as important. Inciting the right behavior for self-protection can often be done through overt and direct communications with your travelers. When your travelers book travel, make it a part of the process to send them a message that the company is aware they are traveling and if possible provide them with bullet points of things to do or avoid that are specific to their travel. In the company intranet sites or in corporate bulletins, provide periodicals on travel safety and give your employees a mechanism to reach out and get their questions answered.

Make it a policy that travelers provide multiple methods of communication, emergency contact information, and any information if they intend on deviating from their planned itinerary. Use mass or targeted notification systems for automated delivering of emergency communications to travelers; consider using a third-party service with a global toll-free number for travelers to reach out to at any time of they have issues. Encourage travelers to notify security after their trip if they run into unusual situations or concerning happenings on their trip, which you can reutilize as intelligence for future travelers.

Crisis Response: Make travel safety and security issues part of your company's all-hazards response protocols. Create a top 20 "what if" or probable incident list based on your business's general travel profile, and create preplanned standard operating procedures for those specific crises. Designate and train a specific travel emergency management team, and if your business is large enough and requires it, consider multiple teams in multiple global regions.

By establishing a travel security program for your business, you create the underpinnings of a successful mechanism by which you can ensure you are protecting your employees wherever they are. Consider the use of third-party experts to assist you in establishing and operating your program where necessary. Let your employees know that the company cares about their safety by communicating regularly, and you'll be impressed by the response from your employees the first time you help get them out of harm's way and safely home.

Kidnap and Ransom Operations

Kidnap and ransom operations (K&R) is separate from your travel program because it does not always involve travel (though often it does). This specific criminal risk around employee safety has different risk areas depending on your position in a company. For instance, all employees may be at risk when traveling in certain parts of South America, but perhaps only a highly public and wealthy executive may be at risk in the continental United States. Your K&R program needs should be assessed by a professional in this discipline and is often available through your company's insurance company. Depending on the industry, how public your company or executives are, if there are any contentious issues, if your industry or company is targeted by activists, and of course your company's travel profile determine your risk level and the specific response needs of your company.

If your company is determined to be at risk, you need to develop and enact a set of policies and plans specific to K&R. The policies should determine who is covered (such as executives, all employees, or employees and their families) by K&R services and what your company will and will not provide in the way of K&R services. These plans must also determine who manages the incident, what the K&R team comprises (such as security, HR, legal), and who has the authority for funds transfer approvals.

K&R planning is not a pleasant process but is necessary. The good news is that almost all insurance companies that provide K&R insurance also partner with a specific firm that will manage the K&R crisis incident beginning to end and act as your on-the-ground negotiator and personal consultant. Additionally, these firms often provide group training for your internal crisis management team. By leveraging their knowledge, planning early, and training on a consistent basis, you will be better situated to successfully manage and get through a K&R situation, compared with getting a call at 2 a.m. one day and never have trained on it before.

Executive Protection

Executive protection (EP) is a generic term used to describe those services delivered to executives or dignitaries who require an additional level of personal protection. Although most people typically automatically associate this with US Secret Service–like protection, there are many levels and different services that can be applied to this type of program.

Before we talk about setting up a program, however, we should discuss need. Simply put, not all businesses need this level of protective service. In fact, most don't. This type of program—whether simply providing vetted transportation services or delivering 24/7 close-in protection operations—should be (as everything else is) assessed based on risk and need. Until a risk assessment is complete, you will not be able to even understand what type of services you need. Are there threats against your chief executive officer because of recent employment actions? Is one of your executives an easily identified public speaker on a contentious issue? Do your executives travel through high-crime areas where carjacking is known to occur? Is one of your executives the target of a negative social media campaign? Depending on the answers to these and many more questions, you need to establish a reasonable and prudent level of services that align to the level of risk assessed.

The assessment is important for more than one reason. One of the biggest is the cost associated with providing EP and how it is allotted. Services that are not deemed necessary for the purposes of supporting a bona fide threat risk against an executive could actually be recorded as direct compensation to the executive involved, leaving the recipient with a significant tax liability. If you are a US-based company, the Internal Revenue Service provides a specific rule in Section 132 of the US Tax Code that creates approved mechanism for evaluating and delivering personal protective security services to corporate executives as a result of need at the office, at home, and while traveling. The rules are somewhat specific, but building a program within these guidelines significantly reduces the tax liabilities of the executive involved.

As mentioned before, not all protection comes at the "presidential" level. In fact, sometimes the need is specific only to travel or while at the office. The following are some services that you can consider as different levels of protective services that can be developed internally or with partners to apply the right level of protection when needed.

Facilitated Transportation: People often forget about the one basic principle of EP: getting your executive in a position where he or she does not need emergent services, either health-related or true protective services. In fact, the most threats our executives face on a daily basis is the threat of personal injury in motor vehicle accidents. Providing driver-related services is a great first step in helping keep your executives safe. Vetted, credentialed, and trained drivers allow your executive to focus on their work, calls, email, and so on instead of trying to operate a motor vehicle while doing all three. A trained and experienced driver can keep your executive out of harm's way and actually increase their safety because of the training they receive on defensive and offensive driving operations. They key here, of course, is to use trained drivers, which does not mean people from a black car service who show up to pick up "the boss." These are individuals who have completed specific driving courses that providing training on accident avoidance, defensive driving, protective driving techniques, high-speed operating skills, and advanced weather motor vehicle operations. This level of service creates a base capability that measurably increases your executives' protection profile simply by removing the risk of self-driving from the equation.

Protection Operations: As the risk increases and the potential for physical harm is identified, you need to consider the use of "bodyguard" services for certain members of your executive team when the need arises. These services can be delivered both armed and unarmed, and in either case they are provided at a level commensurate with the risk of harm. Assessments and planning are necessary to determine the maturity of the threat and the type of coverage necessary to deter or stop a threat. Protection operations is a framework of protection services that encompasses movement planning, site-defensive operations, crisis evacuation, and defending in place planning as well. This type of service must be delivered by a certified and credentialed expert who has received training in this area. Many companies choose to use a third-party service only when they need the specified services, whereas others staff at a minimum level to continuously provide a specific baseline capability of protection, intelligence operations, and transportation serves and use third parties as the resource requirements increase for any given operation.

There are a couple key things to keep in mind when developing your services and plans for protective operations. First, you should never create a false sense of security for your executive. If you claim that you are providing a specific level of protection but actually you have no capabilities, resources, or intention to do so, be transparent in what they can expect. Second, do the appropriate advances and planning necessary to defend against the level of identified or assessed threat. Don't just throw a driver and an off-duty cop with a gun at a problem that demands a multiroute, multivehicle, medium armed protection team. Knowing routes, hospitals, venue layouts, hotel security details, and managed transportation services is part of the planning. Driving the routes at the same times of the day on the same days of the week in advance, and liaising with local law enforcement and response personnel, are all part of the necessary package.

The point of this security is simple: If you are going to provide protective services, understand what is necessary, prepare for your committed level of service, and ensure you have the right resources providing the service.

The Executive 360: The Executive 360 (E-360) is what we refer to as the ability to understand and impact the overall threat of your executive staff. Just because your chief executive officer has gone home for the day doesn't mean he is any less at risk. When he takes a well-deserved and much-needed vacation to his vacation home, how has the threat landscape or risk changed? Is he or she more of a target there?

Creating an E-360 means understanding all aspects of your executive's life and providing the services necessary to protect him or her. Home evaluations the installation of and training on home protection and alarm systems, panic alarms, safe rooms, and even disaster planning (e.g., generators) compose another extended level of service you can consider as part of your overall protection. Some executives appreciate this level of service, whereas others consider it intrusive, but it is your responsibility to explain the options and actions required to create the level of protection the business deems necessary. Remember, as the senior security executive you may work for that executive in some fashion, but the services are being provided at the behest of the company, and in order for you to successfully complete your required objectives, there are parts of the protection program that extend way outside the four walls of the corporate buildings.

Here are a few of the advanced services you may want to consider when creating an EP program with advanced E-360 services:

- Home security, safety, defense, and disaster evaluations and project management
- Vacation security management
- Family threat reviews and remediation
- Family security education
- Executive hometown law enforcement liaison
- Executive and family DNA sampling/K&R kit escrow management

All of these help increase the total security of your executives and create the E-360 certainty of your EP mission.

Intelligence: Intelligence operations is a core component in the life cycle of EP operations. Monitoring social media and keeping tabs on previous targets of interest who have had run-ins with your executives are included in this area. Although many of these services are now offered by experienced former intelligence professionals from various government services, there are simple processes that you can use to alert you to a threat level change, a new threat, or any potential issues that could affect your protectee.

The first line of defense is to ensure that you have policy and processes in place that automatically route calls, letters, or packages to a trained person for inspection before delivery to your protected executive. At a technology level, create multitiered, specific Google alerts that alert you when new information about your protectee is available on the Internet. Use your cyber security data leakage protection technology to create rules that associate words of violence or harm in the same message containing your protectee's name.

Whether or not you are using a third party to provide intelligence operations, create weekly, monthly, and quarterly intelligence operations checklists, with someone assigned to and responsible for providing the service, to drive oversight and assurance into your operations. At an executive level, require that monthly or quarterly reports be generated with the current intelligence and threat levels of your existing protectees. Finally, on an annual or semiannual basis, review with your protectee the intelligence you have for them to have transparency and a voice in the protection they are receiving.

When providing EP operations and services, remember the "Six P's": Proper Preparation Prevents Piss Poor Performance; poor performance could mean a dead executive. Use trained personnel, with the right services for the right level of threat every time.

Business Resilience

The term *business resilience* refers to the triad of operations that ensures the continuity of operations through a consolidated effort of business continuity management, disaster recovery services, and the ability to execute during crisis. Many businesses focus on one or two of these components, but it takes all three to support the totality of operations. The following is a brief introduction to each of the services necessary to a successful program.

The first leg of the business resilience triad is the business continuity program, often referred to as "BCP." BCP is a defined set of processes that starts as an evaluation of how a business operates, how various components of the business value chain may be affected and the downstream residual impact if something were to occur, and dependencies and linkages to each one of the business components and how they may be affected. The second major part of BCP is the operational planning aspect itself. This answers the question, "If this part of the business process were to fail, how would we continue operations?" The final part of the BCP service is the testing, validation, and verification that the assumptions made and planned for will actually work in times of crisis. Sometimes called "tabletop exercises," sometimes full-blown BCP exercises, these tests and evaluations ensure that when a crisis occurs, the functional plans created are truly capable of realistic operations.

BCP experts traditionally reside within the business organization itself, as they have the best understanding of how the business works, are part of business operations every day, and will be there when the business needs to execute against the plan. In fact, this is the preferred method of BCP development. Fluctuations to that structure include providing centralized practitioner consulting services with BCP experts who help train assigned BCP resources in each BU. This helps create consistency, and a specific level of assurance to the standards, while having the function remain within the BU. The final variation is the use of a centralized services group that provides business impact analysis, business continuity planning, and testing and verification as a service to all parts of the business. This reduces the necessity for planning experts within the BU; however, it is still important to have accountable individuals as the liaisons and internal experts as part of the in-BU service delivery team.

The second major component of business resiliency services is the disaster recovery program, often referred to as "DRP." DRP operations and functions are typically the responsibility of IT and facilities. IT delivers recovery operations for technology service platforms and operating centers. From network connectivity through application restores, the process by which IT creates redundancy of operations and the ability to recover operations at the time of the disaster involving technology is a critical part to the disaster recovery program. Whether it's redundant hot sites or on-retainer cold site infrastructure with available lease equipment on demand, your IT organization should be prepared to re-create the technology necessary to operate your business.

From a facilities perspective, disaster recovery involves creating the availability of business operations facilities in general. Whether it's the restoration of normal services in a building affected by a storm or fire, or the establishment of an emergency operations location because of a full disaster at a primary location, facilities must be prepared as an integral component of service operations to create the physical locations necessary to operate the business based on the business continuity plan.

The final leg of the three-part business resiliency program is crisis management operations. Crisis management is the ability to manage through an incident or disaster, relying on previously developed business continuity planning, the disaster recovery capabilities established as part of the planning, and knowledgeable crisis coordinators who can facilitate crisis operations. Crisis management should be an all-hazards approach and use a standard framework of crisis and disaster management; for example, the national incident management system developed by the United States Forestry Service, originally for forest fires and now managed by the Department of Homeland Security, is a foundational crisis management program for the US government. Whatever framework you'd choose to use, you must ensure that members of your entire organization—from your chief executive officer down to individual contributors—are aware of their responsibilities and trained on them as well (at least on a yearly basis).

If BCP, DRP, and crisis management are the three legs to the business resiliency "stool," then it is the integrated use of a technology operations platform that creates the "seat." Specific technology operations platforms have been designed and created for small businesses to major multinational corporations. They are available in locally installed application form or as services in the "cloud" and are designed to help you plan, document, and execute your entire business resiliency program. If a disaster occurs in a certain region of the world, how do you know what assets are in place or what business operations happen at that location? How do you pull up a business continuity plan specific for any part of the business that's affected? Are your crisis operations pulling the right business continuity plans? Are they monitoring and maintaining the return to normal operations or the management of the crisis activities and dispersing that information to the decision-makers? This is the job of a technology operations platform for business resiliency.

When considering and evaluating these plans, here are a few suggestions: First, don't put all your eggs in one basket, meaning, if you deploy the technology into your only data center or a primary data center that doesn't have active backup operations at another location, and the disaster was to occur at that site, you'd be operating from manual processes and printed documentation. Consider the use of cloud services if a multi–data center resilient environment does not exist in your business. Second, consider creating policy that requires the consistent use of centralized technology. BUs often have varying levels of maturity and often employ their own standards or templates. Attempting to decipher different documentation formats during the time of a crisis is a waste of time and a burden on crisis operations. Standardize how all three components of business resiliency operations will be documented, managed, and reported. Ensure that a centralized repository is available for crisis leaders and their backups. Simply having a printed version of a plan with two people who report to the same site is not going to be helpful if it's the entirety of the site that is affected.

If business resiliency programs are not consistent, managed, or well developed at your business, be the leader in creating the total picture. Just having disaster recovery plans or just having business continuity plans that don't reference the business process, the assets, and the recovery of those assets in any specificity will become mostly useless during crisis operations. By the same token, if those individuals responsible for leading through a crisis have not been trained, are not capable of an all-hazards approach, and have not practiced the use of command-and-control crisis operations at a multitier level, then they will be ineffective during a real crisis. As the senior-most executive for business operations protection, it is your responsibility to ensure the business is capable of operations or the recovery to operations when critical issues happen.

Specialties

In closing out this section of the implementation of a corporate security function within your converged security organization, it's important to realize that although we've covered high-level services that help protect and manage the physical portions of your operations, depending on your industry and type of business and the services or products you deliver, there may be additional specialty functions that you must consider as part of your corporate security program. For instance, perhaps you're a manufacturing organization that relies on a global supply chain. Protection specialists in supply chain security assurance may be necessary to help develop a program that ensures the ability of your business to operate continuously through the security of the totality of your supply chain network, including supply chain fraud, supply chain theft, and a variety of other issues associated with supply chain protection. If your company's "secret sauce" is a significant component of your revenue or business operations, then intellectual property protection services may be another specialty that you should consider. Intellectual property protection spans many different industries, from technology to consumer and even media and entertainment. IP protection has its own legal profession and security profession; if you're the individual responsible for ensuring the success of your protection program, take the time understand whether intellectual property protection services is something you need to consider.

There is no one-size-fits-all when it comes to developing a corporate security strategy around public safety, investigations, business resiliency, fraud protection, and all the other things we've talked about in the section. Take the time to evaluate your needs, the industry you serve, and other programs instantiated within like entities, if necessary, to provide a comparison and guide the program you need to create.

OPERATIONAL RISK MANAGEMENT

Whether responsible for risk management or not, the next critical function necessary for you to implement as part of any converged security program is operational risk management. This section takes a look at the minimum components of a framework you should consider having in place to support risk operations for your business, make intelligent risk decisions, and provide meaningful business input into the overall enterprise risk management (ERM) process.

Before you get into the components of the framework necessary to help support overall risk operations at your business, we should focus on the term *operational risk management* and understand the difference between that and ERM. If you were to look for a specific definition on operational risk management, the closest you might come is a description of a life cycle process of risk elements such as risk assessments, risk decision-making, risk control development, and risk management results (e.g., risk avoidance, acceptance, or mitigation). In the context of this book and this section, this is actually a great definition; as the senior-most operational security, risk, or privacy expert in your business, you need to implement a program that helps to define risk, make decisions around that risk, and manage risk specific to business operations that is not within a specialty area (such as tax, finance, or legal) or like technical risks. It's really that simple. Business operations protection management means that, when looking at the entirety of the business operation process, you will find risks that need to be managed. Sometimes it's your decision, sometimes it's somebody else's, but in the end the organization itself must be held accountable and responsible for evaluating risks within its operational platforms being managed.

The confusion that often happens in this area is around the difference between operational risk management and ERM. *Enterprise risk management* is the umbrella term for the evaluation of the totality of risks that affect a business.

As mentioned in the previous paragraph, there are many business-specific risks that need to be evaluated and accounted for. There are legal risks and regulatory risks and financial risks all that have an impact on the business. Then, within the business operation itself there are operations risks—around IT risk, security risk, business process risk—that you support. ERM creates models, measurements, and methods to evaluate and manage the total implication of all the business's risks. Operational risk management feeds into that service.

Risk Life Cycle

The risk life cycle references the totality of the independent functions that help discover, measure, prioritize, and act on risk issues within your environment. This life cycle creates a repeatable, measured, and accountable framework that enables the sustainability of your risk process and, if implemented properly, ensures a fair and equitable baseline by which to measure all risks. As the seniormost security, risk, and privacy operations executive, you are accountable for implementing programs and processes that deliver this life cycle in the areas of operation you are responsible for. Many times, lack of organizational integration or know-how creates independent pockets of how organizations evaluate, think, and react to risk items. For executive management and the business to make informed and sound decisions about risk prioritization, risk action, and resourcing risk reduction efforts, they need a calibrated mechanism that establishes a quantitative measurement capability across all of their business interests.

Governance Risk and Compliance

For many organizations, the instantiation of a framework that creates this life cycle ability is often called governance risk and compliance, or GRC. GRC is commonly used to refer to risk technology and automation platforms that assist in the collection of risk information, the analysis of that information, and the life cycle management of decision-making and risk mitigation programs. Organizations use GRC programs to provide consistent capabilities of how to collect and document information about many different types of business risk. The magic of these programs, however, lies in their workflow and process compliance architectures that deliver transparency, escalation, and accountability of action. Most GRC platforms, when enabled, provide risk notification services, metrics documentation and reporting, risk aging and escalation services, and a host of other risk process workflow actions that help businesses identify, track, and manage the continuing onslaught of identified risks within their organization.

Accountability

The key to any risk program is risk accountability. Risk accountability is the process by which risk is assigned and owned by the business, decisions are assured and validated, and risk mitigation or management processes are adhered to. Without this very important aspect of the risk operational framework, the totality of the work your team does may be all for naught, or you might waste precious hours and resources attempting to resolve an issue that, quite frankly, isn't yours to resolve, nor are you capable of changing. When I meet with security and risk executives and the topic of risk management comes up, I often ask who's responsible for managing the risks that are discovered (hint: it's a trick question). It still amazes me that many say that they are accountable for it. There is a huge difference between being accountable for a risk management program and being accountable for the risk. The only person who can be accountable for the risk is the person who owns it, and typically that is the executive responsible for the business function where that risk resides. Businesses must implement thorough risk management an authoritative process that assigns risk, demands accountability, and tracks quantitatively the reduction of risk as prescribed by your business's executive staff.

To ensure this, you must implement a formalized business risk management process that clearly assigns a risk owner and the executive accountable to remediate that risk. The process should be inclusive by both the risk management program and the business to evaluate the risk and potential remedies, and decide the level to which the risk should be remediated, and then make the final risk remediation decision. Remember, that can be one of several solutions including risk remediation, risk transfer, or risk acceptance. If risk acceptance is part of your overall program—and it should be—the risk acceptance process should be a multistage approval process, whereas risks above a certain measurement must be validated through a risk management organization and ratified by a governance group. As a chief information security officer, chief security officer, or even chief risk officer, our job is not to "approve" or "disapprove" risk acceptances. Our job is to ensure that the risk process is being followed, that the risks are being evaluated under the appropriate standard, and that those risks that need additional level of governance and oversight, however they will be handled, are escalated to the appropriate authorities. By establishing yourself as the authority in your office for the process, not the risks themselves, you force business owners to take a closer look at the risks their business's have and to take accountability in driving remediation efforts for the overall protection of the company or agency.

Enterprise Risk Management

Finally, I want to close this section on business operations risk by revisiting the function of ERM and your responsibility to support its success. As previously mentioned, ERM evaluates the totality of risk issues within a company or agency across multiple risk vectors such as finance, tax, legal, and cyber. ERM is not an audit, and does not evaluate the effectiveness or efficiencies of your control architecture; however, its job is to identify risk items that have a meaningful impact on the risk posture of the company and has a responsibility and the accountability to report if risk remediating efforts seem appropriate, are resourced, and are plausible to reduce the level of risk necessary to protect the business. The implications of cyber risk to many business continues to grow, and in some industries you will consistently be at the forefront of high- or critical risk issues that ERM practitioners need to focus on.

Security practitioners often consider ERM to be yet another audit function rather than the business operations protection entities they themselves are as well. Programs typically come into conflict when either one does not have a clear understanding of the other's intentions, or of the risks or risk remediation programs in play. True transparency, education, and consistent communication allow security, risk, and privacy operations teams to work more closely and better with ERM functions to share information operations about risk reduction efforts in general and to support each other in gaining better insight into the technical and detailed aspects of the risks at hand. As a business executive in your organization, a leader of people, and a senior security practitioner, your job is to support the cohesive intraorganization processes that not only helps identify and manage risk in your own area but also supports the totality of the risk reduction program for the entire corporation.

CONTROLS ASSURANCE

As security, risk, and privacy practitioners, we are often forced into the react, not respond, mode of working. That means that because of our own lack of preparation, a changing threat environment, or a more successful adversary, we are forced to implement actions, controls, or programs that only react to specific unforeseen events. In the respond mode of working, you are able to utilize existing controls, programs, and services to effect the necessary actions to defeat the advisory. The latter is not easy, and it takes an active ability to ensure that the investments and efforts that you have made on behalf of your organization are adequate, valid, and have the efficacy necessary to protect the organization. This is what is called "controls assurance," and it is the fourth pillar that drives operational execution.

To start with, controls assurance is not audit or ERM. Audit's job is to determine whether the company has the controls necessary and to establish whether they are in place and operable. ERM's function is to measure and report on risk, the impact of risk, and programs implemented to reduce risk. The controls assurance function is developed to help you, the security executive, decide whether the controls implemented are not only in place and are working, but that they are necessary in providing the function they were originally implemented for.

We often implement controls for a specific vulnerability or a protection service necessary to defend the business at a point in time; we turn it on, we walk away, and that control just keeps on working (or not). We never look back to reevaluate why the control was put in place. Is the threat that we are defending against still viable in our organization? Is this control even needed? If it is, are there other places within the business that could benefit from leveraging this type of control? Is the control still effective, working, reporting, and stopping bad things from happening? If the control is not needed, can those control costs and associated resources be reinvested in gap areas awaiting remediation?

Those questions are the core essence of what controls assurance is all about. By instantiating a controls assurance function and program, you can be confident that you have the appropriate data to make decisions about your control infrastructure, investments, and certifications and attestations about those controls. The worst situation you can be in is being asked about a specific capability or control and not being confident in the answer. You have to stop and ask yourself, "Am I sure—really *really* sure—that the control not only works, but is even in place?" I once worked for a short time at a company and was asked to sign a certification statement about their intrusion detection program. Although I had been briefed by members of the existing security team that the company did have an IDS that was being monitored by an in-place network operations center, I had not yet begun a controls assurance program and had seen no evidence that IDS was in place and working. So I asked the ISO program analyst who had requested my signature to "show me" the IDS platform. He took me to a security engineer who might have knowledge of it. The security engineer said that they outsourced it to IT and it was monitored by their networks operation center. So I asked him to bring me to the network operations center and show me where it was being monitored. When we got to the network operations center, neither the supervisor nor the analyst responsible for monitoring the IDS (which the security program was actually paying for) had any idea what an IDS even was. When they called someone at home who might know more, he verified that they used to watch it, but because of a network issue several months earlier they disconnected the IDS just in case it was the IDS that was causing the issue (although it was proven that the IDS had nothing to do with the network issue at that time). This meant, of course, that for over half a year the entire global infrastructure was not being monitored for intrusion detection, and they wanted me to blindly sign a document stating that it was operational. Lesson learned.

Even if you are the individual who installed the technology, your position as the accountable executive responsible for that control infrastructure should be "trust but verify." Changes happen, networks move, physical infrastructures (buildings) move, and life goes on—all of which affects the controls that have been implemented over time. The only way to ensure that controls are in place, operational, and effective is to test them. It is through the process of evaluating whether they are still work using supporting evidentiary material like logs and control systems output, or actually testing them through red teaming, that you will ever know how effective they are.

Of course, to start the entire process around controls assurance you really need controls documentation. The effort around documenting the controls must start with the business case of why there were implemented in the first place.

Your continuing controls assurance monitoring program should establish a base level of efficacy requirement against the specific threat area, and that should be your primary metric for identifying whether the control is effective. If the threat environment changes, so should your metric. Other important information to gather includes what categories this control works for. For instance, you may have purchased it for a specific function that it has, but it also protects against 20 or more other areas. You may be using only 10% of the functionality, and so when an issue comes up in another area you can refer to your controls assurance program's available controls listing and potentially reutilize that asset in a different way through the other 90% of the functionality you're not using. Controls verification, investment or reinvestment opportunities, and resource leveraging are just a few of the important outputs of a good controls assurance program.

Another important output is the topic of transparency. Transparency is the underlying factor that helps you evaluate your ability to defend your business. As a senior security executive, your functional responsibility includes your ability to create an operational life cycle of touch points that utilizes the OODA (observe, orient, decide, and act) loop methodology to help your organization prepare, regroup after incidents or issues, and replan as necessary to maintain the higher affective model of being a "responsive organization,", not a reactive organization. Transparency of your controls environment and assurance into the controls' effectiveness are both key to your ability to make well-informed decisions and enable critical decisions, but these are not the only benefits. Transparency works both ways, and your ability to provide a verifiable view into the company's security, risk, and privacy controls environment to your business leadership, internal and external audit functions, ERM, and others who need this information in their own functional jobs or to support their decisions shows your ability to function as an integrated entity, supporting their needs, and demonstrates your leadership skills.

Your controls assurance program enables the services you deliver, your executive responsibilities, and your business as a whole. It demonstrates not only the leadership skills mentioned above but also your skills to manage the business's resources, continue to leverage and create efficiencies when available, and create a truth-in-services assurance level to build confidence in your company's ability to protect itself.

CLIENT FOCUS

Security and privacy issues have become one of the most highlighted areas in business today. Organizations went from never even hearing the word *security* in their relationships with their customers to having contractual security and privacy issues as one of the largest hurdles in the customer acquisition process. We do this for a living, and we know how difficult the issues surrounding security, risk, and privacy considerations are. Nonpractitioners find our space akin to being dropped into another country and not having any language skills whatsoever. As a business leader managing security, risk, and privacy programs, a part of your success is your ability to take clients' complex security and privacy concerns and turn them into a vehicle of trust, a business differentiator for your company's go to market, and essentially a nonissue in general. To accomplish this you need to become client focused and establish programs and services that take into consideration the needs of your business outside of your actual business operations protection responsibilities and create a trust model necessary to operate in today's world.

The importance of being the face of trust, company transparency, and the mechanism of access to your company or agency in the areas of security, risk, and privacy for your peers can't be understated. From sales and field support, client engagement, and trust management programs to metrics for market impact, the ability for your company to compete successfully relies on the way the market and your customers perceive your company's capabilities in your areas of responsibility. Further, when companies do not successfully create this trust connection nor the ability both to articulate their position and to protect their clients' interests, questions and in absence of answers tend to develop. Companies refusing to answer or that cannot answer questions regarding their security posture tends to balloon into significant business obstacles. Successfully creating client-focused programs removes those obstacles before they become a problem.

There are four basic service areas that you can focus on to deliver the quickest and most impactful mechanisms that support client trust. How they are implemented, structured, and delivered are entirely up to you. As with anything else, it depends on the size of your organization, the availability of resources to support different types of business operations, and the success it delivers over time to your company. In most programs I have developed, I created an independent client trust or client security management team whose sole focus is to deliver the services detailed below with direct integration into the company's sales force, go-to-market teams, and customer service entities. In fact, it has been those organizations that received these services that have mostly funded these services as the value goes way beyond my area of operation and directly affects their ability to be successful as well. This is true business integration.

Delivering Trust

The funny thing about trust is that either you have it or you don't. There's really no gray area. Either people believe you based on your actions, deeds, and all the information you present, or they have doubt. If there is doubt, there is no trust. Your job is to create an overwhelming level of professionalism, transparency, information overload, and expertise that delivers trust without ever allowing doubt to enter the process. To accomplish this you need to go back to the basics of delivering transparency and truth of service and how you communicate with your customer base and business prospects. The data you collect, the validation you provide, the legal certification of statements, and the mechanisms used to deliver that data are all very important. The following outlines some service capabilities you may want to implement.

The basis for the remainder of this section starts with how we review, collect, and articulate our business's position on security, risk, and privacy. My guess is that if you looked across business presentations your sales force has created, terms your marketing organization has used, and other statements made by people outside your security organization, your hair would turn white in a moment. In the absence of good documentation people create their own, whether or not it is their responsibility to do so. Broad statements like "bulletproof," "hacker-proof," "24/7," "Fort Knox," "100%," and so on and so forth somehow make their way into business materials where they have no right being. Documenting your security position and capabilities in a variety of areas ahead of time reduces the complexity in the presales process, the sales process, the postimplementation customer support process, and even the audit process. Data you collect, although at times articulated differently, will always be the same information you present in all of those areas because it is the truth, and it is your job to create transparency to that truth. Of course, the hard part is deciding where to start. Here are a few areas where you can begin to collect information; create descriptive information on programs, services, the controls and protection architecture; and begin to compile a catalog that allows you to go create other data sets necessary to support your business:

Security and Privacy Policy: Everyone will ask you for your security policy. Although the detailed aspects of each component of your policy need not be provided most of the time, the high-level outline of your policy, by which standards it was created, and how it aligns to the most common referenceable frameworks (such as ISO, ISACA, NIST) should be included. Sometimes, clients demand that your policy meets theirs, and of course that is nearly impossible. If you were to do that for every client is you would be changing it every day. By creating a view into and a description of your policy and standards environment and how they map back to the standards, you can talk your clients through how it aligns to theirs and how it meets the major categories of standards in most regulatory managed environments.

General Enterprise Security Management: People want to know that security is important to your company. The best way to show them this is to actually show them. This means providing transparency into how your operation works, how security is structured within the company, what oversight programs are in place, and how security, risk, and privacy interact with programs like ERM, audit, and higher-level corporate functions such as your executive committee and the board of directors. This shows your level of maturity and your business's commitment to professional security organization.

Enterprise Security Protection: As most studies show, 80% of all security issues are due to poor security hygiene. General enterprise security management is the ability to document and describe in layman's terms how you perform these general hygiene issues such as logging, patch management, configuration assurance, facilities access assurance, and visitor management. By describing the basic hygienic programs and ensuring the consistency of the controls, policies, and standards that your company attests to, you show that not only have you thought of these issues, you have instantiated programs to ensure their compliance.

Monitoring and Threat Management: One of the first issues that most people fail to describe well is how they monitor their environment and manage threats. From intelligence to security operation centers to outsourced managed security services agreements, people want to know that you actually look at what is happening in your business. Many people suggest that by showing your monitoring program you are potentially revealing things that could put your company at risk. I have yet to meet a practitioner who has had a security incident occur because of his or her presentation of information about the basics of how they manage threats or monitor there infrastructure. In fact, many mature organizations that have full-time critical incident response centers or security operation facilities actually invite clients in for tours. Think of that for a moment. You are a client deciding between two or three companies, and one invites you to sit inside their critical incident response center, review their functionality, and ask questions about their ability to monitor. Who would you trust?

Data Center Security: Data center security, if that is part of your business, is always critical in certification and accreditation processes and a component of most contracts. Whether it is your data center or the one you outsource to, the ability to articulate the security program—from gates and guards to advanced cyber defense posture—is your responsibility. This needs to include factual documents that can be backed up with evidentiary material for audits and so on. But your in-depth articulation of defense, and the implementation of common standards and how they align to your policy sets, as well as the articulation of why you decided for or against any specific control, should be part of your overall documentation.

Business Resilience: Another great hot button for clients is your ability to continue to operate in times of crisis or disaster. Many people show their "disaster recovery" or "business continuity" standards independently. As we learned in this past chapter, the implementation of a business resiliency organization and services is the most effective way to show the triad of business continuity, disaster recovery, and crisis management. It is through those three programs conjoined, or at least aligned, that deliver the most impactful mechanism for businesses to be resilient. Creating documentation that shows the three of these in a common format and converged methodology is your best mechanism for (re)gaining your clients' trust in your abilities to continue delivering services or products to them.

Security By Product: Big-picture security overviews and statements are great, and necessary, but the most complex ones often come up in the area of product–by-product security considerations. Perhaps you are a manufacturing company with 50 different product lines. Perhaps you are technology company that goes to market with 120 different technological applications, or perhaps you are a law firm that has four very different go-to-market practices. Whatever your business is, people will ask specific security-related questions about the products or services that they are purchasing from you, and you need to be ready to answer them. General responses about your overall infrastructure may not be pertinent to or even true for a specific product. In fact, it may not even have relevance or, worse, you could leave out specific security or privacy elements that have been built into a product and that show your advanced stage of security maturity because you didn't take the time to document them. Utilize the business process workflow and controls documentation we've talked about previously in this book. Over time, build up your catalog by going through each one of your product sets and creating an articulable view of each component of the products within your security plan, but do so in such a way that nonpractitioners can understand.

Security Development Life cycle: The last major component is your security development life cycle program, which should describe your security process for developing your product. Most often this is used in the context of developing software, but it can also be modified to support supply chain security, manufacturing line security, engineering security, and even consulting process security. However you create your go-to-market products, security components such as threat modeling, code assurance, supply chain verification, red teaming, and vulnerability assessments should be well described in a simplified process detailing your capabilities for creating a secure product.

These are the basis for establishing transparency and appropriate documentation for all of your company's security programs. Based on this type of information, you can create things such as frequently asked questions, short documentation sets describing the security of each product, and prepositioned and certified statements in language that can be used within contracts. It all starts with cataloging and simplifying the description of the controls within your environment. Ensure that professionals review the data catalog, that people are assigned ownership of the information, that there is an expiration date and the information review process is documented, and that other appropriate entities such as legal services have an opportunity to review, comment on, and certify the information.

Chief Sales Officer and Market Impact

Perhaps you have heard the statement "everyone's in sales" in your company. If you are in a for-profit organization, nothing could be truer. As part of the business-supporting aspects of your role, you have a special job as an ambassador of security risk and privacy for your business to the market in general. In the sections below we talk about how you can support the go-to-market field. In your job as the adjunct chief sales officer, however, this is really about establishing the credibility of your company among your peers, the market, clients, and anyone else who needs to be educated and informed about your company's security risk and privacy practices.

Let's start with your peers in other companies. How you represent not only the security position of your company, but the thought leadership within the industry, your visionary approach to your trade, and your general interaction with other security executives all leave an impressionable mark with current and future clients. Have you ever been at a conference or a peer event where a dynamic security executive is talking about the new program they're undertaking and the overall review of their program, and you think, "Now that company has it together." This is the type of individual you need to be for your company. Through the participation in industry events, the presentation of your approach to security and the unique programs that you may have created, as well as your approachability by and availability to your peers establishes the unique level of trust that is important for your company as a whole; when those companies looking to use your business turn to their own security practitioners to review your capabilities, they will remember you and your program in whatever light you have shown.

There is an obvious good and bad to this chief sales officer strategy. The good is that, if done well, you obviously put your business in a very good position. The bad is that this can become all-consuming. I have been in the position of and have seen peers being consumed by the needs of a strong sales or marketing organization and being overwhelmed by the continuing requests for meeting with clients, speaking engagements, and other similar functions. There is a fine balance between being able to manage the business you are accountable for and providing these adjunct services to support your company's go to market in the position as the "chief sales officer." At times that balance may shift in order to support issues or incidents that have happened within your business, and you become the face of the business in this context, but I would caution you to remember that your job is to manage a security, risk, and privacy organization and its operational entities. All of the speaking, all of the interactions, and all the spotlight mean absolutely nothing if the programs and services you're speaking about are becoming unhinged by your absenteeism.

To avoid this, create the schedule of what you can provide based on your availability and operational requirements. For instance, create a monthly schedule that allows for a specific number of client meetings and speaking engagements, the number of blogs or video blogs you can document and create, or even the number of articles you will write on behalf of your company. Try to plan out at least one quarter and up to six months to show your commitment and be able to anticipate the business's needs. Also, creating bench strength through the use of your direct team and those capable of delivering similar messages at the next level down is also your responsibility. Just as when we talked about important aspects of succession planning, the impact of security on your company's go to market relies not only on you being the "superstar" but also on having many superstars to be able to create that standard messaging an outward face of trust broadly across your operating areas.

Field Enablement

Your impact on your company's field groups cannot be overstated. This thought process of client trust and a client focus works internally as well as it does externally. When your field organization knows that you "have their back," that they can rely on your team not only to defend the company but also to support them when things go bad, you create within your company an incredible level of optimism about your programs. By creating for those who directly interact with your clients and customers a mechanism of access to security resources, security information, and even you, you become an adjunct member of your field organizations. At the most basic level, making available field tutorials, question-and-answer documents, attestation letters, and wikis that can answer questions that allows them to support the customer need is absolutely critical in establishing this client focus. Secondary to this, you and your teams are the experts, both internally and externally, about your company's security issues, and by providing a path for the field to get access to that expertise, you increase their ability to be successful. Consider a telephone hotline, a group email service, Web forms, or even online chat services that connect directly to security experts on your team, which your company or agency's field teams can use if they have a question or problem. At one company I worked for, the average return time for a question regarding security was about 4 months. By the time the field took it, sent it to one group, it got sent to security, they found the right person to answer it, and then it made its way back literally took 4 months. Through facilitated intake and tracking processes, we were able to reduce that to 24 h. Do you think that changed the way the field felt supported?

Transparency, accuracy, information, and professionalism all play into this context of client trust management. Create your own path by starting small, asking your business what it needs based on past experience, and move forward in establishing yourself as your company's chief trust officer.

EXECUTING

Now that you have your five steps to operational execution, the only thing left to do is execute. Earlier in the book we spoke about the criticality of being able to execute consistently and on many fronts. But we did not cover some leadership actions that help support your ability to execute effectively, how you think about operational execution, and how you develop essential actions required for ensuring effective results-driven leadership.

Being the Rock

The first thing about executing as a leader is being self-aware and knowledgeable enough to understand that those whom you lead are actually the ones executing the strategy. What that team needs is an anchor point they can rely on, knowing that not only do they have your trust but you have the vision, the authority, and the skills necessary to help steer them, correct their course, and provide the protection they need to effect their mission. Being their rock means being consistent, being rational, and being that safe place they can go back to for instruction, shelter, and support. Transparency, communication, passion for the mission, and optimism help establish that consistency for those you lead and ensures that the team will take the risks necessary to execute with the passion that excels the organization and will continue to push forward knowing they are anchored to a safe place.

Your business is also looking for that rock—a serious and confident individual with the ability to lead through crisis, act rationally during turbulent times, and have the fortitude to drive through difficult issues. To them, you are not only 911, but the police chief, the fire chief, and the military all rolled into one; they will look to you to be their rock during those times. Getting to that level of business trust takes experience, training, and the willingness to be that leader. Constantly updating your skills, being prepared to accept leadership, and being resilient and determined under pressure are hallmarks of the type of individual whom others can rely on when push comes to shove. Create your own personal, individual development plan that looks at "all" the jobs you have. Evaluate yourself against your delivery requirements and prioritize based on probable business need. Seek guidance from experienced practitioners and become confident in your own ability to deliver. Remember, the business is not looking for you to have all the answers, just the ability to make good decisions, find those who have the right answers, and execute.

Continuous Momentum

Another important component in the ability to execute is to establish the continuous momentum of your mission objectives through action, urgency, and excellence. The roadway to mission success is paved with many obstacles, combatants, and steep hills. Your job is to create organizational momentum by finding ways around obstacles, fighting the fights that need to be fought, and obtaining additional resources to push the mission uphill when necessary. From outright obstinacy to passive-aggressive behavior, you will find a plethora of political, turf, financial, position, privacy, and legal battles that attack your emotional and deterministic health, but knowing that ahead of time and creating self-awareness and self-help capabilities will help you overcome these challenges. Maintaining a positive mental attitude and being *the* example of a can-do attitude can often be the difference between an organization beginning to roll backward and the additional steam necessary to push it over the hill.

Obsessively Devoted to Outcome

Outcome-based leadership is the intersection of vision, perseverance, dedication, and effort. Being obsessively devoted the outcomes to which you have committed your business or agency, the mission that your team has planned and is executing to, and the assurance of a resilient business operations protection plan is all part of flawless execution. The only way to get this type of outcome is to be intimately involved in your operations and mission scope. This does not mean that you must be a micromanager or go it alone; rather, you should seek the inclusion of ideas, experts, and operators that help deliver the mission outcome. Once again, transparency and communication reign through the education of those co-delivering your mission and by you being able to articulate the connection between your decisions, actions, and related outcomes. Being told "no" by superiors is different than accepting no from detractors. I cannot possibly count the number of times that I've been told that it is "not possible to do it in this company." Not only do those people not see the vision, but they are incapable of overcoming their own preconceptions or unwillingness to make the changes necessary to be successful. Focus, passion, and resilience will serve you well in becoming an established outcome-based leader in your company.

Delivering Trust through Action

To continue executing you'll need the support of other business leaders and executives within your company. For them to support you beyond doing what is simply right, or supporting the "new" person, requires establishing a trust relationship. That trust is built on many different aspects depending on the persons and personalities involved; the constant in that trust decision support algorithm that most people make is based on your actions. Can you deliver on what you committed? Do your words and deeds reflect those of a trustable individual? The action in this context is not about your ability to push out work and complete a task (although ability to complete the committed-to task is important); your actions are as a pure executive, a leader, a human being whom others are looking to make a connection with. Simply ask yourself this: Are the actions and deeds that you demonstrate every day in your position those that invite others to trust you? If yes, you can continue to move forward, make progress, and utilize the support and trust of those from whom you have earned it. If not, conduct an honest self-assessment, create a summary of characteristic and leadership traits that you need to work on, and let the training begin.

Creating Your Wake

Finally, after all of this talk about execution, deterministic behavior, and obsession, it is important to remind you that today's actions determine tomorrow's outcomes. As an executive passionate about leadership and driven by my mission, I try to measure my actions through service and love, a concept picked up through my years in the military; yet it took the longest time for me to understand how to verbalize it.

As someone who is constantly driving hard, delivering, and pushing others to the success of the mission, I am always faced with making decisions and being judged by others on how and why I made any given decision. You can be seen as a person who is trying to build a kingdom and who is driven by ego, or as a person who is passionate about what they do, humbled by what they see, and executes with the success of those they work with at the forefront of their mind. We are only one bad day, one bad decision, or one angry moment away from destroying the trust given to us—from using our authority or position in a way that is not consistent with using the filter of service and love as the basis of a mission-centric moral guide. To leave the right wake of emotion when we leave the room—one of trust and the confidence of our partners, peers, or teams—we need the presence and strength of determination to be committed to making the right decisions for the right reasons.

Chapter 8

A Focus on the Business

SUSTAINABILITY

By now you have seen the word *sustainability* throughout this book as a repetitive descriptor of core elements of many parts of your business that you are responsible to deliver on. In fact, it is the responsibility of all executives and the concern of every board member to ensure that the implementation of programs to protect the company/firm/agency is done in a sustainable and measurable way to ensure continuity and broad effectiveness of the overall business protection portfolio.

Your focus on the business starts with how you think about the success of your operation and the availability of what you provide even after you are gone from the position you hold. The focus on the business goes far beyond your abilities as a practitioner and touches on your ability to lead, partner, and provide services outside the traditional business operations protection expert role. Creating sustainability involves not only security program operational service sustainability, but that of the entire business. As a leader in your company—not a security risk of privacy leader, but a true leader—you will help the organization as a whole advance, overcome difficult issues, and lead the business into the future.

In this chapter we visit the topics of partnership, the extensibility of the services you provide, and additional aspects of leadership not yet discussed in this book. It is through constantly revisiting how we sustain our people, our processes, and our technologies in a holistic sense of business that we can often have a greater impact as a business executive in those companies or agencies we serve.

PARTNERSHIPS IN DELIVERY

Many times security programs and executives get marred in specialty silo stigmas or are seen as complex oversight entities with business inhibitor complexes and thus are treated as such when engaged with their internal customers. Sometimes these are well deserved, whereas at others they are blind, uneducated typecasting based on others' previous experiences. In either case, it is your responsibility to create a dynamic set of relationships that deals with, and simply is, more of a partnership than an oversight or enforcement role. This section

Becoming a Global Chief Security Executive Officer.

focuses on how to create a program based on shared responsibility, shared oversight, shared accountability, and an ecosystem of partnerships to make them more effective.

Before we dive in, let's talk briefly about what partnership means. Although there are legal definitions, business definitions, and theologically based discussions of partnership, the most common aspect I've been able to correlate all of these definitions to is the simple statement that a partnership equals a joint interest. Many people confuse a partnership with the equivocal state of action based on that joint interest. But in fact, many partnerships are very uneven in the action-oriented portion of the joint interest; at the end of the day, however, a connection, a relationship, or a collaboration still begins based on some joint interest.

Why then is this important to you as a business security executive? It is because in most cases you will need to explain and make the case for why you and whomever you are trying to convince have the need for partnership. Others in your business may see themselves as very different from you (information technology (IT) and other similar entities often have a very different perspective from yours), and all of them will be suspicious when you start spouting the word *partnership*. Is he looking for a share of the budget? Is he looking to pass off work? Is he looking to make this my problem? These are some of the questions that people ask themselves when deciding whether they want to engage in any type of partnership. It's the "what's in it for me?" and the "what's in it for him?" questions.

As your company's senior-most security, risk, or privacy executive, there are automatically a few partnerships that could make or break your program. If you are successful in aligning interests in understanding, then you can spend more of your time driving the operational action, urgency, and excellence that can more effectively protect your business. Screw it up and you'll spend more of your time defending your program, justifying projects, and creating workarounds to roadblocks and political fights rather than affecting your mission.

Employees

The first place you need to look for partnership is with those you are trying to protect. The "citizens" of the virtual city (large or small) are the first priority. As an executive that may sound way off, but on a day-to-day basis the partnership you build with the employees of the organization you protect is one of your most effective tools in leveraging a broad set of resources to help you accomplish your job. Consider yourself like a police chief of a municipality. If the citizenry of your town do not trust you—if they believe that your department is doing things in an unethical manner, such as targeting one race or another, and that you operate as an unchecked, power-wielding, rights-abusing public figure—how long do you think that would last? What type of support do you think your town would provide for you? How much of your time will be spent on lawsuits, dealing with the press about the state of your department, and dealing with external investigations of how your operation works? Would you actually even be able to do your job?

Compare that with a police agency that is transparent to the community, involved and ingrained in every aspect of it, believes and supports public and community policing, and utilizes the community as an oversight and checks-and-balance mechanism to ensure that they are in synch with the community they protect. Might they perhaps be more willing to trust your decisions? Maybe provide more information knowing that it will be used well? Perhaps they would be willing to accept different approaches to law enforcement to ensure the protection of their families because they know it will be done in an ethical in even-handed way.

It is that type and level of trust that you must get at with the employees of your business. As we mentioned earlier in the book, the best way to do this is through transparency, communication, and engagement. Part of your duties and those of your direct reports should be that public-facing representation of your program. Creating information-sharing capabilities either through a written, electronic, or multimedia mechanism, you should ensure the constant sharing of information and transparency to operations even at the employee level. Further, you should listen to your "public," perhaps through specific forms to brief employees on the business operations programs in a converged manner that protects their future and their work environment every day. Opportunities such as town halls, virtual town halls, and email addresses that go directly to your desk or to someone who can help answer them quickly are simple ways that give you this platform to reach out to your employee population.

Although transparency and communications are important to build trust, with your employees that does not necessarily mean that it establishes a partnership. Remember that the partnership is a joint interest and by establishing a connection between what you do and what your organization does every day and how it affects the employees creates the joint interest. I like to call this the "awakening" of your employees' "self-preservation gene." When an individual can relate to a concept that has a very direct impact on their well-being, whether it be their future employment, physical safety, or another personal condition, they typically listen more closely and react more quickly. Your ability to awaken their self-preservation gene is based on how you tie business operations protection goals to actions you need from them. This starts with a very basic concept of explaining the downstream residual impact of negative-impact issues within the business and tying that back to how it directly affects them. For instance, when explaining why they should not allow people to piggyback (a term that refers to an individual who illegitimately enters a protected facility by getting close to the person who legitimately entered before them) on their badge when they enter the facility, tell them a plausible story of what "could happen," such as a domestic violence issue spilling into the workplace or an individual who is attempting to get into the building to steal client data, and then what could happen as a result of that incident. Finally, explain that whomever allowed that person entry may be considered at fault and that they would most likely lose their job. Of course, this must be in context with your human resource policies, but I think we can agree that in most organizations, if you violated significant security protocol and someone was hurt because of it, you would probably lose your job. With that in mind, add that you know that most people don't think of those downstream risks, and our jobs are not to only enforce security policy but also to educate to ensure that everybody understands their responsibilities and the "why."

In effect, when you educate and enact behavior changes among your employee "partners" you create the beginning of what many people call the "human firewall." The human firewall, whether used in the context of cyber or physical security, is the extension of the services you provide in the areas of security, risk, and privacy, all the way down to where the action actually happens in the business. You can have all of the technology and all of the public safety services known to mankind at your disposal, but if the people responsible for delivering business, dealing with clients, managing technology, and operating within your campus or facilities ignore those services, controls, and rules, then all is for naught. It takes one click of a mouse, once holding open a door, one time not calling and notifying someone of a suspicious activity, and it can be too late for prevention. Through explaining to your employees the why, the downstream residual impact of specific actions, and the "here's what I need from you," you create an educated human control that is intelligent, analytical, and—for 99.999% of the people who work in your environment doing the right thing every day for the company—will help stop bad things before they happen.

Spend the time thinking about your partnership with your employees. Get their impressions and input on their needs. And go out and create the most impressive relationship you have ever had with the "citizenship" of your business.

Information Technology

Obviously, the basis of this book is created around a converged security program, which includes public safety, criminal civil investigations, and other traditional physical security programs beyond cyber security. But even with those programs in the mix, one of your biggest partnerships you must make work is with your IT organization. From controls integration to evidence collection to technology defense operations, your partners in the IT organization are important at all levels. Much of this section is based on the relationship from an information security, cyber operations, and technology protection standpoint, but it is important to remember that all aspects of your converged operation have touch points that are relevant and need to be nurtured and maintained like any other partnership.

First and foremost, when thinking about your relationship with IT, remember that they are by far your largest customer because of size (meaning how much of the services they consume) and shared responsibility in many cases. Whether

IT manages direct in-line security controls such as network devices, firewalls, and end-user computing platforms, or whether you provide a suite of protective services end to end for them, your interaction with IT occurs on a daily basis at a policy, program, politics, project, and even response level. How each of you perceives that partnership and, for that matter, your joint interests determines your ability to operate within their environment, respond to critical issues or incidents that involve technology, and make modifications and changes to the business that involve technology in order to better protect the business.

In that sense, IT also becomes your most critical ally. Just like we described in the previous section on employees, you must be able to make your case as to why security and IT have specific joint interests in the services you provide and vice versa, as well as the technology and platforms they provide to the business. The most effective mechanism I have ever seen used in my 25-plus years in this industry is to educate IT, just like any other human being, on the how and why of what they are being asked. For instance, simply throwing another technology in place in telling them they "have to do it" typically does not work. In fact, without a partnership, that "tell" often turns into 150 reasons why they cannot do it. By spending the time up front, explaining the needs and the downstream residual impact of what could happen if a specific control or change isn't made, how it affects them, and more definitive information like where it has happened before the impact and the probability of it occurring to your organization, makes them part of the solution rather than the order-taker for the "security guy." When you are operating in environments where high-speed decision-making is happening because of all evolving threats, changing threat environments, an escalating risks, this step can often be lost. It must be a conscious effort on your part every day to ensure that this happens.

Again, when you provide oversight and enforcement technologies and services such as threat management and forensics, or you partner in the delivery of an entire suite of IT security capabilities, the platform you create needs to be integrated as part of that partnership and shared interest. Your focus should be creating security as a component of IT quality, not an independent security capability that monitors IT. If we truly are trying to get to a place in this world that embraces and effects prevention as a primary avenue of business operations protection, then a joint partnership in the development of a protected platform is necessary.

This begins with shared visions, shared goals, and shared delivery. Understanding who is better at delivering what aspects for this platform and why is critical to the conversation. Once you have established the shared partnership, and determined why it's important for both of you to create a shared approach, the rest is fairly simple. By creating a RACI (responsible, accountable, consulted, informed) index for everything, from policy to technical operations delivery, you can shortcut the "that's not your job" discussions as part of the platform definition in co-development. It is not to say that these RACIs won't change over time or will be implemented perfectly the first time, but they certainly remove the complexity of action ownership.

With regard to shared platform ownership, the business should see an end-to-end service delivery program, not where they have to go for technology and where they have to go through security. This is accomplished through joint architecture and technical publications. Embrace the use of a single end-to-end project management process that integrates security checkpoints within a standard rather than attempting to have security, risk, or privacy checks and balances conducted outside the normal realm of IT operations. The reality is that IT has many years of experience and process optimization quality delivery assurance. By utilizing a shared process, you ensure an insured outcome.

Finally, put your money where your mouth is—and vice versa for your partner on the other side. If they have a huge technology project or product or project development effort that you are providing services for, stake your bonus or a variable part of your compensation on it. Create joint goals that are measurable and consistent with the shared vision. Likewise, if there are specific metrics of enterprise defense that you're trying to get to and they require change on the IT side, ensure that your partner in IT understands the importance of making that change for the company and have joint goals in that aspiration that both of you agree on.

Bidirectional communication, transparency, listening, and inclusion with your technology partners goes a long way. Having empathy for how you affect IT's service delivery capability, budget, and overall operation is imperative in your relationship and partnership with them. Spend time getting to know their issues, how they impact you, and ask—don't tell—your IT partners how your operations affect them.

General Counsel

Your general counsel is another important business partner. As a service provider to legal function in the area of investigative and discovery services, you are an important part of their overall operation. As the executive responsible for the defense of the business that they are ultimately responsible for protecting from a legal perspective, you are a huge part of the business protection program. You can almost look at the general counsel as another senior executive leader in the company whose job is focused on "business operations protection." It is through this lens of a joint interest, and certainly as a big "customer," that creating an optimal partnership is significantly important to your success within the company.

In my tenure in this career field I've come to realize that it is often the general counsel that helps embody and deliver the ethical roots the foundation of most companies. I've also learned that whether or not general counsel technically understands the entirety of the operations you are accountable for, there is a keen appreciation and understanding of the impact that security, risk, and privacy have in the overall protection of the organization.

At a partnership level, you may think that this overarching protection of the business is the only parallel that creates your joint interests. I would argue that beyond the protection aspects, it is the unique and specific perspectives each individual brings that help create a purposeful partnership. Some of the most important lessons I have learned in business; responsibility, decision-making, and, most importantly, prioritization, have come from a General Counsel. Their specific perspective on impactful issues and the total effect of any one issue has on a business is truly unique. Most people within a business spend their time thinking about how an issue or event will affect the business when that issue is focused at the business. General counsels have the unique ability look far beyond the business at issues affecting legalities, regulatory implications, other businesses within the industry, and another whole set of decision-making criteria that forms their overall perspective. It is through this lens that one can truly learn much and develop their organization using the same concept of inclusion of the rest of the world as part of their decision-making process.

Beyond partnership in protection, and obtaining a specific perspective, your partnership with general counsel can also have an important effect on your career. The job of the general counsel is to give advice, and most often it is good to heed that advice. In the American work culture the term *rabbi*, from the Jewish word for the religious role of a teacher, is often used as a metaphor. The broad definition is a person who can provide good advice, education, and corporate politics, and at times can intercede on behalf of another. If you establish a great partnership with your general counsel, they often can serve as an important pseudo-rabbi; not only you can learn from them, but through an open relationship and plenty of transparency and communication, they can often act on your behalf when you are not in the conversation or room.

A final point I want to make with regard to your partnership with general counsel is the trust that you must put in their ability to make decisions. Many times you may not agree with the direction they are setting forth, or with how they contextualize a specific situation. To be clear, however, the general counsel is much like the attorney general in that they get the last word. Ultimately, they own the translation to the board from a legal perspective, the only legal risk for the company, and they make the decisions necessary to protect the business. Whether or not you report to a general counsel, ensure the internal support process recognizes that the general counsel does get the last word, with one exception; a quantifiable and evidenced based concern of ethics. The most important piece of advise I have received from a general counsel (GC) is this; If a GC has asked, instructed you, or otherwise has acted in an unethical manner, it is your duty to report him or her to the Board of Directors. Think of that for a moment. A GC's most pressing advice was to not allow undo pressure from the most powerful legal or senioe executives for that matter sway me from my ethical obligations. Now that is a GC that many can only wish to work with.

Human Resources

Your relationship and partnership with human resources (HR) also help to support the unique perspective necessary to do your job, specifically for the 99.99% of those people doing the right thing for your business every day of the year. The HR partnership provides continuity and program development as it relates to the impact on the people and organization you are protecting. From disciplinary management perspectives through cultural inclusion for communications, HR serves a multifaceted role wrapped around ensuring a good balance of business and people perspectives. Additionally, your side of the bargain in this partnership is to create context with regard to your discipline and specialty in order for HR to use that as a component of their decision-making process. Just to say something is bad without a description of why, the impact, or what it takes an individual to accomplish that bad act is not enough as part of that bidirectional partnership of education and transparency. Again, from creating policy to affecting disciplinary actions of members of your "community," a partnership with HR makes the enforcement portion of your job significantly easier; it provides validation and tolerance broadly because of their involvement in the overall process.

As a practitioner and executive responsible for sustaining business protection operations across multiple disciplines, HR to be an incredible partner in ensuring that (1) you get the right team on board and (2) you have the right services available to help recruit and retain resources necessary to sustain your operation.

Enterprise Risk Management

Your next important partnership is with your company's enterprise risk management (ERM) program if one exists. Depending on the size of your organization, you actually may be the enterprise risk manager, or the chief of audit, or potentially the chief operating officer. Despite who is responsible for the overall consolidation, classification, and measurement of multidisciplinary risk for the corporation, it is your responsibility to ensure a good partnership exists for your joint and collaborative efforts toward reducing risk. All risk is complicated in its own right; however, cyber defense and technology risk issues have a multitiered complexity that has to be understood from a technical level, a business operations level, and an impact level. It's a skill set that takes years to learn and even more to be able to articulate. Your partnership with the enterprise risk executive is critical for you to be able to explain any given risk and have it well represented in the overall context of the entirety of business risk.

As in almost all other partnerships, the most important mechanism to start this joint understanding is transparency. In the organizations I manage I ensure that not only ERM but also audit have full access to all operational risk management program data that I am responsible for. In governance risk and compliance platforms I provide independent credentials for our partners in those areas to ensure that they have insight into and immediate access to all risk data that they are accountable for translating. This reduces time, instills trust, and often reduces the need for the back-and-forth of "what does that mean?" and "where else do we have that issue?" Being fully transparent, providing unfettered access to data components with regard to risk, and spending the time explaining issues around risk discovery, prioritization, and in mitigation actions is the beginning of establishing an important bidirectional relationship.

Often, on the flip side of the partnership is the experience that the ERM function can bring to you. Like I mentioned before, it takes years to be able to interpret risk and its impact on a business, and even longer to articulate it well. This is something a senior ERM executive does every day. Whether it's to your executive committee, regulatory entities, the board, the audit committee, or just the business at large, ERM executives take complex risk issues and algorithms and turn them into action based on a broad perspective and a unique approach to business imperatives. Your ERM partner can teach you and accelerate your ability to reasonably articulate complex security, risk, and privacy issues, including risk, in a way that is well accepted by the business in other business management functions. That experience and those skills are critical to your future success as a business operations protection expert.

Executive Committee

The next key business partnership you need to have is that of your executive committee. Commonly referred to as your "CEO direct reports," these are the men and woman who run the business you protect every day and consume your services. Some of the most difficult relationships/partnerships to make and maintain in the business, and your ability to change the way the business operates, change the mind-set of how the business thinks, and make an impact to the overall operational defense of the corporation, often rely on the level of partnership you can create with members of the executive committee.

There are two different types of partnership when it comes to your executive committee, and they are both important to understand. The first, of course, is the one-on-one relationship that you have with each committee member. Remember that executive committee members are humans too (for the most part), and in order for them to "do business with you" they prefer to get an understanding of who you are, your ethos, how you operate, and how much you can be trusted. Sometimes this happens in one meeting and sometimes over the course of many. Your job is to figure out which are the most important relationships to have based on their level of influence in the company, how they align to the things that you are trying to drive or change, and the secondary influence you need to have on others with whom your relationship is perhaps lacking.

The second type of partnership with the executive committee is with the entirety of the committee as an entity itself. That is to say, the relationship and partnership you have with each individual executive can be severely different then the relationship and partnership you have with that person when they are among their peers inside the executive committee. At a one-on-one level your focus is to engage as a person and create trust, alignment, and a service-minded approach, enabling a connection between two partners. In the context of the entity, your focus is to create a perspective and partnership based on business effectiveness, expertise, and ability to execute. As an entity, the responsibility of the collective committee members is to make broad business-affecting decisions based on the input and the experts they bring to the table. To be a good partner, you need to be that expert when you get to that table, which includes being well-prepared, knowledgeable, and able to interact in an effective manner.

In both situations, an important aspect of your partnership is confidence. As we mentioned previously in this book, the business is looking for a rock, a foundation that they can depend on when dealing with issues that involve the security of the business and during times of crisis. Confidence does not mean cocky; confidence comes from preparedness, the ability to engage, the ability to execute, and a self-awareness of your limits and knowing what you know and what you don't.

On the flip side of that partnership is information about the business—and, more specifically, about the business you protect—that you're able to obtain from both the individual and the entity. Business is what they do, and as an entity, the business is them. Understanding and listening about the future of the business, critical issues that are important for them to make the right decisions about that future, and the specific direction given to help go execute that strategy are all part of that bidirectional aspect of the partnership itself. Given the opportunity, earn that trust, earn that relationship, and be the partner they are seeking; ensure that your ears are open to listening to the other side of the table.

The Board

The last critical partnership that we discuss in this book is the board of directors (BoD) or a similar entity. Of course, there are many more "partnerships" that you will need and develop over time, but as a next-generation business operations protection executive, the basis of the partnerships previously covered and the BoD form a valuable and holistic partnership approach from day-to-day operations through the corporate business management and regulated governance oversight. The BoD provides the latter, and your relationship and partnership with them is important because of their broad perspective to protecting the company and a diverse set of interests as whole.

A board, which can also be called by several different names (such as board of governors, board of trustees, or board of regents), are staffed by the "directors" (depending on the bylaws set forth by each company) and serve several oversight and authoritative functions. These functions, such as policy and objectives, senior executive officer appointments, fiduciary and financial governance and oversight, and executive compensation oversight, create a broad and holistic perspective of the company, its performance, and its commitments to the company's stakeholders, including shareholders, investors, and the employees. It is through this perspective that your partnership is viewed and relied on as a component of their input for understanding things like risk impact, sustainability, and detailed areas in your specialty.

Your end of the partnership is actually not that complicated, even though at times the number of opinions and directions on how to present something, what information to provide, and the level of anxiety that seems to abound around any given board meeting. Predominantly, your job is to provide an honest, open, and factually supported assessment and opinion on issues pertaining to the security, risk, and privacy operations facing the business. Your part of the partnership is not to say everything is OK when it is not, and your job is not to be the "paid paranoid" who speaks of only the bad issues and not in context with the totality of the business; rather, your job is to provide a baseline of information the board can use in support of a variety of decisions necessary to do its job. This baseline should be a consistent method by which the board is provided the data in context with a framework that they are all familiar with (such as the National Institute of Standards and Technology Cyber Security Framework) and in a nonpractitioner format that simplifies issues, such as a business scorecard. Your part in this partnership is to provide simplified, factual expertise in a manner consumable by intelligent business experts that speaks to the goals the organization is trying to obtain, the risk the business is managing in your area of responsibility, and plans and opinions of emerging threats and issues that the company is facing.

That word *plans* in the last sentence is a bit loaded because potentially it has huge implications. It is important to remember that, as in any good partnership your partner isn't expecting you to have solved every problem. Should you be aware of them, should you be knowledgeable, and should you understand the impact of them against your business? Yes. Do you need to have solved them all, have definitive answers, and be capable of stopping every possible bad thing coming at your business? No.

Unfortunately, security executives often feel it is their job to go in and "defend" their position or "sell" the BoD that everything is OK. When that happens, the executive unfortunately degrades their confidence and their ability to be open and honest because, for the most part, every person in that room knows that there is no way possible that a company can protect itself against every threat. The BoD wants to know that you understand the issue and are capable of developing and delivering "plans" in a practical, prioritized, and business-rational approach that meets the needs of the business and stakeholders in an honest and open way.

Your partnership with your BoD starts with you being confident, knowing the status of the defense of the company, the prioritization of the programs in place, the threats facing your business and the industry, and how you think about priorities and objectives over the coming years. How you deliver that message, how you show the data that demonstrate the effectiveness of your businesses programs, and how you engage is a matter of practice, experience, and a bidirectional conversation at these meetings as to how the BoD wants to be provided with the information. The partnership begins with your approach.

Finally, with partnerships being partnerships, the flip side to the partnership is the wisdom that the BoD can impart to you if you chose to listen. Often provided in the context of questions, at other times as directive conclusions to a topic area, the years and years of business and leadership experience that most board members bring to the board room is almost incalculable. Different industries and different perspectives, from startups to multinational corporations, their opinions and actions come from a career's worth of incredible experiences that made them the successful businessperson they are today, spanning decades of job experience. Listen, interpret, and internalize their wisdom and it will soon add to yours.

YOUR NEW JOB: A MARKETING GURU

There may have been a time when leading a security organization wasn't affected by the totality of the people who make up your business, but in today's world—where security, risk, and privacy are all critically interlinked in every part of the business—it is the people whom you engage with every day that will be a large part of your success. The "human enterprise" needs and expects leaders who understand and thrive among the people they lead, and the business of business operations protection requires a leader with skills in human behavior management to create understanding, action, and momentum. Many of these skills are most aligned the world of marketing, where perception can be reality and where optics drive perception.

The tone, tenor, and presentation of topics, facts, and our own passion are all up for individual and group evaluation as we present our case, tell our stories, and create dialog to engage, be engaged, and impact the actions of others. There have been many studies of and articles written about the first 30 seconds you meet someone and the impression you make on those you interact with. Those lessons are described as the "30 golden seconds" to simply get you into the conversation, because if an individual or group is not open to a conversation then there is no conversation, and you simply become just another lecturer.

With some careful planning, practice, self-awareness, and basic marketing skills, you can become the next great "security marketer." This concept isn't about being a "salesperson" or "spin master," but rather creating a tool set that ensures a more human connection to better your chances at creating change in a human enterprise. From your presence to creating successful mechanisms of understanding to some basic mechanism of engagement, the following section can help you develop a new skill and hone other skills needed to create the optics necessary to deliver the right perception.

Your Presence and Presentation

I once took a sociology and psychology class that talked about the human condition and the needs of most healthy human beings. Something that has stayed with me all of these years was the lesson that people all have a basic need to be liked or loved (not necessarily both) and, whether or not they understood it, also needed to be needed. Now, assuming I'm a healthy human, I can attest that it is much better working with a group of people who, for the most part, "like" me and consider me useful. I will attest that I have been in front of several people, groups, and audiences where I most certainly did not get those "warm fuzzies," and let's say the return on those time investments were less than profitable.

Although we cannot please all the people all the time, we can certainly create circumstances and opportunities that lead to a better engagement and a better outcome. Before you even verbally connect, market your wares, or begin your life-altering dissertation on the criticality of security, risk, or privacy, there are things we can do to create perception and a presence around us that invites and engages others into a communicative environment that is open to their success as well as ours.

One of the first lessons we all must learn is the concept of being approachable. As people who grew up in a normalized society, went to school, work in an everyday environment, potentially have a spouse and children, and may even participate in local civic groups or on a sports team, most of us believe that we are approachable. But our individual personas take on a very different context inside the workplace as a person who is a senior leader, who has authoritative control in a specialty that is often little understood (seen as an enforcement position), and who is probably fairly passionate about what they do. These "perceptions" often lead to assumptions that make us less approachable.

The simplest way to overcome this type of perception is to create a clear set of optics that demonstrates the exact opposite, and that starts with a positive mental attitude and demeanor. First, humans are very perceptive. Before we even hear a word out of someone's mouth we are judging our ability to engage with them through their demeanor, posture, facial expressions, the many other nonverbal communications. What does your body language say? Do you mentally feel that no one wants to listen to you and therefore you don't make eye contact, you don't smile, you don't invite people into your presence? Remember that most people are like you, and don't like to be rejected. Simply acknowledging that someone walked by you with a wave, saying hello to someone in a hallway, or smiling at someone whether you intend to engage them at that moment or not creates a memory and connection with your persona that says "he or she is approachable." This type of nonverbal engagement cannot be simply an echo of what someone does to you but rather your own engagement into their world. Don't be the individual who says hello only to those who say hello to you first or wait to see if they make eye contact. The fact that you are confident enough to invite people into your presence with a smile and acknowledgment of their being is another telltale sign that you are approachable and confident individual. Just like in many other areas, confidence carries, even through nonverbal communications.

Approachability and nonverbal communications are also as a visual aspect. How people see you has an impact. Are you dressed like them? Do you look like you can barely dress yourself? Are you dressed in a three-piece suit while speaking to a development organization with people who are wearing jeans and flip-flops? How you dress in the context of where you work, whom you are speaking to, and the presence you are trying to create are all important. Lack of personal hygiene or a self-managed persona can lead to people simply wanting to avoid you. Dressing four levels above what anyone else in the room is wearing can also cause people to want to avoid you. Later we will cover knowing your audience and how to market yourself to that audience for that given context, basic confidence, and how to care for yourself.

The last area around approachability is the concept of humility. Someone once told me if you take yourself too seriously then no one will take you seriously at all. Or, said another way, if you're too important in your own mind, you are not approachable. We all have important jobs in our own realities, and recognizing that every person matters, every connection is important, and every time you get to talk to another person is a fortunate opportunity you have makes you a more humble person. A sense of humility is not only good for leveling ourselves and our expectations; it also puts you on par with those to whom you speak and creates a level of social comfort that makes you very approachable.

Once you become approachable, the next trick is to be a person whom others want to listen to. Don't consider this a discussion about topics, but rather how one delivers a message. Think about it for a moment. When you hear great speakers or you are drawn to listening to someone's message, other than the message, what is it that grabs your attention? Is it the fact that they are passionate about what they say? Are they knowledgeable? Do they seem to be speaking right to you? Are they a great storyteller and do their stories relate to you? Are they positive in how they talk about an issue or negative?

There are many ways to become that person whom others want to listen to, but there are several occupational hazards being a security, risk, privacy professional that often limit our ability to do so, because often our messages involve bad news. But it is not all bad news that we deliver, and even when we do speak about issues in our business that require attention, it can be done in a way that has less "oh no" and more "oh yes." Let's take a look at a few of these critical areas.

1. *Be Positive:* Certainly difficult at times, but in general, when you engage with senior leaders, employees, or even customers, remember that being positive attracts listeners. You can take an issue that needs to be remediated and start by talking about the downstream positive results that can occur if it's remediated. Focusing on the positive—like how people are working together to resolve an issue, how you will be able to reuse the efforts in other areas, or what a big milestone it is for the company—are all positive spins on a potentially negative situation. Not everything can be positive and you need to be sensitive to that, but always focus on an issue's silver lining and people will want to continue to hear your story.
2. *Be Confident:* Just like in other areas, confidence carries. Whether it's public speaking, presenting at a meeting, or engaging in conversations in a hallway, when you speak confidently about whatever subject or topic you're discussing, people feel like they are in great company, being educated by an expert, and learning something. Confidence also carries passion, and people

like to feel that excitement and passion that others have in whatever they are speaking about. This does not mean we have to be off-the-wall crazy when speaking or promoting a specific topic or be arrogant like a know-it-all. Remember, being humble is still a value that connects people, but being passionate and loving what you do, and knowing about what you're talking about, creates an anticipatory connection for those who want to hear more.

3. *Be a Thought Leader:* The difference between being someone whom others will listen to and being the person whom others want to listen to is being the speaker or conversationalist who can teach and enlighten. Articulating and repeating the facts of the specific topic is only one part of the equation. Being knowledgeable about your career and discipline, understanding the future of the market you serve, and being able to shed light and share ideas as an educator are important parts of being an engaging speaker or presenter. When you master this people will come to hear you speak just because they know that they will depart the conversation or session with more information than when they got there.
4. *Be a Storyteller:* Everyone likes a good story. It's even better when it's personal and other people can connect. Some of the best speeches I remember are by those who not only told a good story but interjected it with their own personal experiences that matched mine. Telling a story not only makes it personal but makes it digestible. You could be talking about a complex issue of next generation Internet protocol controllers for the Internet of things and deliver it with a discussion around how refrigerators will use the technology and link to your Gmail. Being a storyteller reduces the complexity of complex issues, and articulating a topic with a good story behind it creates a positive connection with your audience that keeps them coming back for more.
5. *Be Connected:* Getting back to that question of have you ever heard a speaker who seems like they are speaking right to you? That does not just happen; rather, they build it into their model of engagement with their audience. Great speakers do things like ask questions, ask their audience to think about something, and ask their audience to ask themselves questions. By making your target audience—whether in a meeting or in an auditorium—interact with you, either in their mind or directly, you create a direct connection that drives home the feeling of them being involved in the conversation, you caring about what they think, and you speaking with them rather than at them.

These five steps are simple guidance for you to establish a framework of how to connect with your target audience and keep them coming back for more. It doesn't mean that every time you speak you will encompass everything described above, and that is really the next lesson: remember not to use the same performance for every audience. Every audience requires a different approach, a different tone and tenor, and a different delivery because the message you are trying to leave behind, the point you are trying to get across, and the outcome of the engagement should be different for each audience. When you are delivering business metrics about security program effectiveness you will have a very different delivery than when speaking to a room of your peers on the topic of next-generation technology deployment. When speaking in the hallway to an employee who is feeling overwhelmed with the amount of work they have, you will have a very different delivery and approach than when speaking at an all-hands meeting with all of your employees in attendance. Part of being an engaging individual is spending the time up front considering what the person or people you are speaking to need to get out of the conversation, what you need to get out of the conversation, and how to create a positive outcome for both.

Above all, be present. Conversations between people are just that, conversations, and being personal and connected and present means as much to any other human as being charming and engaging. As a leader, executive, and an authoritative part of management, the simple fact you can engage one-on-one or one-on-many with a level of respect and humility makes you approachable, likable, and someone whom others will want to connect with. It also keeps you grounded and reminded that we all wake up every morning and put our pants on one leg at a time.

Changing Corporate DNA through Human Behavior

I would be remiss if we closed this chapter without talking about one of the most important functions that you will have as a security, risk, or privacy executive in your company, and that is often changing how a business functions and how people operate for the betterment of the protection of the overall business. Many referred to this is changing the "DNA" of a company, which is often a concerted effort to adjust many different behaviors of the company and the people within the company that make up things like corporate culture, operational habits, core perceptions, and legacy ethos. These are not easy things to change, but over time they may have become inhibitors or promoters of behaviors, actions, and mindsets that are the root cause of dysfunctional or nonsecure operations.

The first thing that you have to know going into this is that you need to be mentally prepared, because it is not going to be easy. You can have all the evidence you need and the budget to go implement changes, and you can still fail miserably because of human perceptions, actions, and attitudes. Having a level of mental toughness, knowing that it will take convincing, time, and effort to change the DNA of your company, and having the will to see it through, confidence in your plan, and trust in your team's ability to deliver are the first steps in a positive mental attitude will ensure that you are mentally prepared to change your company's DNA.

One of my favorite things I like to hear when I start this process is a famous quote you always get: "They'll never do that here." Sometimes that comes from practitioners who work for you who have run up against the wall a thousand times in their career and have simply given in, or from an angry executive who likes the way they are doing business, does not want the boat rocked, and is going to be a road bump in the way. The reason I like it so much (and typically smile internally when it is said) is because I know I am going to change it, and when I do I will remember the words of that individual and will have proven to myself again that people, businesses, and organizations can change if they have the right leadership.

The one simple way to overcome the naysayers is to show them the road map, be transparent, and have the answer for the what, the why, and the how. Have an open, direct, and simplified conversation that articulates where we're trying to get to and the things that will get us there. They may not agree—they may even try to get in the way—but they can also choose to be part of the solution rather than the problem, and being educated and aware of the path to get there is a first component necessary to get them on your path.

Mentally you also need an end goal. Just like anything else, when you try to change the DNA of a company you are trying to reach a specific outcome. You have to be able to tell yourself and your team what the outcome is. How will you know that the business has changed? What are you trying to change? I remember that a key outcome in one company was to make sure that the business engaged me directly before I had to go to them when they were making decisions about business strategy. The first time a business unit president came to me and asked for our services before making a business decision I knew we had attained the DNA change we were attempting to create. Choose your target state and write down how you and your team will know that you have completed that portion of your mission. When it happens, make it a team win and celebrate.

These DNA changes do not happen overnight. Most take years of a multipronged effort to educate the organization and implement process and technical changes that support your effort. These changes do not need to be monumental, such as stating that one of your outcomes will be that "employees in my business no longer allow piggybacking through doors" or "employees in my business no longer click on links." Each one of those things, although they seem small, have major effects on the overall security posture of your organization, and there are many of these in both the physical security realm as well as the cyber realm. Although these two are simplified, you will probably have a list a page or two long of everything you would like to see changed around your business an embedded as part of the culture and DNA of your company. Just making a list is not going to get you there, and often it will remain just a list unless you take action. Once you've created your list, your next step is prioritization. Remember that your overall end goal is to better the security posture of your business, prioritize short-term wins that help your team and the business create a sense of accomplishment, and that the world can change. Then prioritize those items that have the largest effect on your overall risk posture and depend on the human firewall. Finally, for each of the behavioral changes on the list, document the path by which you intend on taking your business there. These can be education, awareness, enforcement actions, technology, and a whole host of other projects, programs, or linear efforts. Just make sure you have a plan to get there, and as you begin to execute, remember that it is a journey.

Media Is Your Friend

What's a topic about being a marketing guru without addressing the need for some enhanced use of media? In the broad sense of the word, *media* simply means mass communication, which can include print, video, or voice through traditional paths such as television, radio, and newspapers or digital delivery mechanisms such as the Internet. For your purpose, media is simply a mechanism for delivering your message, educating your employees, and creating mechanisms for engagement from your internal consumers to your external clients. Because of the ease of access and the ability to create different types of media formats, practitioners can now simply use technology available to them (like a personal computer) and create a quality video message, such as a video blog or a recorded podcast, and immediately extend their message far beyond the office they work in, the groups they can physically meet with, or the emails that they blindly send to a large distribution list. Practitioners now have the opportunity to utilize media as a directed tool that expands their voice, delivers their message, and creates the persona of being engaged, committed, important, and personal.

In a changing world where children seem to come out of the womb with smartphones and Nintendo devices attached, you as a leader must adapt to the way that people learn and the generations you serve. People want to consume information in very different ways, and by altering how you deliver your messages you create an opportunity to capture a larger percentage of the target population's interest in doing so. From both an end-user awareness perspective as well as a normalized education and communication platform, traditional mechanisms of communicating involved a "once-a-year" type of approach or a "once-a-quarter" meeting that people attended on occasion. This type of format has diminishing returns and that starts the minute that the PowerPoint they just read is closed or they start walking out of the auditorium doors. The use of media in your communication strategy presents to you an opportunity to be where your message needs to be, when it needs to be there, and in a format that is consumable by multiple audiences. If you can create this on-demand availability of information and utilize it as a push-and-pull delivery mechanism, you create an evolving and constant cycle of touch points with your targeted consumer that creates a constant presence of security, risk, and privacy communications in their everyday life, not just once a year. Let's take a look at some of the opportunities that you have from a format perspective of how people consume:

Print/read: blogs, articles, newsletters, emails
Video: video blog series, infomercials, video-based learning
Audio: podcasts, audio blog series

Mobile: mobile device–specific push mechanisms and formatted content
Social software: internal or external social connect apps
Social visual communications: image-based simplified smart communications
Activity streams: RSS streams/tweets
Digital signage: digital advertising such as on campuses and in cafeterias
Gamification: online quizzes, fun programs, and so on aimed at teaching

As you can see, there is no shortage of ideas on how to communicate across generations and using the different preferred methods of your target audience. Remember that you can start small and grow your multimedia efforts and leverage one against the other. For instance, you may write a blog for in internal executive blogging site that employees like to go to. Leveraging that blog, you can simply record it as a podcast and published the MP3 file for people to download on their way to work or perhaps on a break if they are interested in hearing what you have to say. Using the same script, you can do it in video format by simply recording to your PC or using a fairly inexpensive video camera and posting the video as a video blog for those who prefer to watch it. You now have one script, three ways to consume it, and around-thc-clock availability, every day of the year. That's extending your communications capabilities intelligently. Create a list for the year or by quarter of what you want and need to communicate. Remember that it does take time, so ensure that you account for that within your schedule and make it a part of your job. If you don't write well, seek help from someone who does, such as personnel in corporate marketing, public relations, or corporate communications. One or two messages a month turns into 36 to 72 available touch points per year.

When considering changes in your end-user awareness program for the purposes of education and training, consider short interactive segments that are visually represented in just a few minutes multiple times a year. When we force-feed employees a 30-page PowerPoint on why security is important, it's difficult to consume, memorize, and interpret what it means to an individual. When you provide them with a 2-min explanatory video twice a month, they hear and interpret the message independently from all of the other messages and tend to retain that information longer. Shorter segments, purposefully delivered, consistently applied: That's how you change people's minds.

Developing Your Skill Set

Communication and engagement are not necessarily natural skills that everyone have, and for many they're actually pretty scary. Whether it's getting up in front of a crowd to deliver message or trying to record a video, these are skills that need to be developed and honed over time, and practicing in your mirror is not necessarily going to get you there.

One of the first things you can do to increase your skill set is to get feedback. As a mature leader, you have to accept some constructive criticism along the way—so I suggest you get used to it. You do not want to waste your efforts trying to communicate when it may be your style, your delivery, or your words that make you difficult to connect with or awkward to watch. Have a trusted person or professional critique your skills in person or through recordings. Ensure you do it in several different venue types and then make a list of the critique items and work on those using a coach or another means, such as joining a Toastmasters club.

Another great way to educate yourself on presentation styles and content delivery is by watching others. YouTube and the Internet have made this extremely easy and are one of the best tools you can use to help define your style and create some self-motivation. Look at speakers you like, speakers in your own field, videos in the same market areas, and videos about entirely different subjects. Learn how the presenters connect with their audience, how they weave their stories, and how they succinctly deliver their message. Take notes and rework your own messaging, and practice through imitation.

Communicating is like anything else: Muscle memory is necessary to be able to do it when needed, as needed, with the necessary impact. Training both internally and externally is important to sharpen your skills. Training can mean educational and coaching, but it can also mean creating opportunities to practice. Look for small speaking engagements or opportunities to create a video and go for it. Different crowds and consumers require different content and different delivery styles. Create those opportunities by asking to speak at an event, speaking in your community, or creating video content about an important message for your employees.

Being the advanced security leader of the future means being a business leader of the future. You cannot bifurcate your responsibilities as a business operations protection executive into security responsibilities and business responsibilities; they are conjoined and critically important to each other. The focus that you have on the enablement and success of your business directly affects the success of the strategy you bring forth to protect that business. From operational sustainability for the corporation through the partnerships you create, you are forming the basis by which others will execute and the behaviors those whom you lead will follow. Create silos and your people will create more. Integrate through partnerships deep into the business and your people will become part of the business. Create the example, be the guide, and blaze the path. No one could ask for more and you should demand no less.

Chapter 9

Your Career as a Chief Security Officer

The military often uses the phrase, "movement is life." It is a phrase that has multiple meanings and multiple outcomes. When you are under attack, the phrase represents your need to continuously move from position to position to avoid being detected or pinned down, and to continuously head in the direction you need to go. When attacking, if you detect movement on the other side, it simply means they are not dead yet and the enemy is still at hand. In a survival mode the phrase represents the necessity for a positive mental attitude and that, if you are moving and breathing, no matter how little, you are not dead yet. So keep moving.

Though a stark comparison to the life we live in the civilian world and as commercial business executives, the lesson still applies. As a next-generation security executive in the role of a converged security leader, you need to apply the lesson of "movement = life" by learning how to continually re-create yourself, expand yourself, be a learned person, and continuously adapt to the missions in the environments you operate in. There are key considerations in the self-development, education, and executive skills needed to be a world-class security leader and a converged security expert.

Beyond lessons in movement, chief security officers (CSOs) need to embark on lessons in self-brand management as they continuously develop and expand their career. Your individual brand as a security executive supports not only your current duties but also your position in the industry, your opportunities for employment, and even perceptions necessary when developing political capital internally as well as external to your business. In this final chapter we cover important components of market and marketability, and actions an individual must take to help develop their persona as an effective executive and security leader.

CREATING YOU AS THE CSO

If you would have asked me in my late teens and early 20s when I was in the military, or even later when I was a federal police officer, if I would ever see myself as a CSO, I probably would have had to ask what that even was. Our careers take us down many paths, and if you are reading this book then either one of two things have happened. The first possibility is that you are an executive in security, risk, and privacy, and you are seeking to develop new skills through self-education and industry awareness. The other option is that you are considering becoming a CSO and are taking the steps necessary to prepare yourself for what I believe to be one of the best careers any practitioner could ask for.

In either case you have figured out something very important; that is, we all create our own capabilities through direct accountability and responsibility for self-development planning, road maps for career success, and strategic career alignment to get us where we want to go. Nobody will take you by the hand and create you as the CSO. You may be mentored, suggestions may be made, and—if you're lucky—education might be paid for, but at the end of the day it is you who create the acumen, learn the business, create your own development plan, and execute flawlessly in your position as a senior security leader driving next-generation business operations protection programs.

Of course, to get there, you need to know where you are going. To that end, you need to establish your "end goal," that is, what you are trying to attain from a career perspective and as a practitioner. That end goal will undoubtedly change several times during the course of your career, but in the here and now, the present tense, where you have to establish a path to reach your trajectory, you need to consider what you're developing yourself for, including things like what level of leadership you want to attain. Do you want to be *the* CSO? Is the top position really what you want—with a 24/7 job, potentially massive ongoing travel schedules, and all the headaches associated with being in the top spot? Or would you rather focus on a career leading a specific portion of an organization, such as a business unit–level security executive or a chief security technology officer, or perhaps operating as a chief operating officer for a large security program in a multinational corporation? All are very rewarding and important positions.

Other aspects of a career you should consider are things like what industries you would like to work in. Or are you trying to develop yourself holistically and work across multiple industries to get the broadest set of experiences possible? Is there a certain leadership team you would like to work with? Is there a specific company you've always dreamed of working in? Taking the time to step back and evaluate your options, your passions, and your aspirations is a necessary first step in creating you as the CSO. Document your decisions and review them with a trusted advisor with industry experience. Create self-imposed brackets of time (years) to attain the next level in your plan and start to document the road map for each plan section.

Every year during your self-evaluations and your planning cycle in your current job, pull out your road map and see whether you are achieving those development areas necessary to keep your forward momentum going. If not, readdress and realign to manage your success. Human capital management experts suggest that professionals should readdress their overall strategic career-planning road map every 3–5 years. However often you do it, make sure that you document and hold yourself accountable.

Your Road Map as a Total Person

The job of any senior-level security, risk, or privacy leader, like many senior executive positions, is incredibly stressful, demanding, and at times consuming. Beyond the normal stress of any senior position is the constant level of emergent issues that you are responsible to respond to. At any minute of any day (and more often at four o'clock on a Friday afternoon) the phone will ring and you will be called on to lead the business through the crisis du jour: cyber attack, internal fraud, ethics violation, privacy breach, domestic violence, regulatory violation, hurricanes, threats to an executive, distributed denial of service attack, supply chain outage, plane crash, regional political destabilization, and on and on. Some days you are the hero and other days simply the garbage collector.

Simply knowing your job as a practitioner and being a "good leader" are not the only preparatory areas necessary to deal with such a wide range of issues and responsibilities of the next-generation security executive. Later in this chapter we touch on road map items necessary for both you as an executive and you as a practitioner. In this section we look at you as the person. To deal with this extraordinary responsibility and stress, you need to be well grounded, and how you merge important personal aspects and perceptions into the road map is important because they are the real glue that holds you as "the total person" together when the balance between life and work becomes stretched and stressed.

Family

One of the first discussions you need to have is not necessarily one you have with yourself. If you have a family or are planning on having one, you need to take into consideration the family discussion. Time and time again over your career you will hear the concept and mantra of having a good life–work balance. Although I am most certainly not the expert in this, I can tell you that it is a constant effort to understand what that independently means to you, what it means to your family, and how to obtain it. Careers in any discipline have a tendency of taking over a major portion of your life, especially if you have an aggressive can-do/will-do attitude, are highly competitive, or you simply just love your job. As a CSO, the level of difficult is increased by four because of the around-the-clock global responsibilities, the emergent nature of your response requirements, the continuous level of external influence that affects security issues with your business, and the overall criticality of how time-to-issue management can affect your business.

If you have a family, it is your responsibility to have an open discussion about what a work–life balance looks like, what measures you will have in place to evaluate when things are getting out of control, and to ensure you set the right expectations of the requirements and duties of this career. When you are on another conference call at two o'clock in the morning, or you are sleeping in the office because of an ongoing investigation that needs immediate resolution, or you're traveling multiple weeks in a row away from home, knowing you have the support of your family and your partner can significantly reduce your overall stress. Conversely, letting your partner know that they have a say in what normal and reasonable will be, and that you will prioritize the family needs within that framework, helps to create the give and take and the flexibility necessary on both sides to be able to perform these duties.

Your Moral and Ethical Compass

When creating your personal success road map, something that not many people speak of is the development of personal decision points that support and maintain your personal moral and ethical beliefs. As an individual it is a good and valuable trait to understand what moral and ethical standards you hold closest and hopefully model your life after. I cannot tell you what your moral or ethical beliefs should be, nor can anyone else. As people we are influenced and taught different reasons, concepts, and beliefs across many social, religious, family, and educational boundaries. It is through these concepts that we build our lives, live our lives, and pass on to others. At times during your career these moral and ethical standards will be challenged, and as a person you will be challenged to understand how to deal with it.

To start, take the time to write down what is important to you. What are your 10 "golden rules?" More important, when will you know that they have been breached? This is simply an exercise in establishing self-governance. Taking your list and applying a basic standard of what you will not allow yourself to do, what you will not allow others to do to you, and what you will not stand for from other people in each of these moral and ethical areas will help you address the situation if it ever comes to light.

Remember, situations will happen in which you feel very uncomfortable and at times they will begin to approach that line of what you believe is right or wrong. They may be perfectly acceptable for the company you work at but totally unacceptable to you. If that continually occurs, at some point you may have to make a decision if that is the organization you want to continue to work in. At other times the behavior of others whom you are responsible for protecting may not meet your personal standards but you have to be mature and capable of segregating their actions in your presence and enforcing your standards on others, which may not be appropriate.

Mind, Body, and Soul

If being the next-generation global security leader is about creating an impactful and sustainable business operations protections program for your business, then self-sustainability must also top the list of personal road map development for you as the CSO. Sustainability means that to operate at the levels and pace necessary in your chosen career, you not only need to develop excellence in your mastery but also in yourself as well.

The concept and connection between your ability to perform your job and the management of your mind, body, and soul is not new. Since humans have been documenting themselves, understanding the basics of making sure that we take care of ourselves in order to be able to take care of others or provide other services for the betterment of society (like our jobs) has been a principle in almost every culture. But what does that mean to a CSO?

First, it means having a healthy outlet to manage stress, whether you have a great hobby that can occupy your mind, an incredible family unit that does things together, you're into meditation or reflexology, or you find peace and solace through your religion or work within your community. Whatever it is, having a healthy mind means having the ability to manage stress and creating mental health in doing so. Figure out your method of getting away, separating work from play, and creating downtime. There are no checklists, no perfect methods, no frameworks to follow here. Every human is different and every human relieves stress in a different way. Figure out what yours is to make sure you have the ability to separate, deescalate, relax, and enjoy life.

Next, the physiological issues associated with a high-stress job like the one you have selected means that your body needs to be in shape to handle it. I know, you've heard it over and over again, but it's worth restating. It's really simple: When you have healthy body, you have a better physical mechanism for dealing with the biology of cyclical mental and physical stress, enabling you to perform at higher levels for longer amounts of time and thereby positively affecting your mission. Whatever keeps you in shape, do it. On one of my leadership teams I had three Ironmen and two marathoners. I am neither. However, I typically run a 5K three to five times a week, and strength train as well. A moderate level of physical discipline for any person helps drive their personal and professional performance in a multitude of ways. Lead by example and ensure that you have the physical sustainability to perform the duties required of your position.

Finally, the point bringing it all together is how we feel about ourselves and what we do every day. That aspect of "soul" that is the essence or embodiment of those qualities or traits you hold to a certain standard for yourself. Whether it be for yourself or for others, how you fuel yourself and your soul matters. I once attended a seminar that was being given by a US Navy SEAL who was speaking on matters of leadership and personal excellence. When he got to the topic of mind, body, and soul he challenged everyone by asking two very simple questions. First, with regard to the concept of what we believe are those qualities and traits that fill our soul, how do we feed them? If we believe in nonviolence, are we constantly watching violent movies? If we believe in treating others with respect, do we listen to music that uses derogatory terms for people and less than colorful words? Do we feed ourselves the right inputs that ensure that we are developing the "soul" each of us wants?

The second question was about how we deliver on what we say is important to us. He asked, "Is what we do in our deeds evidence of what believe our personal standards are?" This can be a tough question to answer sometimes. Did I make a decision out of anger at another person rather than what's best for the team or the company? What did I do to ensure that what is important to me shows in how I live and work every day?

These are all great questions for us to think about as we create our own personal road map. How do we get to the next step? Simple. First, conduct an honest self-assessment by examining your actions and your heart regarding what is important do you, what you know what you should do, and how you are attaining it. Next, create a summary of those characteristics you believe are important to you as a person, as a leader, and as a practitioner. Establish your comparative gap assessment list and prioritize. Choose the top one to three and make decisions on how you will get there, and let the self-training begin. Mastering yourself is your first step in mastering your career as a CSO.

The Executive Road Map

Where you start your path to become a CSO ultimately dictates the road map you create for yourself. There are two distinctive paths that you must travel that have very different training and acumen development necessities: you as the executive and you as the practitioner. It is not necessary to start your paths at the same level or time in your career. I have seen many excellent CSOs decide that is what they were going to become very late in their career, such as coming to the profession after being an individual contributor within the security, risk, and privacy space for a good number of years or coming from a successful executive career in another specialty. As long as you know where you are on each path, know the necessary steps to accumulate the acumen required to succeed, and have the ability to develop your road map and train to it, anything is possible.

Starting with the executive road map, as you think about the positions that lead to the executive level, there are necessary skills that should be obtained, which the next position in line builds on, creating foundational and career-enhancing abilities required by a CSO. The following five career levels are indicative of those typical positions that you can fulfill and that provide important career knowledge and executive acumen development.

Practitioner

Whether you begin your path to becoming a CSO as a newly hired college graduate or you have made the decision as a senior executive with 20 years of experience to move to this career field, you need to develop basic skills and an understanding of what it is you will be leading. In the next section we dive deep into what key takeaways you should have in each area of a converged practitionership to be a CSO, but the basic fact remains that you need to understand the world of security, risk, and privacy. Leadership absent a solid understanding of who or what is being led is management, not leadership. Spending the time necessary to develop critical understandings, concepts, and capabilities that are educational and on the job training specific to the position are the first steps in becoming a next generation security executive.

Manager

Leadership and management are two very different things. Being a great executive requires great leadership skills, but leadership is all about leading people, and leading people requires a solid knowledge base of how to manage resources and work output in the workforce. Managing resources requires a new level of skills that aren't just about the people, but are necessary to fulfill people management positions, which will serve you well in all aspects of your career. The following are a few of those skills you should accumulate in a management or management-like position that allows you to learn, develop, and practice these basic skill sets:

- General planning
- Problem solving and decision making
- Effective delegation
- Effective listening and communicating
- Meeting management
- Self-management

In most management positions these are key attributes necessary to successfully fulfill the position and are often part of the management training programs of most companies. As you can see from the list, each skill set is just that—a basic skill set that can be applied to management practices, leadership, and general business positions. But to be an effective manager, you must master these.

Entry-Level Leadership

The next important level of development is the entry-level leader, or what some experts refer to as the "leadership transition" phase of one's career. As a manager, we learn how to manage resources. In fact, most of my organizations have "manager" positions that have no direct reports because they are managing programs. When you cross that chasm between resource management and people leadership, you embark on a new set of skills that are prominently focused on enabling you to become an "influencer" of people. In this early level of leadership, there are a handful of skills that prepare you for executive leadership, where decision-making becomes imperative, but as important are how you relate to people and how you influence the execution of work necessary to effect the mission. The following are examples of the skill sets you learn at this level:

- *Self-Awareness:* Handling different situations; learning appropriate attributes that help you lead yourself before you lead people
- *People and Group Relational Skills:* Establishing rapport; encouraging, communicating with, and guiding people
- *Strategic Thinking:* Process development for obtaining a specific goal or state and what tools and resources are necessary to obtain the goal
- *Solution Creation:* Defining the problem space and creating a functional response through the use of the teams one leads to effectively solve the problem

Depending on the size of the company, the typical role of entry leadership is often a "director" position with organization-specific responsibilities across a more narrow set of programs. In some organizations, as an entry-level director you will be required to attend leadership training, whereas in others there is no such program. As you grow into more senior positions throughout your career and even into the role of CSO, make sure that you set your entry-level leaders up for success by creating opportunities for internal or external education about the basic skill sets necessary to be a good leader. Although there are natural-born leaders, not every leader comes with every skill set when they are born.

Expanded Responsibility Leader

The next phase in executive development is providing extended responsibility to those who have mastered the entry-level leadership positions. What you have learned up to this point are the basic tools necessary and have applied those to a specific realm of authority. It is important to learn several new skills and challenge your leadership capabilities by learning to lead beyond your own organization and across other organizations and geographies. This is a time when you learn to be a leader in the business.

When an individual obtains a senior director position in one of my organizations, I always take the time to sit down and have with them a discussion about expectations. When an individual is given this expanded responsibility, it is not only because the position that they are in warrants that level of leader, but also because I believe that they have the capability to be an executive in the organization, and this position is the one step before becoming that executive leader. I emphasize in the conversation that this is their opportunity to build skills and learn to lead as a business executive. I commit to provide them with the training necessary, but their responsibility is to step up to the plate, reach far beyond their comfort zone, and take the skills that they have been taught to the next level.

I typically remind them that I expect them to be accountable and responsible at the business level and lead efforts and programs that are not insular to their specific discipline across multiple boundaries within the company and across the world. I expect them to create business skills that they may have not had before, such as financial acumen and deep company-specific, go-to-market knowledge. My job is to give them the new tools in their leadership tool kit and opportunities to use them. Their job is to recognize those opportunities, grab them with both hands, practice their skills, and demonstrate to the company exactly what type of leader they are. Some of these "fundamental executive competencies" that they must learn and master at this level include the following:

- Interpersonal skills
- Oral communication
- Integrity/honesty
- Written communication
- Continual learning
- Mission motivation

Executive

The final level of development in your process to becoming a CSO is learning those skills necessary to be an executive within your company. At this point in your career you've learned to manage people and learned basic and advanced competencies of leadership. Now, as you prepare yourself for an executive position leading a complex business protection organization, you need to embark on the final skills necessary to effectively lead your business.

These skills can be learned in conjunction with the competencies at lower levels or can be introduced at entry-level executive positions as a staff member or direct report to the CSO in another large business. Your focus should be *obtaining the skills necessary* to be the CSO—*not being the chief security officer*—and then practicing those skills. If you have gaps in core requirements necessary to lead security programs, consider working in a level I or level II executive position in a large security program below the CSO to continue developing the required skills. The following is the final set of skills required of any senior executive position:

- *Leading Change:* creativity and innovation, external awareness, flexibility, resilience, vision
- *Leading People:* conflict management, diversity, developing others, team building
- *Being Results-Driven:* accountability, customer service, decisiveness, entrepreneurship
- *Acquiring Business Acumen:* fiscal leadership, human capital management, business management
- *Building Coalitions:* partnering, political savvy, influencing/negotiating

Your road map can only be developed by you, and by taking a progressive step-by-step approach to developing the acumen necessary to perform the CSO job, you give yourself the edge by not just learning about the skills but also by putting those skills into practice over time.

As a Practitioner

The second part of your bifurcated road map of your career as a CSO is your skills and capabilities as a security practitioner. People often talk about executive positions in the context of being the president of the United States, stating "you don't have to know every part of the business, you just have to surround yourself with great leaders that do." There is some truth to that, even in the context of being a CSO. But we are not the president of the Free World, and our task and mission context are most often operationally focused, specific to the areas of security, risk, and privacy. Would you want the cabinet-level secretary for your country's Department of Health and Human Services to know nothing about medical administration management, health care, or health sociology? Of course not. Preparing yourself to manage and lead business operations protection programs should be your focus, not just being able to talk about them or be a great leader who hires people to do the work for you.

Basic decisions around strategic protection principles, emergent issue management, and discipline-specific sustainability management require that you know your area of responsibility with an acumen equal to the task of making decisions for your company. The following four categories outline those areas in which a CSO should have a reasonable level of expertise to manage that business. Depending on the path you took to get here, you may have to learn all of those at once or over a career, or have accumulated the majority of them and simply must focus on a specific gap area. The diversity of skills necessary to deliver a competent and effective program is broad and, quite simply, this job is not for everyone.

Evaluate your practitioner capabilities in each one of these sections on a simple scale of 1 to 5 (1 being almost no knowledge and 5 being an expert). Then determine at which level you believe you need to be at in order to lead a global security organization. Next, create your own personal development plan to gain the skills to get there. There are professional education opportunities through organizations like SANS, ASIS, and ISMA as mentioned before in this book. There are also universities that have executive-level educational programs for security practitioners, such as the Tucks School of Business at Dartmouth College, the Kellogg School of Management at Northwestern University, George Washington University, the Wharton School of Business at the University of Pennsylvania, and George Mason University. Whatever your course of knowledge learning is, commit to it and obtain the skills necessary for each one of the following areas.

Technical

In this context, *technical* is referred to as information and cyber security. As an executive you do not need to know how to configure a firewall or program a script for analytical data collection, but there is some basic rudimentary knowledge necessary to be successful. The most broadly accepted common body of knowledge that ensures that you as a leader have the knowledge necessary to understand threat, technology, programs, and practices are the eight domains promulgated by the company ISC^2, which certifies security professionals, including the Certified Information Systems Security Professional (CISSP), the most common certification. The domains include the following:

- Security and risk management
- Asset security
- Security engineering
- Communications and network security
- Identity and access management
- Security assessment and testing
- Security operations
- Software development security

Beyond understating these domains and how they act in concert to create a holistic cyber defense portfolio, there are other important concepts and practice areas that you need to have a firm grasp of because they will be part of your everyday operations. Consider the following in your expanded list of technical knowledge priorities:

- Threat management and threat defense
- Operational framework implementation and management (such as ISO 27XXX, ISACA, and NIST CSF)
- Security intelligence operations
- Cyber monitoring operations
- Cyber incident response planning and crisis management

These suggested knowledge areas for your technical development plan are consistent with the typical duties of a converged CSO and most certainly for those who have extensive responsibilities in large multinational operations.

Risk

As a CSO, the entire underpinning of your strategy and operational priorities should be based on risk management. How you determine the risk level of the business, how you plan resource allocation, and how you create budgets and use political capital to force organizational behavior change and action rely on your implementation of a core risk program. Understanding how to implement business-integrated risk frameworks and deliver integrated enterprise risk components necessitates that you obtain basic skills in managing risk.

There are several notable risk certification processes that span IT risk management to information security risk management to traditional business risk. Consider the following as your recommended base core knowledge areas of risk management, risk processes, and risk operations required to adequately arm you with the skills necessary to deliver base operational risk services to your business and to obtain the right level of risk information to run your business:

- Risk governance and assignment
- Risk baselining/identification/assignment
- Controls oversight and management
- IT, security, and business operational risk assessment
- Third-party and supply chain risk management
- Controls assurance
- Risk migration and mitigation
- Risk and control monitoring and reporting
- Board of director risk process assurance

When prioritizing your individual development road map, start with higher-level concepts like frameworks, governance, and program development. Then focus on reporting, the needs of the board of directors, and extended programs like controls assurance that use risk processes to establish and measure the efficacy of control frameworks. Finally, get your hands dirty with identification and measurement processes so when working with your teams you can support operational program development and also have the skills necessary to speak to the business on how risk scores and risk prioritization are developed.

Converged

The future of convergence is here, and whether you are coming out of government as a career physical security or law enforcement expert or you have been a chief information security officer for years and are expanding your practitioner capacity and capabilities for the next generation of CSO jobs, developing converged security skills specific for commercial entities are a must.

Physical security management is a broad practitionership that deals with issues from guards, locks, and alarms to environmental security architecture, global investigations, and legal matters. ASIS, a multinational leader in training, certification, and career education development, has created a certification that meets the basic bodies of knowledge listed below: the Certified Protection Professional (CPP)®.

The CPP program and certification provides education and board certifications in the following areas:

- Security principles and practices
- Business principles and practices
- Investigations
- Personnel security
- Physical security
- Information security
- Crisis management
- Legal aspects

Those base skill areas create the minimum bar for job-specific knowledge necessary to manage converged security functions such as corporate security programs. However, as the size of the company that you work for increases, the number of employees in the business increases, and the geographic complexities of your job increase, you will need to attain a higher level of converged security expertise. The following are topical areas that most CSOs must manage or have the ability to manage in large and complex businesses:

- Business resilience (business continuity/disaster recovery)
- Facilitates security technologies
- Public safety management
- Travel security
- Advanced workforce protection (active shooter response)
- Executive protection
- Credentialing
- Forensics

Remember, we are talking about a body of knowledge, not expertise. Understanding the "what" of forensics or executive protection rather than demonstrating the "how" are two very different things. Knowing how to protect the physical security aspects of your company and its employees requires knowing what expertise needs to be brought to bear and what actions should be needed for specific circumstances. In fact, in many of these practice areas, it may not be your company's assets providing these services, but rather partner contract companies that supply you with the specific skills necessary at the time of need in the geography of need. It is up to you to understand what each of these practice areas are, what level of service your business requires, and how to create a service delivery framework to implement the appropriate operational capabilities.

Privacy

Although most large corporations have specific specialties in the area of privacy law, and often an independent chief privacy officer, the majority of operational privacy protection operations will most certainly fall to you. Privacy, data governance, data security, cyber operations, and physical business protection are not mutually exclusive, and understanding how privacy affects your ability to defend, your responsibilities in ensuring your company meets regulatory protocols required for your type of business, and how to implement leveragable controls, processes, and operations that support the privacy needs of your business and customers requires you to develop a base level of knowledge. In some forward-leaning companies like Intel, the CSO, chief risk officer, and chief privacy officer are entirely a converged function, and many companies are starting to ask whether or not this is a more effective model.

The International Association of Privacy Professionals, the world's largest information privacy organization, has created common bodies of knowledge and certification programs that align to the needs of today's leaders who are responsible for ensuring the development, deployment, and adherence to privacy protection programs globally from both a legal and operational perspective. The following outline is their suggested base areas of acumen if you are responsible for ensuring the efficacy of the privacy efforts at your business:

- Jurisdictional laws, regulations, and enforcement models, or rules and standards
- Essential privacy concepts and principals
- Legal requirements for handling and transferring data
- Development and implementation of a privacy program framework
- The privacy program operational life cycle

As the executive responsible for creating the underlying principals and programs that your company's privacy positioning, certifications, and attestations will be based on, it is critically important that you develop a core knowledge base of privacy principals, laws, and operations. The success of those programs and your company's legal positioning is often at stake.

CONTINUOUS LEARNING

In the world in which you will operate as a global Chief Security Executive, changes to the threat environment, available defensive programs and technologies, and your business happen daily. The core body of knowledge you needed yesterday to be the "expert" in the field will change tomorrow, and you need to take on a self-development attitude of continuous learning. Continuous learning is the applied strategy of change management and learning both in the individual and group settings. As a person, one must constantly reevaluate his or her job, position, and required skill sets, because over months and years, new requirements will be mandated, new programs developed, and new opportunities made available.

As we embrace change and adjust our mission requirements, we must adjust our assumptions of the skills needed to successfully lead ourselves and others through that change and on to operational excellence. This can be accomplished through position description realignment–based changes, expectations, and added responsibilities. By tracking your own personal skill levels in each of your core discipline areas, modifying that list on a disciplined periodic basis, and holding yourself accountable to expanding your skill set and base of knowledge to meet the needs of your position, you will continuously grow personally, professionally, and as a leader. Progressive self-development is a quality of true leader and a desired attribute of a seasoned executive.

YOUR BRAND

Have you ever stopped to think about your brand? Your independent brand image as "the" CSO influences not only your individual success in your job and in your career but also the success of the organization you lead. In this section we focus on perceptions, actions, and outcomes security executives must pay attention to, strive for, and develop to create a personally successful brand.

Before we begin to review what makes a successful brand, we need to talk about what a personal brand is and is not. For starters, your brand is not self-promotion. That's right, it's not about promoting you, but rather is a representation of your value as a leader, of the values you deliver to your company, and of the value others can obtain through you. You have to think about your brand as an asset, not a projection of self-worth. You should view this "asset" as tool that others who associate with you or with whom you have a relationship can actually benefit from through your work. Your brand is a reflection of how others interpret their experience with you as a person and the wake you leave after interacting with others. Do you know what wake you leave? Do you have an impression of what your own reflection is?

If you can't answer those questions, then it's safe to say you probably don't have an equitable brand. As a senior security executive, your brand helps you to establish credibility and trust, and often buys you the political and professional capital necessary for the latitude in making decisions and taking action required to do the job of a CSO. However, personal brand development doesn't happen overnight; in fact, sometimes either you have already established a brand (for better or worse) that you are not aware of, or, unfortunately, you assume the brand that was left by the person who vacated the position before you.

Your first step is to figure out what that perception is. Although painful sometimes, it is imperative you get a realistic look at what others think of you. This is best coming from a trusted peer, your boss, or even HR, but stay away from subordinates, because they tend to tell you what they think you want to hear. Once you have your brand inventory, decide whether the reflection being transmitted is your perception and is true to the values you believe are important. Once you have this inventory you can begin to work on those negative attributes that need repair and add new brands to your portfolio.

There are some key brands that are important to consider when fulfilling the position of CSO. They are important because, as the individual responsible for managing the company through crisis, handling sensitive investigations, and acting as the chief enforcement officer for the company, you are simply expected to have them. It gets back to those important values that you represent and that a position of critical authority within a company is expected to have. Here are a few of the key "brands" you may want to measure yourself against:

- *Loyal:* To the company, to the mission, your team, and to the people you protect
- *Ethical:* Delivering your services with a solid understanding of what is right and wrong and standing up to moral obligations when necessary
- *Integrity:* Being an honest and morally principled leader and executive
- *Knowledgeable and Professional:* Being an expert in your craft and committed to delivering those services in a courteous, ethical, and businesslike manner
- *Confident Leader:* Leading from in front with passion and excellence
- *There to Serve:* Delivering your services with a sense of humility, understanding, and empathy, and the will to protect the business, shareholders, employees, and customers you serve every day

If these are not in line with what you believe your brand should be, perhaps you may want to reconsider what is important to those who consume your services and employ you as the senior-most person protecting their business.

ESTABLISHING YOUR BRAND

The number 1 rule in establishing your brand is simple: Acting doesn't count. Again, the purpose of your brand is to reflect positive attributes of who you are and the value you deliver. Self-promoting unattainable or inconsistent attributes and behaviors becomes transparent quickly and will soon devalue your brand, often taking years to overcome.

If "acting doesn't count" is the first requirement, then living your values is the second. Since your brand is a reflection, then we have to ask ourselves the following questions: What deeds do I do that reflect the key brands I want people to see in me? Do I lead with confidence and excellence? Am I loyal to the people I work with? Do I show integrity in the decisions and actions I take? Are there things I should change, and do I make an effort to change them? Self-reflection is an important part of how we enable our brand. It uncovers gaps, it forces us to apply self-pressure, and, just like combing your hair in the morning, it helps reflect the image that needs adjustment.

Once you are on the path to a good reflection by living your values through your actions, attitude, and deeds, you can then start to project a more honed version of that brand through some planning and strategic actions that can modulate your brand more effectively than your actions alone.

To begin, you need to determine your area of expertise. This is the professional aspect of what you are known for. Sometimes it's better to have a niche and other times to have broader knowledge. At some points in your career, based on what you are working on, the market may determine your expertise brand. For instance, as a practitioner one of my personal brands is converged security. There was a period of time when my team was actively creating new capabilities around the use of intelligence-led security. My brand morphed into that area, and the market had dictated it because it wanted to know more about that topic. You can have multiple brands and that's OK—just know what they are, how to use them, and how they will benefit those you serve and lead.

Your next action is to get out there, introduce, and test your brand. Consider writing and publishing articles, blogs, and white papers or perspectives. The fact that you can document your specialty or professional brand only further mirrors those other values and brand attributes of leading from in front, knowing your job, and being passionate about what you do. Writing also separates you from others as a professional in your field; the more you are published, the more you are read, and the more others gain perspective and insight through your brand.

Brands and perceptions are sometimes led by what is not present as much as what is, and your social media profile may speak volumes. Your next course of action should be to formalize a consistent brand across Facebook, LinkedIn, and Twitter or similar media portals internal to your company. You brand values and shared content should be in line, and you should be active across whichever medium you engage in.

Finally, consider speaking publically at events inside your company; within the security, risk, and privacy profession; and within your industry as well. Developing speaking and presentation skills that share your expertise, are aimed at educating others, and show your passion and values act as an incredible reflector of your personal brand image.

Your brand isn't just "nice to have," it's a requirement for your success as an executive and as a leader. Your personal brand builds equity, establishes rapport, and delivers a message of trust, professionalism, and ability for your team and your company. You also owe it to yourself after years of hard work and dedication, making it to the position of a global Chief Security Executive, to have the right reflection of the committed professional you are.

Conclusion

Becoming the Global Chief Security Executive is a book designed not only to show you a window into one of the most exciting careers in the discipline of corporate security, risk, and privacy executive leadership, but also to provide tangible constructs for you to expand your knowledge, develop yourself, and exceed in this career field. From aspects of what the next-generation converged security leader will be accountable for to what the business needs from you to how to build a world-class program and a world-class team, this book can be used as an instruction set, a personal reminder, or a checklist as you continue to develop yourself, others, your program, and your business.

A few years before writing this book, I was a speaker at a security executive leadership dinner, with a couple of friends of mine on either side of me as co-speakers. The three of us are an entertaining trio, but the passion for what we all do is always palatable when we do these joint speaking engagements. Toward the end of our session, someone from the audience asked the question, "Why are you all so passionate about being a chief security officer?" Without skipping a beat, my friend to my left, who to this day is the chief security officer of one of the largest technology companies in the world, said simply, "It is because we are the only things standing between them and society. Look around this room; this is it. Billions of computers in the world, millions coming online every day, economies and societies depending on technology to manage our way of life, and the people in this room are the chosen few to lead the people responsible for protecting our society." You could've heard a pin drop in that room.

That moment still sticks with me today. The poignancy of the fact that there is such an incredible need for what I have chosen to do as career, and for what I hope you are choosing to do as a career, cannot be lost in all the noise around what a chief security officer is, who they should report to, what skills are necessary, and what the best job out there is. They are all important jobs. No matter what industry, no matter what country, no matter what size business, the leadership necessary to defend modern society is a critical gap in the job market today and will be for years to come. The training necessary, the character necessary, and the fortitude required takes a committed individual with a passion for service to a greater need. Businesses need these people, countries need these people, and society will depend on them for years to come. Is that person you?

Beyond being a committed individual of great personal strength and character, the global chief security executive of the future needs to learn a new set of skills across the boundaries of their practitionership and their business. As security careers migrate from traditional and siloed positions in information security, risk management, corporate security, and so on, to what they really need to become—business operations protection executives—security leaders have the opportunity to retool, relearn, and expand their personal and professional skills and lead from out front as next-generation security executives. Convergence is not only necessary to ensure a consistent and capable approach to discovering, managing, and addressing a broad spectrum of business-affecting security, risk, and privacy issues; it's just good business sense. Integration and consolidation of operational business protection programs reduce costs, drive transparencies, enable oversight, and reduce artificial political and organizational boundaries that constrict the effective development and use of a business's global protection resources.

Your have the opportunity to lead in one of the most exciting careers in today's business. Not only does the opportunity exist because of the expansive need, there is also the opportunity to help shape and develop the future of our career field. With some estimates putting converged business operations protection programs at less than 5% of the total number of security programs in the commercial markets and growing, through training and preparation you have the opportunity to lead your business, your market, and your team in a transition to become an effective and leading-edge global security program.

As they say, nothing in life worth anything comes easy. To achieve high performance, and manage high-performing teams, we all must follow a simple path of preparing ourselves, training ourselves, executing with urgency and action, regrouping and remeasuring, then replanning and starting all over. Being a next-generation security leader means being a learned person. Understanding our discipline, our specialties, the external and internal threat environments, and how to manage our own business, leading the businesses we work for, and being that rock that the business can rely on during critical times in crisis is the job. It's the reward. And it is your future if you so choose.

If you do choose this career, then exude leadership and share your successes, trials, tribulations, and failures so that others may learn and become partners in fighting the good fight. Remember that global business operations protection is a career marathon, not a race with an even perceivable end goal. As long as there are societies, there will be a need for police to help protect the people. As long as there are businesses and economies, there will be a need for leaders who manage the protection of those businesses. Your job is to wade through all of the information, all of the fear, all of the issues, and create a reasonable and manageable approach to what is known as risk. Prioritization and principles are both your friends. Any forward steps in protecting what is yours to protect is momentum, and momentum means moving ahead.

My hope is that this book has provided you with a new perspective, new insight, and a few new tools for your tool kit. My hope is that you accept this challenge of becoming a next-generation global security executive and that you pursue it with a passion for righteousness, excellence, and the betterment of the society you live in.

My final words of advice are these: Be resilient. Be determined. And apply the necessary pressure to yourself and to the rest of the world to succeed at your mission.

Welcome to the ranks of the next-generation global chief security executive. Be a leader—you decide what type.

Index

Note: Page numbers followed by "f" and "t" denote figures and tables, respectively.

T

Printed in Great Britain
by Amazon